Betrayer's Waltz

ALSO BY JENNIFER BOWERS BAHNEY

Stealing Sisi's Star: How a Master Thief Nearly Got Away with Austria's Most Famous Jewel (McFarland, 2015)

Betrayer's Waltz

*The Unlikely Bond Between
Marie Valerie of Austria
and Hitler's Princess-Spy*

JENNIFER BOWERS BAHNEY

McFarland & Company, Inc., Publishers
Jefferson, North Carolina

Library of Congress Cataloguing-in-Publication Data

Names: Bahney, Jennifer Bowers, 1967– author.
Title: Betrayer's waltz : the unlikely bond between Marie Valerie of
 Austria and Hitler's princess-spy / Jennifer Bowers Bahney.
Other titles: Unlikely bond between Marie Valerie of Austria and Hitler's
 princess-spy
Description: Jefferson, North Carolina : McFarland & Company, Inc.,
 Publishers, 2017 | Includes bibliographical references and index.
Identifiers: LCCN 2017039344 | ISBN 9781476668727 (softcover : acid
 free paper) ♾
Subjects: LCSH: Marie Valérie, Archduchess of Austria, 1868–1924. |
 Hohenlohe-Waldenburg-Schillingsfürst, Stephanie Juliana, Prinzessin
 zu, 1896–1972. | Women spies—Germany—History—20th century. |
 Princesses—Biography.
Classification: LCC DB89.M37 B35 2017 | DDC 327.12092/2 [B]—dc23
LC record available at https://lccn.loc.gov/2017039344

British Library cataloguing data are available

ISBN (print) 978-1-4766-6872-7
ISBN (ebook) 978-1-4766-3044-1

© 2017 Jennifer Bowers Bahney. All rights reserved

*No part of this book may be reproduced or transmitted in any form
or by any means, electronic or mechanical, including photocopying
or recording, or by any information storage and retrieval system,
without permission in writing from the publisher.*

On the cover *left to right* Marie Valerie around the time of the Great
War (Library of Congress Prints and Photographs Division, George
Grantham Bain Collection); Princess Stephanie von Hohenlohe,
1937 (author's collection)

Printed in the United States of America

*McFarland & Company, Inc., Publishers
 Box 611, Jefferson, North Carolina 28640
 www.mcfarlandpub.com*

For Chip,
my mentor and friend

Acknowledgments

I would like to thank the following people and institutions for helping to make this book possible: Charlotte Simmonds, whose flawless knowledge of both "old" and "new" German helped translate Marie Valerie's diary and other important documents; Jenny Fichmann, who combed through Stephanie von Hohenlohe's documents at Stanford University's Hoover Archives when I could not travel to California; Lily Szczygiel, documentation technician with McGill University's Osler Library of the History of Medicine, who scanned and emailed photos from a rare album documenting Franz Salvator's visit to a World War I military hospital; Daniela Pümpel with the University of Innsbruck, who sent information on Franz Salvator's honorary doctorate; research volunteers at the Austrian Red Cross who unearthed important documents pertaining to Marie Valerie and Franz Salvator's roles during World War I; the British National Archives for their invaluable declassified MI5 files on Stephanie von Hohenlohe; the Warwickshire County Record Office in Great Britain, which sent me many valuable letters and documents pertaining to Marie Valerie, Empress Elisabeth, and Lady Mary Throckmorton; author Karina Urbach (*Go Betweens for Hitler*, Oxford University Press, 2015), who graciously answered research questions I had regarding Stephanie von Hohenlohe; the great Hitler biographers I have cited throughout this book; the libraries who have digitized their materials, making my research that much easier; the rare book sellers who still make certain hard-to-find titles available; and to Archduke Markus Salvator von Habsburg-Lothringen for putting up with my myriad questions about the grandmother he never knew in order to help keep her memory alive for generations who might otherwise never learn her name.

Table of Contents

Acknowledgments	vii
Preface	1
Prologue: "Doubt exists in the Hohenlohe family"	3
Part I: *Verblassendes Reich*/Fading Empire, 1890–1924	7
1. "She can't marry within the family again"	8
2. "Will she be a good little woman?"	16
3. "Everything is good, terribly good"	26
4. "I could only think, when a man was talking"	31
5. "Are we not the same as all other Germans?"	35
6. "We felt ourselves more deeply united on the inside"	41
7. "Antisemitism is an uncommonly diffused sickness"	50
8. "I tread the path that it is my duty to follow"	57
9. "The whole world suffered in consequence"	72
10. "There was danger in the air"	86
11. "We hope that God's mercy will give us better times"	91
12. "One could only envy her"	98
Part II: *Stehendes Reich*/Rising Empire, 1927–1939	109
13. "She first came to our notice in 1928"	110
14. "Hitler is going to rule Germany"	121
15. "One blood demands one Reich"	127

16. "Sincere thanks for the great understanding"	137
17. "Austria will be ours"	146
18. "One of these days there will be a big scandal"	156
19. "Worse than ten thousand men"	171
Epilogue: "We recall the 'Princess' Hohenlohe"	175
Appendix I: Marie Valerie's Diary, 1881–1890	183
Appendix II: Stephanie von Hohenlohe's Draft Memoir Passage on Lord Rothermere's Tactics	193
Appendix III: Stephanie von Hohenlohe on Lord Rothermere and Nazi Leaders	198
Chapter Notes	201
Bibliography	211
Index	215

Preface

After completing my first book, *Stealing Sisi's Star*, I was left with unanswered questions about the fate of Empress Elisabeth of Austria's two daughters, Marie Valerie and Gisela, and how they fared through the Great War and beyond. It was, after all, their father, Emperor Franz Joseph, who declared war against Serbia after the assassination of their cousin, Franz Ferdinand. Soon, the whole world would be embroiled in the fighting that would bring an end to the Empire, and the life of imperial splendor they had known.

From my research base in the United States, I was unable to glean much information on Gisela, who quietly lived most of her adult life in Munich, Germany. Marie Valerie, the "favorite daughter," however, kept a thorough diary, *Das Tagebuch de Lieblingstochter von Kaiserin Elisabeth 1878–1899*, which was published in the German language. I was unable to find an English translation, but did seek out the next best thing—a brilliant Ph.D. student who spent time in between working on her thesis to decipher it for me. I believe some of the English diary translations in this book are the first ever to be presented. Marie Valerie also took on a formal court role in Vienna after her mother's death, and there are many more official documents pertaining to Marie Valerie than to Gisela.

As I researched Marie Valerie's life from pampered Austrian Archduchess to young wife and mother, I came across a startling theory—that her husband and cousin, Franz Salvator, the man she carefully vetted and for whom she renounced her rights to the Austro-Hungarian throne, fathered a child with a young mistress who had a fascinating history of her own.

The mistress was a teenager named Stephanie Richter, a Jewish girl from Vienna, who had her sights set on the world stage. She was determined to break free from her middle-class upbringing, and her affair with Marie Valerie's husband put Stephanie on the path to wielding considerable power in her dealings with Adolf Hitler in the 1930s. She even had a hand in orchestrating Austria's *Anschluss*, or amalgamation, with the Third Reich in 1938.

I say "theory," because a lack of DNA technology in 1914 made it, of course, impossible to say definitively whether Stephanie's son, Prince Franz Josef Rudolf Hans Weriand Max Stefan Anton von Hohenlohe-Waldenburg-Schillingsfürst, was fathered by Marie Valerie's husband. There are revealing clues in Stephanie Richter's writings, however, and even in her son's considerably lengthy name and the lifelong relationship between Stephanie and Franz Salvator, that confirmed to me that he was, indeed, the boy's father. Notwithstanding the fact that Emperor Franz Joseph, himself, arranged Stephanie's shotgun marriage to Prince Friedrich Franz von Hohenlohe-Waldenburg-Schillingsfürst. It was virtually unheard of at the time for an unknown Jewish middle-class girl to marry a Germanic prince, let alone to have it be arranged by the Emperor. When one examines all of the puzzle pieces, I believe the evidence is irrefutable.

One of the things that perplexed me while writing this book was how Stephanie Richter could deny her Jewish ancestry in order to voluntarily collude with Adolf Hitler. She was well aware of the draconian measures the Nazis were taking against the Jews during her time in Berlin, yet she continued to promote antisemitism even when she was in the United States and free of Hitler. Stephanie did not leave any writings to explain why she would betray her own blood; she denied her Jewish background until the end, even having her own son do so for her.

While researching this book, I was fortunate to have become acquainted with Archduke Markus Salvator von Habsburg-Lothrigen, Marie Valerie's grandson and the proprietor of the Kaiservilla in Bad Ischl. The estate is the scene of a great deal of Austrian history with far-reaching repercussions: the site where the Archduke's great-grandfather, Emperor Franz Joseph, proposed to Duchess Elisabeth of Bavaria; the summer retreat where his grandmother, Marie Valerie, got to know her cousin and future husband, Franz Salvator; the hideaway where Franz Salvator would abscond with his mistress, Stephanie Richter; and the place where Emperor Franz Joseph signed the declaration of war that would become the basis of Adolf Hitler's rallying cry for German domination. This book does not seek to give complete biographies of Marie Valerie, Stephanie Richter, or Adolf Hitler; rather, it attempts to examine the extraordinary times in which these singular historic figures lived, from imperial Vienna through World War I to the cusp of World War II, and to chronicle how their actions and betrayals affected one another as well as millions of innocent people who were devastated by Hitler's insidious path of destruction.

Prologue: "Doubt exists in the Hohenlohe family"

—FBI Report on Stephanie von Hohenlohe

Vienna, 1914

The old Emperor of Austria-Hungary, Franz Joseph, rose slowly from his office chair to greet his contrite son-in-law and an apprehensive female guest. Both callers were married to other people, yet stood together as a couple in the grandeur of the Hofburg Palace for this imperial audience. It was unusual for the Emperor's son-in-law, Franz Salvator, to visit the aged monarch without also bringing along his wife of 24 years and at least a few of their nine children. But the middle-aged Archduchess Marie Valerie had not been invited on this trip to the royal residence where she had grown up. In her stead was 24-year-old Princess Stephanie von Hohenlohe-Waldenburg-Schillingsfürst. Stephanie, who was known for bending the truth to suit her needs, had told Franz Salvator that she was just 17.

Although she felt uncertain, Princess Stephanie found the Emperor to be unexpectedly kindly and warm.

"There was an atmosphere of welcome and sympathy, and a friendly smile that removed at once all embarassement [sic] and inhibition," Stephanie would write many years later.[1]

The princess had just months before given birth to a son, whom she had named after the Emperor. Now she stood before the dignified octogenarian who had, with a trembling hand, inscribed a photograph for Stephanie's child, little Franz Joseph von Hohenlohe.

"He must have thought me a silly, scatterbrainy, inarticulate young woman," Stephanie would write of her meeting with the Emperor. "I had come to say some things, but they seemed so painfully petty."[2]

In an exceptional maneuver, the Emperor himself had been instrumental in arranging Stephanie's marriage to Prince Friedrich Franz von Hohenlohe-Waldenburg-Schillingsfürst on May 12, 1914, just two months before the Austro-Hungarian Emperor would declare war on Serbia. Stephanie's child had been born a little more than seven months after her wedding day. The union had been a morganatic one since Stephanie Richter was a commoner from a modest, Jewish working-class family, and the prince was from the dynastic Germanic house of Hohenlohe with its many branches, one of which was closely related to Britain's Queen Victoria. The melding of lives from such very different cultures was nearly unheard of in class-conscious Vienna. And yet Stephanie, who was not particularly beautiful, well-bred, or accomplished, had managed to elevate herself to become a German princess of the Austro-Hungarian Empire.

Stephanie had not received a wedding befitting a princess, however. Instead of a jewel-studded royal celebration in Vienna, Stephanie and her prince had quietly married at Westminster Cathedral in London with only the bride's mother present. There were no ornate carriages, cheering crowds, or fanfare typical of an aristocratic wedding. And there was a surprising lack of sentiment on such a momentous day. The bride and groom showed little affection—they stayed in separate London hotels—and Stephanie described the prince in less-than-romantic terms: "Not tall—and I like tall men—but certainly very well-proportioned."[3] It was said that Stephanie paid more attention to her pet Pomeranian than to her new husband.

Prince Friedrich was an undistinguished Austro-Hungarian military attaché on assignment at the Tsar's court in St. Petersburg, Russia, with a known gambling habit that found him constantly in debt. He had been obliged to obtain approval from the ambassador in Russia and the Ministry of Foreign Affairs in Vienna before he could marry. He also required the blessing of the head of his family's house, Prince August von Hohenlohe. Even though Prince Friedrich was quite obviously "marrying down," all gave their approval for one simple fact: the Austro-Hungarian Emperor wished them to. Franz Joseph was desperately trying to avoid a regal scandal.

* * *

The fact was that the father of Stephanie's child was not Prince Friedrich at all, but Archduchess Marie Valerie's feckless husband, Franz Salvator, the man who now stood by her side before the Emperor. The entire Hohenlohe family may have been on to the ruse. According to an

FBI report on Stephanie from 1941, "Doubt exists in the Hohenlohe family that her son, Prince Franz, is in fact a Hohenlohe."[4] Despite the suspicions, if the Emperor wished the union, there was little anyone could do to stop it. Emperor Franz Joseph most likely nominated the prince because he was not the Hohenlohe family's eldest son and was, therefore, somewhat expendable. Prince Friedrich was also unattached and of a compatible age to marry. And, there were those nagging gambling debts that the Emperor could easily wipe clean. To Stephanie's benefit, the prince would give stability, respectability, and a title, all of which were meant to keep her content and quiet. She must never proclaim Archduke Franz Salvator as the real father of her child.

Emperor Franz Joseph had one goal in all of these machinations: to protect his favorite daughter, Marie Valerie. Now that he had successfully cleaned up Franz Salvator's domestic mess, he had a world war to contemplate.

But the newly-fabricated Princess Stephanie von Hohenlohe, satisfied though she may have been with her novel royal status, would not simply disappear into the aristocratic woodwork. The same desire and unique ability to fraternize with the rich and powerful would eventually lead her to the doorstep of Germany's future Führer, Adolf Hitler.

PART I

Verblassendes Reich/Fading Empire, 1890–1924

1

"She can't marry within the family again"

—Emperor Franz Joseph

July 31, 1890

An unusually solemn air hung over the tenth and final carriage that made up the imperial wedding procession for the Emperor's favorite daughter as it wound its way through the verdant Upper Austrian spa town of Ischl. The townspeople had decorated their homes with festive ribbons and flowers for the occasion and were now lining the route, cheering and vigorously waving handkerchiefs to wish the bridal couple well. Yet, despite the outward show of celebration, a melancholy mood filled the opulent carriage that transported the 22-year-old bride, Archduchess Marie Valerie, who was serene in intricate white Bohemian point lace.

The bride was considered to be rather mature for such an occasion. Her older sister had been just 16 when she had married, as her mother had been before her. Yet, this was a true love match, not a strictly dynastic one, and Marie Valerie had had the freedom to agonize over her decision for years. The Archduchess had wanted to make absolutely certain that she was in love with her groom and that he was God's chosen man for her. There was no room for error.

Next to Marie Valerie sat her mother, Empress Elisabeth of Austria and Queen of Hungary, considered one of the most beautiful women of her time for her ivory skin, floor-length chestnut hair, and 20-inch waist. On this day, Elisabeth wore an understated pearl-gray gown that reflected the gloom she felt, despite the fair weather and blooming edelweiss that dotted the surrounding mountain landscape like so many stars. The hearty alpine flowers had just begun to show their noble white and yellow faces

1. "She can't marry within the family again"

for the summer, and folklore dictated that they represented devotion when presented to a loved one. Certainly, their presence was a propitious sign for the bridal couple.

And yet, Empress Elisabeth was deathly pale and dabbing tears from her eyes with a lace handkerchief as if she were en route to a funeral. She had told her daughter in the days leading up to the marriage, "I can hardly conceive what my life will be after we are parted by your marriage. The time between now and your wedding is like a condemned man's last hours."[1]

Elisabeth was satisfied that her daughter was marrying the man of her own choosing, and had even encouraged the relationship with Archduke Franz Salvator when Emperor Franz Joseph had frowned upon a morganatic marriage with a close family relation, proclaiming, "She can't marry within the family again, where will we end up?"[2] The bride's father had favored a dynastic union for Marie Valerie with one of Europe's eligible Catholic crown princes, but although Franz Salvator was a Habsburg

Marie Valerie married Franz Salvator in Bad Ischl's Parish Church of St. Nicholas on July 31, 1890. The engraving's original is credited to Alois Greil (author's collection).

cousin, the fact remained that he was a minor prince from the less prosperous Tuscan branch. Elisabeth paid no mind to this fact—Marie Valerie's dowry from the state was said to be worth around £50,000 ($8.6 million in today's U.S. dollars), and she would be able to count on an additional "very large yearly allowance" from her father, the Emperor.[3] Despite his initial concerns, the Emperor now sat beside his soon-to-be son-in-law in a carriage ahead of the bride as it made the 20-minute ride from the Kaiservilla to the parish church of Saint Nicholas.

Rumors had swirled throughout Vienna that Marie Valerie was being courted by the likes of the Crown Prince of Saxony, Prince Miguel of Braganza, and even Russia's Tsarevich Nikolai Romanov. And indeed, she confided in her diary, "I owe it to Franz [Salvator] and myself to get to know other young men, so that I will not encounter the 'right' one when it is too late."[4] But Elisabeth had thwarted the Emperor's dynastic ambitions, telling her daughter that she could marry even a chimney sweep if it would make her happy.

Happiness was something that had eluded Elisabeth for most of her life. She felt as though she had been forced into marriage as a teenager because her first cousin, who had become the Emperor at the age of 18, had asked for her hand, and one did simply not tell an emperor no. Even though Elisabeth would come to look on marriage as an institution akin to slavery, she had little objection when her eldest daughter Gisela became engaged at 16 to 26-year-old Prince Leopold of Bavaria. Although Leopold was also a cousin, he became the Emperor's choice for Gisela since so few eligible Catholic princes existed who met his approval. Elisabeth, known for her self-centeredness and dislike of domestic life, had no interest in helping her eldest child compile her wedding trousseau; that task was left to the Empress's staff. But when Elisabeth's youngest daughter, the one person whom she considered to be her life's blood, came of marital age, the Empress spared nothing to ensure Marie Valerie's fulfillment. Elisabeth managed every detail of Marie Valerie's trousseau, from her jewelry to the French corsets that would see her through her first months of marriage. Little surprises were also arranged for the favorite daughter; following a fireworks display the night before her wedding, Marie Valerie stepped out onto the balcony of her writing room to hear the *a cappella* strains of a men's choir performing a favorite poem written by her mother:

> O, ask not of tomorrow
> Today is yet so beautiful
> Scatter in the valley all sorrow,
> Let it be blown by the wind![5]

1. "She can't marry within the family again"

* * *

Marie Valerie lacked her mother's arresting beauty that had been captured in the Empress's youth by court painter Franz Xaver Winterhalter; instead, Marie Valerie possessed a muted version of Elisabeth's dark eyes and shy smile. She also inherited her mother's tall frame and impossibly slim waist which she highlighted with tight corsetry, the aesthetic promoted so ardently by the Empress. According to a contemporary newspaper account, the Archduchess "is not a pretty woman, her features being too decidedly irregular for that, but she possesses a great charm of manner, and has her mother's willowy figure, slender feet, perfect hands and exquisite look of refinement and unequaled distinction."[6]

Marie Valerie's sister Gisela, older by 12 years, looked strikingly like her father, the Emperor, with piercing blue eyes and full cheeks and lips. Although neither young woman was considered beautiful by the day's standards, each did her best to imitate her mother's fashions and famous braided hairstyles with face-framing fringe.

As the church of Saint Nicholas and its enormous clock tower came into view, Marie Valerie attempted to comfort her mother, but there was no solace for the aging monarch, now in her 50s. Marie Valerie had been raised to feel responsible for her emotionally fragile mother's happiness and had done everything in her power to be a conscientious daughter. In fact, the night before the wedding Elisabeth had thrown her arms around Marie Valerie and whispered through her tears, "I thank you for always having been a good child to me." Marie Valerie wrote in her diary that this had been one of the most beautiful moments of her life.[7]

Elisabeth's emotional health had always been precarious at best, but the past year had been especially difficult because January marked the one-year anniversary of the suicide of her son, Crown Prince Rudolf. Subjects throughout the empire had observed the occasion, with commemorative services taking place in most parish churches. Marie Valerie, Gisela, and their mother had donned thick black crepe veils to obscure their grieving faces as they made their way to the memorial service at the village of Mayerling outside of Vienna, where Rudolf had been found dead the year before.

The Palace had tried to cover up the real reason behind the 30-year-old's death, but it soon came to light that Rudolf had shot and killed his teenage mistress, Mary Vetsera, and then himself in the head at his hunting lodge, leaving behind a wife, Crown Princess Stephanie, and young daughter, Archduchess Erzi. Marie Valerie had recorded the palace physician's description of the scene: "Girl stretched out in bed, hair loose over her shoulders, a rose between her folded hands—and Rudolf in a half-sitting position, the revolver on the ground, fallen from his stiffened hand, nothing but cognac in the glass. He laid down the corpse, long ago turned cold, the skull cracked, the bullet in one temple, out the other. Same wound in the girl. Both bullets found in the room."[8] According to Erzi's governess, a woman known only as May T., the five-year-old child was made to look upon her father's corpse, which had been laid out in the Hofburg. An artist had been brought in to mold a wax piece to disguise the disfigured side of Rudolf's face destroyed by his bullet. Erzi was overcome by the sight and cried, "That is not my father!"—a position the young Archduchess maintained up to the time May T. left her service, "some twelve years after the tragedy."[9]

Her son's death had plunged Empress Elisabeth into a depression far deeper than any Marie Valerie had seen her mother grapple with before, and Elisabeth became particularly cold and distant toward her granddaughter, Erzi. Doubtless, Elisabeth ignored Erzi on Marie Valerie's special day; the girl's presence was a direct reminder that Elisabeth had lost her only son, the monarchy's future, and now she was losing her favorite daughter just 18 months later.

Once the team of horses came to a halt outside the nearly 550-year-old church, Marie Valerie and her mother made their way gingerly down the carriage steps, under the double-eagle emblem that paid homage to Habsburg rule with the words *Pietate et Munificentia Caesar* and into the church narthex. Church bells and imposing pipe organ chords filled the air, played by Anton Bruckner, the composer Marie Valerie so admired and financially sponsored. Archduchess Erzi, now seven, led a procession of flower girls who formed a tiny honor guard to rain down flowers on the bride as she entered the church.

Relatives and close friends lined the pews, including Gisela and her four children, and Marie Valerie's court lady Clarissa, Countess Komis von Göncz-Ruszka, known affectionately as Zummel. Habsburg cousin Franz Ferdinand took his position—he would not become heir to the Austro-Hungarian throne until the death of his father six years in the future. Franz Salvator's mother, Marie Immaculata, smiled amiably from her station even though she had been admonished by Empress Elisabeth in no uncertain terms not to meddle in the young couple's new life. Elisabeth felt that her own mother-in-law, Archduchess Sophie, had come between herself and Franz Joseph early in their marriage, irreparably damaging their relationship. Elisabeth did not want the same for her favorite daughter.

1. "She can't marry within the family again"

In addition to family and friends, Marie Valerie had wanted to invite as many townspeople from Ischl and surrounding villages as could fill the church to show her appreciation for their support. Several hundred invitation cards had been distributed to commoners, allowing them to partake in this once-in-a-lifetime celebration.

The other imperial children, Gisela and Rudolf, had had truly royal weddings in Vienna's grand Augustinian Church with all of the proper court ceremonies observed and monarchs from throughout Europe present to witness the pomp. Such a show of courtly splendor was not what Marie Valerie desired for her wedding day. She had chosen the bucolic town of Ischl, nearly 270 kilometers away from the big city, very purposely. On this day, there would be no High Holy Mass for heads of state; just a simple blessing and sacrament.

Marie Valerie had sentimental memories of summers spent in the Kaiservilla at Ischl, the Neoclassical imperial home where her parents

The spa town of Bad Ischl at the foot of the Salzkammergut Mountains (author's collection).

14   Part I: *Verblassendes Reich*/Fading Empire, 1890–1924

The Kaiservilla at Bad Ischl, summer retreat of Franz Joseph (author's collection).

were engaged so many years ago. Marie Valerie cherished the town so much that she dreaded the inevitability that it would become the possession of Crown Prince Rudolf and his wife when the Emperor died. That possibility was "so terrible that I would like to put the beloved villa to the torch," she confided in her diary.[10] Elisabeth knew of her youngest daughter's love of the Kaiservilla and made sure that Marie Valerie, not Rudolf, would one day inherit the estate. Now that Rudolf was gone, the point was moot.

As she made her way into Saint Nicholas and observed the numerous relatives and villagers before her, Marie Valerie was delighted to spot her beloved English governess, Lady Mary Throckmorton. The matron's presence was a happy contrast to Elisabeth's despair, and Marie Valerie breathed easier as she walked purposely toward the altar where the Bishop of Linz (a man of no small girth made to look even larger in his voluminous robes) stood with her handsome, yet apprehensive groom.

Franz Salvator was a 24-year-old captain in the Seventh Regiment of Dragoons who was buttoned up in his formal high-collared uniform for the occasion. He cut a slim and serious figure, with hair neatly slicked and deeply parted on the side, a modest mustache framing his upper lip. He was boyishly handsome, just on the edge of maturity, and Marie Valerie had been taken with his gallant appearance and charmingly shy nature as

1. "She can't marry within the family again"

he grew into adulthood. And now, here he stood before her, ready to pledge his life and future.

This was the man for whom she had just a month before renounced her birthright to the Austro-Hungarian throne. The legal ceremony had taken place in the Hermés Villa, the exquisite palace in the Lainzer Tiergarten that had been built in 1881 as a gift from the Emperor to his beloved wife. A solemn Marie Valerie was photographed in her mother's apartments in a white gown with diaphanous draping at the neckline, long white gloves with diamond bracelets at each wrist, a double-strand of diamonds adorning her neck, and an intricate tiara topping her carefully braided coiffure. Clearly, this ceremony had been as significant as the wedding itself.

A Habsburg family law obliged her to sign the official documents "[t]o avoid dynastic quarrels and obviate the partition of the patrimonial property of the house of Austria.... By this engagement she undertakes not to raise for herself or for her descendants of either sex any pretensions to the eventual succession to the throne."[11] Since Rudolf was now gone, the Emperor's brother Karl Ludwig was the heir presumptive, and Marie Valerie's signature proved that she would never contest his place as next in line.

Yes, Marie Valerie was certain that Franz Salvator was the right man, and she had signed the papers to prove her love and commitment. Now it was time to make the union official in the eyes of God.

2

"Will she be a good little woman?"

—Archduke Franz Salvator

While making her tearful goodbyes following the splendor of the day, Marie Valerie's new husband helped her into the honeymoon carriage draped with colorful alpine roses and forget-me-nots. The team of horses, sporting floral wreaths around their strong necks, pulled away from the Kaiservilla and toward the quiet lake town of Offensee some 24 kilometers away.

Once they left behind the cheering crowds at the bridge leading out of Ischl, Marie Valerie found herself alone with her husband for the very first time. The trip would take several hours by coach, and her nerves began to overwhelm her. But Franz Salvator gently took her hand and "spoke tenderly to me until I gradually felt myself calmed in the knowledge of our deep happiness."[1]

Hours later, as the imperial hunting lodge in Offensee finally came into view, the bridal couple were met with still more flags and wreaths. Marie Valerie was undoubtedly exhausted from the wedding ceremony and long drive, yet she immediately sat down to write her mother a letter to be carried back to Ischl by the returning coachman. Even now as a married woman, Marie Valerie would think first and foremost of her mother, Elisabeth.

Once this obligation was complete, Marie Valerie stole herself to inspect the honeymoon suite. To her surprise, it wasn't decorated with masculine leather and pine like the rest of the lodge; instead it had been "all draped in pink, the beds beneath a pink-colored sky and pink blankets, as well as the curtains and the [prayer] hassock between the windows."[2]

And if there were any doubt as to the purpose of this pink bedroom that had been appointed to appeal directly to the bride's aesthetic tastes, on the dresser stood a picture of a stork carrying a baby.

* * *

Consciously, Marie Valerie would do all in her power to stave off the inevitable wedding night. She and Franz dined alone, then took a long walk along the lake, and she described in her diary feeling a sense of dread that grew stronger as the night lengthened. Marie Valerie had desired to linger by the lake to observe the romantic moonrise, but Franz felt that it would take too long, so they finally made their way arm-in-arm back to the lodge.

The new couple sat in silence for some time until Franz asked, "Will she be a good little woman?"[3] Perhaps he hoped that speaking to her in the third person would lessen the impact of the deed she was now obliged to perform.

The couple took their leave to the pink bedroom and knelt next to one another on the hassock to say their evening prayers, but Marie Valerie was feeling far from collected. In her diary, she described the supplication as "heart-felt, thankful and also slightly agitated…. I shed a few tears again on his breast in unspeakable trepidation."[4]

Marie Valerie then gazed "into his deep clear eyes" and was "enfolded by" his soul. Not taking into account his military service and the sexual education it often afforded high-born young men, Marie Valerie believed she was "the first woman he has ever touched," and asked God then and there to help her with the great responsibility she had been given to safeguard his happiness and "pure soul."[5]

* * *

Marie Valerie hadn't been obliged to marry. She fancied herself a writer, like her mother, and penned a drama titled *Ein Goldstuck* that an American paper reported in 1891 would be "presented shortly."[6] She was also a musician who had "composed a number of pretty songs."[7] Not marrying would have been unconventional for an Austrian Archduchess, but not completely out of the question given her mother's poor opinion of the institution. Elisabeth had raised Marie Valerie with her liberal views on what constituted a woman's role, and undoubtedly wished her daughter a very different life than one of traditional wife and mother.

Marie Valerie had considered her options carefully when deciding whether to marry Franz Salvator, but ultimately chose the conventional route in keeping with her deep Catholic faith. She wrote in her diary, "then I saw that I must choose between woman and artist—on the one hand,

A young Marie Valerie dressed for a costume ball (author's collection).

inclination and a sense of vocation, on the other hand, the recognition of my inability made the choice an easy one ... more in line with Papa's sensibility.... My struggle is no longer for greatness but only toward the ideal of a true woman—a German woman with heart and mind, edu-

2. "Will she be a good little woman?"

cation and soul."[8] By calling herself "a German woman" in her diary, Marie Valerie was confirming her German Nationalistic tendencies. She would grow to see herself as Germanic first and a member of the ethnically-diverse Austro-Hungarian Empire only second.

* * *

Marie Valerie was born in Hungary on April 22, 1868, just ten months after her parents were crowned the country's King and Queen. The coronation had come about thanks to the Austro-Hungarian Compromise that Elisabeth had promoted fervently.

Franz Salvator in his dress officer's uniform (author's collection).

The Empress, originally from Bavaria, never felt at home in protocol-conscious Vienna and fell fanatically in love with the struggles of the Hungarian people, most likely in a bid to spite her controlling mother-in-law who never liked or trusted Hungary's ethnic Magyars. Elisabeth collaborated with radical Hungarian reformer Count Gyula Andrássy, and convinced Emperor Franz Joseph to give Hungary special rights within the Empire that included dual capitals of Vienna and Buda. Franz Joseph had gone against his advisors and his better judgment, and had acquiesced to his wife's wishes. His reward was a return to the marital bed, which had been all but abandoned, and the birth of Marie Valerie. The child's arrival sparked initial rumors that Andrássy was the true father, rumors that always greatly disturbed Marie Valerie, but nothing of the sort was ever proven. Marie Valerie would grow to hate Andrássy and her mother's fanaticism toward Hungary: "I held out my hand to [Andrássy] with great brusqueness," a teenaged Marie Valerie wrote in her diary. "His detestable familiarity makes me so sick that almost involuntarily my voice turns cold, almost scornful.... Surely he hates me as much as I do him, at least I hope so."[9]

* * *

November 4, 1868

Empress Elisabeth sat stiffly at her desk in her lavender writing room of the royal Hungarian palace of Gödöllő. The Hungarian people had gifted her the 100-room manor now that she was their crusader and Queen. Little Marie Valerie had been born seven months earlier at the Hungarian palace where no royal child had been born for generations. The decision to give birth to her child here was Elisabeth's statement that she favored Hungary over any other part of the Empire, especially Vienna. She desired for her new daughter to be raised a Hungarian, speaking the language and observing the traditions. Marie Valerie became known as "The Hungarian Child" and "The Only Child" by the royal courtiers who saw how obviously Elisabeth favored this baby over her other children, Gisela, 12, and Rudolf, nine. Those two and another daughter, Sophie, who died as a toddler, had been spirited away from their young mother at birth and raised by Elisabeth's mother-in-law, Archduchess Sophie. Elisabeth, now in her 30s, refused to let that happen again, and kept the new child continuously by her side.

In just a few weeks' time, the Hungarian people would celebrate their Queen's name day with a music-filled torch lit procession along the Danube River and across the Chain Bridge leading from Buda into Pest. But before the celebrations, Elisabeth had work to attend to. She had to find the perfect governess for her new child.

Elisabeth's sister, Queen Marie of Naples, had recommended an English governess by the name of Lady Mary Throckmorton. Queen Marie knew of Mary through

Empress Elisabeth of Austria and Queen of Hungary at the height of her beauty. She was 29 years old when she posed for painter George Raab in 1867 in full Hungarian coronation regalia. Marie Valerie was born just ten months after the coronation (author's collection).

the noblewoman's maternal grandfather, Sir John Acton, 6th Baronet, who had been commander of the Neapolitan Navy. English governesses were considered to be the best in the world among 19th-century European royals who looked for "a gentlewoman, accustomed to good society, conscientious and reliable"[10] to handle all aspects of childrearing. English governesses were also known to take a more liberal view of girls' education, which must have appealed to Elisabeth's progressive values, values that were shared by many royal European mothers. Of her search for a governess for her five daughters in the 1870s, Alice, Hereditary Grand Duchess of Hesse, wrote to her mother, Queen Victoria, "You say rightly, what a fault it is of parents to bring up their daughters with the main object of marrying them. I want to strive to bring up the girls without seeking this as the sole object for their future—to feel they can fill up their lives so well otherwise."[11]

In choosing Mary Throckmorton, Elisabeth was relying on her sister's word-of-mouth alone. Without even so much as an interview, she dipped her pen lightly in ink and composed a letter in English on imperial letterhead offering Lady Mary the job:

Dear Miss Throckmorton,

Through my sister the queen, who is one of your warmest admirers, I ... heard so much of you, that ever since dear baby is born, I had but the one wish, that I might be so happy, as to see you take charge of her education. Have I any chance of seeing this, my fondest wish, once fulfilled? She is such a lovable little creature, that I trust you would not repent devoting her your life. As she will be 12 months in April, I thought in case you are inclined to comply with my request, this would be the best time for your coming. At this age children begin to attach themselves already.... Pardon me, Dear Miss Throckmorton, for intruding so on you, and treating you already as quite an old acquaintance. With eager anxiety I am looking forward to your answer. May it please to be a good one for me and my beloved little Valerie.... I am, dear Miss Throckmorton, with sincere sympathy,
Yours
Elisabeth[12]

Marie Valerie would, indeed, attach herself to the governess in a relationship that would last a lifetime.

Mary Elizabeth Throckmorton was born at the grand Georgian home of Buckland House in Berkshire in 1832 to Sir Robert George Throckmorton and Elizabeth Acton. Noblewomen like Mary who chose not to wed were in great demand as governesses for royal children because they possessed the good breeding and education in reading, languages, manners and music that royal mothers desired. Yet, despite their professional allure, English governesses were still known in their home countries by the early 19th-century terminology for unmarried women: spinster.[13]

The 36-year-old Mary was officially hired as Lady-in-Waiting to Elisabeth, and was issued royal documents proclaiming her new position with the Austrian Crown. The formal papers stipulated her salary at 630 Gulden per year (approximately $7,000 in today's U.S. dollars), plus her own apartment in Vienna's Hofburg Palace, although she would spend most of her time raising Marie Valerie at Gödöllő Palace in Hungary. As May T., the governess to Rudolf's child Erzi, would write, "truly 'tis more glory than gold one earns by serving Royalty."[14]

The first place that Lady Throckmorton and her imperial charge, Marie Valerie, would meet, however, was at Bad Ischl in June 1869. Elisabeth wrote that the family would be at the Kaiservilla beginning in May, and bade Mary to meet them there.

"The house there is very simple," Elisabeth wrote. "Baby has cut four teeth and is weaned this week."[15]

As a child, when Marie Valerie was traveling with her mother and separated from Lady Mary, the girl sent thoughtful telegrams to her governess. One telegram from 1874 wished Mary happiness on her birthday, while another in 1876 gave best wishes for Mary's name day.

As a child, Marie Valerie loved to draw and created numerous pictures of people, flowers and animals for Mary Throckmorton, whom she called her "Aunt Minny."[16] When she was 12 years old, Marie Valerie put pen to paper to sketch a picture of her gray Angora cat, Minet, for her governess.

Much of Marie Valerie's childhood was conventional for an Archduchess who was taught to serve her people. At this stage in her young life, her "people" were the Empire's children. According to her Hungarian tutor at Gödöllő, "In the evenings they played blind man's bluff at the desire of Marie Valerie, then they got busy again, colouring and cutting out figures for the picture book the kind-hearted princess wanted to give to the little patients in the children's hospital."[17] When riding in her open carriage, Marie Valerie would throw candy to children along the route, and if she ran out of supplies before each child received a treat, Marie Valerie would beg her attendant for coins to throw instead. She also enjoyed ice skating at the palace in the winter and had a best friend with whom to share the fun: "In a corner of the upper garden an artificial skating rink was set up, where the princess and her close friend, Duchess Aglája Auersperg would skate happily all day long."[18]

Marie Valerie used the French spelling, *Aglaë*, when referring to her good friend, who was regarded as a sort of adopted sister. Aglaë was born the same year as Marie Valerie to the aristocratic Auersperg family, and was considered "among the great beauties of the highest Austrian nobility." According to *The Illustrated American*, the Auerspergs owned vast estates in Prague and the family was "one of the oldest in the empire, and the heads of it have been hereditary grand marshals of Carinthia [southernmost Austria] ever since 1463."[19] Photos of the two girls portray them forehead to forehead with matching high-collared dresses and braids. Court rumors swirled that once she became a teenager, the beautiful Aglaë caught the eye of Marie Valerie's brother, Crown Prince Rudolf, who was then married to Princess Stephanie of Belgium. Marie Valerie's best friend then had to be banished from court in order to avert a scandal. There is no solid evidence to prove this story, and Aglaë went on to marry Count Ferdinand Kinsky and have seven children. She named one child Marie Valerie and another, Rudolf.

* * *

From the moment of her birth, Marie Valerie was coddled and fussed over by her mother to an extent that alarmed Empress Elisabeth's attendants. Now that she had helped achieve Hungarian independence, Elisabeth channeled her once political fanaticism toward her youngest child. Elisabeth's lady-in-waiting Countess Marie Festetics wrote, "There is no moderation in her, and she suffers from this ecstasy rather than gaining happiness from it—a trembling fear for [Valerie's] health, then again the feeling that attempts were being made to turn the little girl against her."[20]

Marie Valerie began keeping a diary when she was nearing eight years old. On May 12, 1878, the ten-year-old child decided to take her journaling seriously. "I said to Botz [one of the archduchess's governesses] in passing today: 'Botz—I will always write in my diary the good and bad things I do just like Marguerite' ... and that's what I'm doing! Marguerite is not a real child or at least I don't know her, but I am reading a book that is called: 'Le journal de Marguerit' and she writes the way I am going to write from now on."[21]

Marie Valerie had a favorite large wax doll given to her by her mother that Marie Valerie named Feri. Feri was said to resemble a four-year-old boy, and the Archduchess wrote about him as a brother. "I have a small brother Feri and another brother Rudolf then a sister Gisela there are four of us in total. we [sic] love each other very much," she wrote in a child's hand.[22]

Marie Valerie was a sensitive and perceptive child and soon grew to realize that her mother's happiness depended on her actions. She also saw how her mother's suffocating love alienated her from her real brother and sister. Rudolf, who was starved for his mother's attention, grew outwardly hostile toward his younger sister. Marie Valerie felt further ostracized from her family because Elisabeth only allowed her to speak and correspond in Hungarian. The Archduchess once begged her father, whom she adored, to speak German with her so she could feel close to him. Of her mother, Marie Valerie said, "her unbridled love and exaggerated, groundless concern place me in such an embarrassing and false position."[23]

Empress Elisabeth loved to provoke, and used her youngest daughter to shock the stodgy Viennese court. When Marie Valerie was small, Elisabeth bought a monkey with the intent to make it Marie Valerie's playmate. The macaque frightened the courtiers, which no doubt thrilled Elisabeth. Soon, however, the Empress's "monkey passion"[24] would give way to a more pitiable figure in Marie Valerie's life: a disabled African man, small in stature, named Rustimo. The Shah of Persia had "gifted" Rustimo (referred to then as a "blackamoor") to the Empress, and a delighted Elisabeth endeavored to make him Marie Valerie's new playmate. Marie Valerie "was afraid of him and took some time to grow accustomed to him, while the whole household was up in arms, the tutors, masters, and ladies in waiting refusing to ride in the same carriage with him or have anything to do with him."[25] To the hyper class-conscious Viennese, the dark-skinned boy was less than human. A photo taken at the time shows a tense Marie Valerie, about seven years old, playing checkers with the boy in Austrian dress, whose boots hover several inches above the ground.

Marie Valerie mentions Rustimo just once in her published diary as she recounted her daily schedule: "Get up between 7:30 and 8, breakfast, the bishop comes at 9 o'clock, [history tutor Dr. Karl Ferdinand Kummer] on other days, from 10 till 11 I speak French, at 11 I study either with Kummer or the bishop. At 12 o'clock I dress to go out or if we do not go out, then I have free time for my diary or 'Le journal de Marguerite' or whatever, preferably, I act out something like 'Bürgschaft' or 'Count of Habsburg' both by Schiller. At 2 o'clock I have half an hour or arithmetic, at 3 o'clock we dine, then I speak English until around 5:30, then it is a piano lesson, then it is English or French reading. At 6:30 … we have a dancing lesson until 7 which is supper and then [board games] with Rustimo. Papa comes from 7:30 till 8. Then I go to bed."[26]

To quell the outrage of allowing her daughter to fraternize with a "heathen," Elisabeth eventually had Rustimo baptized as a Christian. Elisabeth wrote a mocking account of the occasion to her mother, Princess Ludovika of Bavaria: "Today was Rustimo's christening in Valerie's salon…. Rudolf was godfather. It was solemn and ludicrous, there were tears and laughter."[27] For posterity, Elisabeth had a stately photo taken of Rustimo with Crown Prince Rudolf.

By the time of Marie Valerie's wedding in 1890, Rustimo had fallen out of favor with the Empress and was dispatched to a charity institution over a hundred kilometers away in Ybbs. By 1892, Marie Valerie's former playmate—and Empress Elisabeth's dupe—had died of unknown causes.

* * *

As a child, Marie Valerie never witnessed a properly-functioning, healthy family unit. She wrote in her diary, "O dear God, how sad is our family life, which seems so wonderful to outsiders.... Encounters with my parents made up of small but unbelievably irritating embarrassments—Mama constantly tells me her troubles. And I no longer look at Papa with eyes of fervent admiration."[28]

As her parents' estrangement deepened and the feuds intensified, chatter was common among the staff. One morning, Mary Throckmorton asked Elisabeth's lady-in-waiting Marie Festetics whether her "night's rest had not been disrupted?" Marie asked why Mary wanted to know, and "with a sweet-sour expression, she told me that Their Imperial and Royal Majesties had quarreled, and the Empress would not open the door to him and barricaded *le passage*!"[29] Such gossip galled Marie Festetics, who was devoutly loyal to Elisabeth and had no patience for court intrigue.

In addition to the frosty family relations, Empress Elisabeth kept Marie Valerie from Vienna where she might bond with her brother and sister. "The Hungarian Child" couldn't bring herself to resent her mother; instead she turned her anger toward the country of Hungary itself for keeping her family apart. On special occasions like Christmas when she was reunited with her entire family, Marie Valerie found the time spent to be awkward and uncomfortable—they were a family of strangers who hardly knew what to say to one another. Perhaps this is why Marie Valerie formed such a tight bond with her English governess who devoted her time and efforts to developing the young Archduchess's mind and spirit.

After Marie Valerie reached maturity and her governess's services were no longer required, Lady Mary Throckmorton would continue to visit court and write letters back and forth to her Archduchess. Two days after Christmas 1888, a now adult Marie Valerie sent a joyous telegram to England: "I am happy to tell you that I am engaged to the Archduke Francis Salvator."[30]

3

"Everything is good, terribly good"

—Archduchess Marie Valerie

For a growing Marie Valerie, summer days spent at Ischl meant visits by the large Tuscan branch of the House of Habsburg Lorraine. Archduke Karl Salvator and his wife, Princess Maria Immaculata of Bourbon-Two Sicilies, had 11 children. Archduke Franz Salvator was third-born and second son behind his older brother, Leopold Salvator, with whom he would remain close throughout his life. At Ischl, the Austrian and Tuscan cousins romped through the Imperial Park and down the wooded sloping hills to the river, before returning pink-cheeked and grass-stained to the Kaiservilla.

The Tuscan Habsburgs came about thanks to legendary Austrian Empress Maria Theresa, the only woman ever to rule Habsburg lands. Her forward-thinking father, Holy Roman Emperor Charles VI, had passed the Pragmatic Sanction of 1713, allowing Habsburg rule to continue through his future daughters if he had no sons. The Sanction would lead to great conflict and even war within the Empire, whose people were not quite ready to be ruled by a woman. But it would ultimately prevail and save the Habsburg dynasty from dying out; Maria Theresa was born at the Vienna Hofburg in 1717, six months after the death of an older brother, Archduke Leopold John, who had lived just seven months.

At the age of 18, Maria Theresa married Francis Stephen of Lorraine who became hereditary grand duke of Tuscany in 1737. Thus, the house of Habsburg-Lorraine was born, but the Tuscan branch would remain distinct from the imperial line in Vienna. Maria Theresa ascended to the Habsburg throne upon her father's death in 1740 and would go on to successfully rule for 40 years while giving birth to 16 children (one of whom became the ill-fated Queen Marie Antoinette of France).

As the Habsburg cousins passed through their childhood years on the way to maturity, Franz Salvator began to take particular notice of his imperial cousin, Marie Valerie.

* * *

January 28, 1886

Strains of Johann Strauss's *Zigeunerbaron-Quadrille*—debuted by the Strauss Orchestra for the Imperial Court Ball and conducted by the master's brother, Eduard—filled the Hofburg Throne Room. Some 2,000 invited guests crowded the parquet dance floor between Corinthian *stucco lustrous* pillars and beneath dozens of exquisite crystal chandeliers. The sovereign Habsburg family, including Marie Valerie and her mother, the Empress, had made its glamorous entrance around 9:30 p.m. Emperor Franz Josef considered the social occasion to be "a rather arduous pleasure" since he would be expected to exchange pleasantries with the crushing number of very important guests.[1] The reticent Empress usually chose to avoid such overwhelming social occasions, but had taken up a renewed interest now that 18-year-old Marie Valerie had begun attracting suitors.

In attendance were the population's highest-ranking politicians and church leaders, along with officers of the Vienna garrison. The aristocratic young ladies present, attired in their finest Worth gowns and heirloom jewelry, looked forward to participating in the *Cercle*, when they would vie to be introduced to the Empress herself. Until they were properly presented to the monarch, they would not be permitted to make their official debut to aristocratic society. But Elisabeth didn't make it easy for them; she was known for barely opening her mouth when she spoke, possibly due to extreme shyness or in a bid to hide the less-than-perfect teeth over which she felt extremely self-conscious. Thus, even brief conversations with the Empress, could be "slow and awkward."[2]

Also among the distinguished throng were the Tuscan Habsburg cousins. Franz Salvator, undoubtedly wearing his crisp officer's uniform, timidly approached Marie Valerie, kissed her gloved hand, and led her to the center of the crowded floor to dance the stately quadrille in 2/4 time. Empress Elisabeth intently observed the encounter, dissecting the couple's body language, and later told her daughter, "I have a sort of inkling that one day Franz Salvator will be your husband."[3]

* * *

Throughout 1886, Franz Salvator and his elder brother Leopold continued to visit Marie Valerie and her good friend and cousin, Princess Maria Teresa of Bourbon-Sicily, called Mädi. In Marie Valerie's diary entry for October 12, she wrote of Mädi rejecting Leopold's advances, "as he is her cousin, even if rather nice."[4] Despite using this excuse herself, Mädi encouraged Marie Valerie's relationship with Franz Salvator, calling the Crown Prince of Saxony (one of Emperor Franz Joseph's choices for his daughter) "horrible ... and thinks he only would marry the Emperor's daughter."[5]

Elisabeth also encouraged the relationship with Franz Salvator. She sent 50 bottles of Bordeaux and a "whole load of hearty plate-things" to Göding in southern Austria where Franz Salvator was living with his army regiment. Marie Valerie was afraid that such overtures might "awaken hopes" in him that she could not fulfill. On November 3, as she continued to wrestle with her feelings, she alluded to receiving a disturbing letter from Franz Salvator's mother, Maria Immaculata.

"So a mother's heart does beat in Arco [the township near Lake Garda that was home to the Tuscan family]," Marie Valerie wrote in her diary, "one which mistrusts me as it feels everything that has happened simply served as my amusement for the summer, I merely toyed with her son and could destroy his life's happiness which the dear God appears to have laid in my hands.... Was I really playing games with Franz? God knows I didn't intend to."[6]

December 6, 1886

The Empress would work to solidify the budding relationship by arranging a serendipitous meeting of the young couple at the Burgtheater, where the Austrian National Theater was staging a production. Franz Salvator had been too reticent to visit Marie Valerie and her mother in the red-and-gold imperial box the night before. During the Monday night performance at approximately ten minutes after seven p.m., Marie Valerie and her mother left their private seating to tiptoe down the red carpet to the room occupied by Franz Salvator. Thoroughly enjoying the intrigue, Empress Elisabeth slipped through the restricted archway and slowly cracked the door. There sat Franz Salvator, alone in the corner, startled by the intruders. He did not recognize the Empress at first. She beckoned him with her index finger, whispering softly, "Come." The confused officer, now catching a glimpse of Marie Valerie behind her mother, jumped to attention and greeted his imperial aunt. After a brief chat, Elisabeth turned the attention to her daughter, with whom Franz Salvator had been avoiding eye contact.

"Isn't that right? Valerie has grown?" Elisabeth asked.

"Yes, grown some more," Franz Salvator answered, finally acknowledging Marie Valerie. The Archduchess wrote in her diary that he had "such a blissful expression that my heart leaps up and I feel that everything is good, terribly good."[7]

* * *

It would take two more years for the couple to become formally engaged, much to the disapproval of Marie Valerie's brother, Crown Prince Rudolf. The troubled Crown Prince had been married himself for the past seven years to Princess Stephanie of Belgium. Stephanie had been 15 when Rudolf had proposed, not for love, but because she was one of the few Catholic princesses available in Europe and he found her tolerable. The wedding had to be postponed a year when it was discovered that Stephanie had not yet reached puberty.

His marriage was not a happy one, but it was a dynastic match, and Rudolf believed that his sister should also marry in keeping with her station instead of joining with what he saw as a practically impoverished and insignificant cousin.

Neither Elisabeth nor Marie Valerie were fond of Stephanie. The Empress called her a "mighty bumpkin" and made fun of her "long, fake tresses" and "cunningly watchful eyes."[8] Marie Valerie found Stephanie tedious, and made it her goal to become a very different wife than her sister-in-law.

"Stephanie is actually not very nice and her love for Rudolf is more than love and not particularly pleasant," she wrote in her diary. "She says everything he says without any independent thoughts or desires."[9]

Stephanie was known to be vain, ultra-conservative, and to love the pomp of her new position as Crown Princess and future Empress of Austria. Rudolf was a liberal intellectual like his mother, who had written academic books and anonymous political newspaper articles questioning the future of the Habsburg monarchy. He was interested in Europe's destiny, not in celebrating the old guard. After his only child, Erzi, was born in 1883, Rudolf turned away from his wife, patronized a plethora of courtesans, contracted a sexually transmitted disease which he passed on to Stephanie rendering her sterile, and became dependent on alcohol and painkillers to quell his physical and emotional pain. He reportedly petitioned the Pope to seek an annulment of his marriage, but the process was stopped in its tracks by the Emperor. Seeing no way out of his misery, an ailing and addicted Rudolf began to entertain thoughts of suicide. Just over a year after Marie Valerie announced her engagement to Franz Salvator, Rudolf died at his own hand, leaving the Austro-Hungarian succession in question.

After Rudolf's death, his wife and daughter would continue to be tolerated by the royal family, even though Empress Elisabeth directly blamed her daughter-in-law for Rudolf's suicide.

Marie Valerie recorded in her diary that Crown Princess Stephanie "kept asking all of us again and again for forgiveness, for she must surely have felt that her lack of devotion contributed to driving Rudolf to this horror."[10]

Elisabeth told Marie Valerie "she was ashamed of [Stephanie] before the people. If one comes to know this woman properly, one must excuse Rudolf for looking elsewhere for distraction and a narcotic to ease the emptiness of the heart in his own home. It is certain: Things would have been otherwise had he had a different wife, one who understood him."

Marie Valerie recorded an incident in which Elisabeth confronted Stephanie directly, with great vitriol: "You hated your father, you did not love your husband, and you do not love your daughter!"[11]

Stephanie's entire future would be marred by Rudolf's actions, which left her in limbo; she was still the mother of a Habsburg Crown Prince's daughter, which entitled them to certain imperial rights, but salic law did not permit the girl to inherit the throne. Mother and daughter would continue to live in Viennese splendor at the Hofburg, but Empress Elisabeth would all but avoid and ignore them for the remainder of her life.

Unbeknownst to her, however, Stephanie had a namesake in Vienna who would find a way to break free from convention in a way that Vienna's court constraints would never allow the Crown Princess. By the time of Rudolf's death in 1889, a young girl by the name of Stephanie Maria Veronika Juliana Richter, a product of middle-class Jewish parents who named their daughter after Crown Princess Stephanie, was just beginning to learn how to use her charm and wit to manipulate people—people who would one day include the Habsburgs, members of the English aristocracy, and the highest-ranking German politicians.

4

"I could only think, when a man was talking"

—Princess Stephanie von Hohenlohe

Gmunden, Austria, 1905

Just north of Bad Ischl, where Marie Valerie had married 15 years earlier, lay the spa town of Gmunden on Lake Traunsee. The town was part of the Salzkammergut area that housed the prized Habsburg salt mines and countless briny therapeutic baths. As they did every year when the weather turned sultry, the hard-working people of Vienna and surrounding areas congregated in the leisurely town for a much-needed summer respite. Among the holiday goers were 14-year-old Stephanie Richter and her family.

Stephanie had been born in Vienna in 1891, the product of an affair between her mother Ludmilla, a Jewish woman from Prague, and a rather poor Jewish money lender named Max Wiener. Ludmilla's husband, lawyer Johannes Hans Richter, called Hans, was serving seven months in prison for embezzlement when Stephanie was conceived outside the marriage. Despite realizing that he wasn't the child's father, Hans agreed to raise Stephanie as his own upon his release, and may have been compensated by Max Wiener to do so. Stephanie was reared a Catholic in keeping with Hans Richter's Moravian Catholic background; Ludmilla had converted to the faith from Judaism when she married Hans.

Although she never conceded to being of Jewish descent or publicly acknowledged Max Wiener as her true father, Stephanie would honor both Hans and Max, along with the Austrian Emperor and Crown Prince Rudolf, when one day naming her own son: Franz Joseph Rudolf Hans Weriand Max Stefan Anton von Hohenlohe-Waldenburg-Schillingsfürst.

Once his affair with Ludmilla was over, Max Wiener had married another woman and they had a daughter, Regina, who would become a writer and change her name to Gina Kaus. In the 1920s and 30s, Kaus wrote plays and novels. But unlike her half-sister Stephanie, Kaus would feel the full force of the future Nazi regime that Stephanie would help promote; in March 1938, Gina and her family fled Austria on the same day as the *Anschluss*, when Hitler's Third Reich annexed Austria. The Nazis would go on to burn Kaus's books, along with works by other prominent Jewish thinkers and subversives.

Gina Kaus kept up with Stephanie for a time, but did not speak highly of her half-sister's interest in powerful men, writing, "I've always had a certain interest in my half-sister Steffi, who was ... a whore working in the highest circles. Back then she had a whole circle of the highest-paid women who were primarily occupied with high nobles, and she made me a fine offer. I declined and that was the end of our acquaintance."[1]

A prominent Viennese doctor, Hans Simon, seemed to back up Gina Kaus' claim that her sister Stephanie took money for escorting prominent men. In 1941, Dr. Simon presented the U.S. Immigration and Naturalization Service with information about Stephanie, who was under surveillance due to her dealings with Adolf Hitler. John T. Seely with the department's Special Inspection Division typed the words, "As regards her earlier career, Dr. Simon tells us that she was known as Stephanie Richter, who had been a common prostitute who more or less [before World War I] specialized in political clients."[2]

Gina never forgot her half-sister and the privileged life Stephanie continued to lead in Europe, while Gina was forced to flee the Nazis and start over. After exile in Switzerland and Paris, Kaus found her way to Hollywood via Ellis Island, where she wrote an anti–Hitler comedy for Columbia Pictures, *The Wife Takes a Flyer*. One of the characters is referred to as having a "Mata Hari" personality, after the Dutch woman who was executed for spying for Germany during World War I. Mata Hari was also a name that would be used to describe Stephanie von Hohenlohe through her work with the Nazis.

But in 1905, Stephanie was still a diminutive, curvy teenager, about 5'5" with sable hair, pronounced eyebrows framing large, deep-set blue eyes, and a prominent nose that created a distinguished Grecian profile. Many years later, a Prague newspaper would describe her as without "any noblesse in her features."[3] Her looks were the least of her charms; she had a star quality about her that attracted plenty of male attention when she performed graceful ice routines at the skating club back home in Vienna. That charisma became even more evident on a sweltering summer day in Gmunden.

4. "I could only think, when a man was talking"

Looking for a diversion from the swimming, horseback riding, and tennis matches that had filled her summer days, Stephanie entered the town's annual beauty contest. She carefully combed out her hair, donned the best outfit she had brought along on holiday, and took her place in a line of fair-haired youths with classic Germanic features. When it was her turn to parade in front of the judges, Stephanie's smile, and especially her laugh, which at least one future admirer said should be bottled and sold, attracted all attention away from any other contestant. Stephanie's undeniable charisma and grace won the day, and she was crowned a beauty queen.

Stephanie's confidence soared on that day, and she determined that she would make something of her life in the upper echelon of society. Her mother must have spotted the potential in her teenaged daughter and gave her every opportunity to excel. She sent Stephanie to the south of England to study language and culture, gave her piano lessons at the Vienna Conservatoire, and enrolled her in ballet lessons at the Vienna Court Opera school of dance.

By the age of 15, Stephanie had made it her goal to one day marry a prince, despite the fact that it was nearly unheard of for a Viennese Jewish girl to cross over the closely guarded socio-economic boundaries. She was no romantic; rather, Stephanie was pragmatic, and made it her mission to obtain a title one way or another. Stephanie received some invaluable help toward her goal from a member of the nobility who also happened to be one of Hans Richter's legal clients: Princess Franziska (Fanny) von Metternich, a relative of revered Austrian politician and statesman Prince Klemens von Metternich. Stephanie referred to the widowed princess as "The Grande Dame," and the teenager absorbed the aristocrat's lessons on social graces. Princess Fanny most likely did not know that Stephanie was Jewish, a fact that could easily have tainted her altruistic attitude toward her protégé in early 20th-century Vienna. And Stephanie, for her part, wasn't telling.

Stephanie described Hans Richter as a devoted father, but while she was still a teenager, the increasingly religious and sickly Hans withdrew from the family and became a lay-brother with the Catholic Brothers of Charity. Now no longer benefitting from an attorney's salary, the family found themselves in dire financial straits. Family members were still permitted to call on Hans at the order, but the visits weren't always pleasant. Hans once asked Stephanie to leave because he was upset by the "worldly" sound of rustling taffeta caused by her skirt.[4] Stephanie essentially no longer had paternal emotional support or financial stability, and began to seek it out in other men.

* * *

Under the auspices of Princess Fanny, the teenaged Stephanie Richter threw herself into Viennese society where she "flirted outrageously with all the eligible young men."[5] Stephanie learned how to hone her charm and skills at flattering those in power and soon caught the eye of a Polish nobleman named Count Josef Gizycki. Gizycki was a handsome, abusive womanizer who had recently undergone a tumultuous divorce and custody battle with Eleanor Medill Patterson, granddaughter of American newspaper magnate Joseph Medill. The split had been so fierce that even U.S. President William Howard Taft and Russia's Tsar Nicholas II became involved in solving the custody dispute after the Count kidnapped his own daughter. The Count was also three times Stephanie's age, and she wisely refused his proposal of marriage. His courtship was followed by those of a string of privileged older men, but Stephanie always turned them down.

Stephanie saw her personal financial status blossom at this time thanks to the charity of her millionaire uncle, Robert Kuranda. He had made his fortune in South Africa by "commandeering goods, horses and equipment,"[6] and generously shared the spoils with his family members back in Vienna. Stephanie, now a shrewd young woman, managed to invest her money wisely and put the family back on a course of prosperity. She took advantage of the high life by traveling extensively with her Aunt Clothilde, who took Stephanie on a tour of Europe where the industrious young woman became adept at languages, culture, and ingratiating herself into society.

Even though she was growing into an independent woman with her own money and connections, Stephanie would forever define herself by the powerful men whose company she loved to keep. These men fascinated her and attracted her so completely that she would one day write, "I came to the conclusion that apparently I could only think, when a man was talking."[7]

Around 1911, Stephanie met one of the most powerful men in all of Austria. He was a member of the ancient Habsburg Dynasty and son-in-law to the Emperor himself. Archduke Franz Salvator was 45 years old and the father of nine children. His tenth, a baby girl, had died that same year following a difficult birth. Stephanie was 20 when they met, but she told Franz Salvator that she was still a teenager.

5

"Are we not the same as all other Germans?"

—Adolf Hitler

April 20, 1889

Shortly after Crown Prince Rudolf's death, while the Habsburgs mourned his loss and contemplated the future of the throne, a baby boy entered the world in the Upper Austrian border town of Braunau on the Inn. At 6:30 p.m., just above the pub in a small lodge where his parents had rented a suite of rooms, the child's mother Klara held the baby close against her for the very first time. Mother and child would soon share the same hypnotic blue eyes that people commented seemed "to bore through them."[1]

The location of the boy's birthplace, across the border from Germany, would become monumentally important to his future world views. As a small child, he could make out the Bavarian town of Simbach just over the bridge spanning the Inn River. At some point in history, someone had declared that this river separated Austria from Germany, but the boy wanted to know why. Both peoples spoke the same mother tongue: German. And yet, they remained two different countries.

"Are we not the same as all other Germans?" he would ask. "Do we not all belong together?"[2]

The boy's mother, Klara Poelzl, was the third wife of Alois, a minor civil servant who was 23 years her senior. Alois had been born illegitimately and baptized Schicklgruber after his mother. He worked for the customs service and took Klara, who was his second cousin, in as a foster daughter to help care for his ailing first wife. While Klara managed the household, Alois took up with a hotel cook, eventually separated from his first wife, Anna, and married the cook when Anna finally died. After his second wife eventually left him and then died herself from tuberculosis, Alois married his young foster daughter, Klara. They would apply for and receive a dispensation from the local bishop to marry due to their close blood relation.

But Alois would not pass on his baptized name of Schicklgruber to his new young wife. When he had been in his 40s, an astonishing thing had happened. A man claiming to be his real father testified to the fact before a notary and in the presence of witnesses. The man was 84 years old, and there is no record of why he finally came forward to claim his adult son after so many years. But on November 23, 1876, the parish priest at Döllersheim opened the baptismal registry, scanned the pages until he found the name Alois Schicklgruber, crossed it out, and wrote in the new, legitimized name: Alois Hitler.

Baby Adolf would be born in the lodge and christened in the Catholic Church 13 years later.

* * *

Adolf Hitler's middle-class family moved often to different homes around Linz before settling in the Austrian village of Leonding with its magnificent view of the Alps. He was sent to school to become a civil servant like his father, but Adolf had no desire for what he saw as a tedious government job. At the age of 12, he told his father that he wanted to be an artist, a revelation that had a stunning effect: "my father for the moment was struck speechless,"[3] he wrote.

Alois was said to have had a volatile temper and often beat Adolf and his half-brother, Alois Jr., with a whip. It seems that even as a child, Adolf inherited his father's unstable temperament. Alois Jr. described his half-brother's disposition: "He was quick to anger from childhood onward and would not listen to anyone. He would get the craziest notions and get away with them. And my stepmother always took his part."[4] A fed-up Alois Jr. ran away from home as a teenager, leaving Adolf to face his father's wrath alone.

Young Adolf told a friend that after years of abuse, he finally made up his mind not to cry when his father whipped him. He described a harrowing scene: "My mother, frightened, took refuge in front of the door. As for me, I counted silently the blows of the stick which lashed my buttocks."[5] Adolf said that his resolve not to cry during the incident dissuaded his father from beating him again. Of his parents, Adolf would write, "I had honored my father, but my mother I had loved."[6]

Klara Hitler was described as a kindly but sad and weary woman who had been worn down by her circumstance. In addition to living with an explosive, abusive husband, she lived with the heartache of having lost her first three children in infancy. As if to make up for the loss, she smothered Adolf, his sister, Paula, and younger brother Edmund, with an obsessive, maternal love. Klara tried her hardest to shield the children from Alois' bullying, but she was ultimately rendered powerless and sank further into despair.

Paula remembered her mother as "a very soft and tender person, the compensatory element between the almost too harsh father and the very lively children who were perhaps somewhat difficult to train. If there were ever quarrel[s] or differences of opinion between my parents, it was always on account of the children. It was especially my brother Adolf who challenged my father to extreme harshness and who got his sound thrashing every day.... How often on the other hand did my mother caress him and try to obtain with her kindness what the father could not succeed [in obtaining] with harshness!"[7]

Then, in 1900, Klara's worst fear came true—five-year-old Edmund contracted measles and died. The loss also devastated Adolf, and the ensuing grief and stress would serve to further separate the family instead of unite it. Adolf and his father, an Austrian patriot, began to argue over politics and over how poorly Adolf performed in school. But there was one subject that held Adolf's interest: history. He had a favorite teacher who used the students' "budding nationalistic fanaticism as a means of educating us, frequently appealing to our sense of national honor."[8] Adolf learned to hate the House of Habsburg and the vastly different ethnic groups that made up the crumbling Austro-Hungarian Empire. He and his mates wore the German national colors of red, black, and gold instead of the red and white of Austria. They refused to sing the imperial anthem, opting instead for *"Deutschland über Alles"* ("Germany above all things"). And when they greeted each other, they shouted the German greeting "Heil!"

Adolf began to be recognized at school for his sketching talent with pencil and paper, a fact that bolstered his argument that he should become an artist. Father and son would continue to clash heatedly over Adolf's contention, until his father suffered a stroke and died at a nearby tavern when Adolf was just 13.

Klara was left alone to raise Adolf, a younger sister, and two half-siblings. Despite the financial hardship, Klara tried her best to continue Adolf's schooling toward a civil servant's career until fate intervened. A lung ailment required Adolf to drop out of regular school, and his mother allowed him to spend his days as he liked—sketching, painting, and visiting museums.

Adolf had one close friend during his youth, a musically-talented upholsterer's son named August Kubizek, nicknamed Gustl. They first met around 1904, when Adolf was 15 and both boys jockeyed for standing room at the back of the Landestheater during the evening performances. Once the boys struck up a conversation, they realized that they shared an affinity for Wagnerian operas, especially the medieval German romance *Lohengrin*.

The more time they spent together, the more Gustl realized that Adolf was "exceedingly violent and high strung. Quite trivial things, such as a few thoughtless words, could produce in him outbursts of temper which I thought were quite out of proportion to the significance of the matter."[9] Adolf also proved to be a jealous friend who demanded all of Gustl's spare time. "I had to be at his beck and call," Gustl would write.[10]

Unlike Gustl, who worked long hours as an apprentice in his father's upholstery shop, Adolf had no desire for a "bread-and-butter job,"[11] and spent his days leisurely sketching and dreaming. In the evenings, the two friends strolled along the Landstrasse, the central shopping district in Linz. It was there that Adolf first took notice of a tall, slim, blonde woman walking arm-in-arm with her mother, and became instantly infatuated. He learned that her name was Stefanie Isak, daughter of a high government official. Adolf made it his mission to wait for Stefanie at 5 p.m. each evening in the hopes that she would gift him with a glance.

"You must know, I'm in love with her," he told Gustl.[12]

Adolf idealized Stefanie as the perfect German woman who would one day be his wife, despite the fact that he had never even spoken to her, and that she had begun to be escorted by a handsome young lieutenant. Adolf saw this as an irritating inconvenience and fantasized that Stefanie was merely biding her time as he gathered his courage to speak to her. "[H]e was convinced that Stefanie had no other desire but to wait until he should come to ask her to marry him," Gustl wrote. "[H]e drew up an exact programme for his future which would enable him, after four years, to ask for Stefanie's hand."[13] Adolf never did actually speak to Stefanie, opting instead to seriously consider kidnapping her and even contemplating suicide if she didn't return his ardor.

* * *

In May 1906, 17-year-old Adolf left his friend, Gustl, and his imagined girlfriend, Stefanie, to travel six hours by train to Vienna. After announcing that he would become a professional artist, his struggling mother had agree to pay for Adolf's trip to visit the imperial art gallery, attend operas

5. "Are we not the same as all other Germans?"

and marvel at the architecture along the Ringstrasse. For the first time in his young life, Adolf experienced a city illuminated by electric lights and teeming with automobiles, as well as horse-drawn carriages.

"In the center and in the inner districts you could really feel the pulse of this realm of fifty-two millions, with all the dubious magic of the national melting pot," he would write. "The [Habsburg] Court with its dazzling glamour attracted wealth and intelligence from the rest of the country like a magnet."[14]

While in Vienna, Adolf wrote Gustl several postcards about the opera, Vienna's architecture, and the weather. He also wrote of Stefanie, referring to her by an agreed upon male moniker that only Adolf and Gustl understood: "I simply must see Benkieser again," Adolf wrote. "I wonder what he is doing?"[15]

Adolf returned to Linz with a wider vision of the world and a fervent desire to be a part of it. According to Gustl, his friend immediately started making plans to attend the Academy of Visual Arts in Vienna, and to take the entrance exam in the fall of 1907. Before he left, however, Adolf sent a letter to Stefanie Isak, the woman to whom he had never even spoken.

"Once I received a letter from someone telling me he was now attending the Art Academy, but I should wait for him, he was going to return and marry me," Stefanie said years later. "I don't remember what else the letter said, and neither, whether and how it was signed. At the time I just didn't have a clue as to whom I should attribute the letter to."[16]

With dreams of artistic greatness swirling in his mind, Adolf found a sublet apartment in Mariahilf, a poor district of Vienna, and moved into a small, back basement bedroom for ten kronen a month, or about $5 in today's U.S. currency.

It was a ten-minute walk to the imposing Academy of Visual Arts on the Schillerplatz, with its statue-topped columns that resembled a Greek temple. Adolf's submitted artworks had been deemed good enough to allow him to sit for the entrance exam. On the morning of October 1, 1907, Adolf took his place at the drawing tables, along with 112 other hopefuls. Adolf was supremely confident, writing that he was "convinced that it would be child's play to pass the examination."[17]

For three hours in the morning and three hours in the afternoon, the candidates completed "composition tasks" from groups of themes, including "Expulsion from Paradise, Hunting, Spring, Construction Workers, Death, and Rain."[18] His renderings did not impress the professors, however. When the results were in, Adolf was one of 85 candidates who was not accepted into the academy. Adolf said the rejection "struck me as a bolt from the blue."[19] He returned home to Linz defeated and questioning his future. For the time being, however, he would care for his beloved mother, whom he learned was battling breast cancer.

Klara had noticed a lump in her breast as early as 1905, but did not bring it to a doctor's attention until two years later. By that time, the cancer had advanced, and the family's physician, a Jewish doctor named Eduard Bloch, recommended a mastectomy. The doctor recalled a distraught Adolf crying, "Does my mother have no chance at all?"

"Only then did I realize the magnitude of the attachment that existed between mother and son,"[20] the doctor said.

After possibly administering a barbiturate to coax his patient to sleep, the surgeon removed Klara's breast and found that tumors had inundated her chest wall. Her recovery was slow and painful, and Adolf pleaded with the doctor to save her life. Doctor Bloch decided on an experimental chemotherapy treatment which proved to be excruciatingly painful. He reopened the mastectomy scars, dipped gauze into a corrosive iodine-based medicine called iodoform, and packed them into the open wounds. Klara shrieked through the treatments that lasted for 46 consecutive days and left her barely able to swallow. Adolf could only watch hopelessly as his mother suffered, then finally expired on December 21, 1907.

At the age of 18, Adolf was now orphaned and virtually destitute. With no other options before him, he decided to return to the city to pursue his artistic dreams one way or another.

"In my hand a suitcasefull of clothes and underwear; in my heart an indomitable will, I journeyed to Vienna,"[21] he wrote. He carried with him about 1,000 kronen (about $500 in today's U.S. dollars) cobbled from his maternal inheritance and orphan's allowance.

It was there, in the heart of the Habsburg monarchy, that Adolf would come under the political spell of those who blamed all of the working man's misfortunes on one particular group that made up the multi-ethnic capital—the Jews.

6

"We felt ourselves more deeply united on the inside"

—Archduchess Marie Valerie

June 26, 1911

Heavily pregnant at the age of 43, Marie Valerie had made the 140 kilometer trip from her home at Wallsee Castle to the one place she felt most at ease—the Kaiservilla at Bad Ischl. In addition to the familiar comforts, the Archduchess required a closer proximity to her obstetrician, Dr. Plskacek. He had visited her at Wallsee months earlier when she had started to feel unwell, and informed her that the baby was situated horizontally in the womb, which could cause serious complications during the birth.

Marie Valerie knew she was taking a risk having a child in middle age, but desired one nonetheless if it was God's will. It had been four years since the birth of her last child, Mathilde, when she wrote in 1910, "Hoping for a child once again, thoughts of death without fear of death which now seems to me more as the destination."[1] Maire Valerie had reason to be preoccupied with thoughts of death; in the early 20th century, women were still dying in childbirth at an alarmingly high rate from bacterial infections, hemorrhaging, and toxemia. Even over-zealous doctors were shown to be responsible for patient deaths due to often unsanitary and unnecessary procedures. Ironically, less well-to-do women who were delivered by midwives often had better outcomes.

From the moment she married, Marie Valerie had desired a large family. Unlike her mother, Empress Elisabeth, who loathed pregnancy and childbirth, and had a strained relationship with each of her three living children, Marie Valerie believed it was her duty as a Catholic and a German-Austrian woman to have as many children as she was able. In Vienna at the time, there was a great push for German women to concentrate on family in order to keep up with the birthrates of the Czechs, Poles, Croats, and other nationalities that made up the Austro-Hungarian Empire. It was seen as a German woman's duty "to be prepared to make sacrifices for her people and to bear more children."[2]

After their honeymoon, Marie Valerie and Franz Salvator had moved to Lichtenegg Castle near Wels in Upper Austria to be near his regiment, the Fifteenth Dragoons. They welcomed their first four children into the Lichtenegg home, but Empress Elisabeth rarely visited her daughter, and when she did, she never stayed long.

"It is precisely because I like being here that I must not stay," Elisabeth told Marie Valerie with her flair for drama, "for the sea gull is out of place in the swallows' nest. I will take a photograph of your home at Lichtenegg back with me; I am content with that, and I will commend the swallows and their nest to the protection of the great Jehovah."[3]

As Elisabeth's faith moved away from the traditional Catholic belief in the Father, Son and Holy Ghost in favor of a terrible, vengeful Jehovah, Marie Valerie's grew stronger. She became particularly close to the Mother Superior of Sacré Coeur convent in Vienna. Mère Mayer was a member of the Sodality of Our Lady, a Roman Catholic Marian Society devoted to the Blessed Virgin Mary. She told Marie Valerie of her desire to establish a convent to the west of Vienna on a plot of wooded imperial land in Pressbaum. Marie Valerie convinced the Emperor to donate the land to the order, and was present at the laying of the foundation stone on June 9, 1891.

In 1892, when Marie Valerie became pregnant for the first time, Elisabeth's depression got the best of her and she did not share her daughter's joy.

"She sighed about my condition, it was difficult for her to feel with me the happiness which, strangely, in spite of her motherlove for me, she cannot understand at all," Marie Valerie wrote in her diary. "She told me … that the birth of every new human being seemed to her a misfortune, since one can fulfill one's destiny only in suffering."[4]

Despite her mother's lack of support, Marie Valerie named her newborn daughter after Elisabeth, and called the girl Ella. Marie Valerie would go on to have three more children in the next four years, before Franz Salvator's father gifted the growing family the larger medieval Wallsee Castle on the Danube River in 1897. The 14th-century fortress, built atop a former Roman camp, featured a red-roofed inner keep and tremendous square clock tower encircled by a long, barrel-vaulted structure with crenelated turrets. It was truly a home fit for an Austrian princess.

* * *

6. "We felt ourselves more deeply united on the inside" 43

Back in the comforting surroundings of her apartments at the Kaiservilla, Marie Valerie labored and prayed for many painful hours before finally delivering her tenth child, a baby girl she named Agnes. The baby was immediately baptized and struggled for eight hours until her

The growing family, around 1905. Marie Valerie would go on to have two more children. The last child, Agnes, born in 1911, would die several hours after birth (author's collection).

cries weakened, her movements slowed and she at last became permanently still. The doctor presented the swaddled and lifeless child to Marie Valerie and Franz Salvator who poured out their grief.

"My good old Franz cried at my bedside so bitterly that I still had to speak comfort to him," Marie Valerie wrote. "Perhaps it was mixed in for him with the thought that this abnormal pregnancy could have cost me my life. We felt ourselves more deeply united on the inside than we have done for a long time."[5]

The still newborn was dressed in lace and placed on the changing table amongst white roses before her older siblings were brought into the room. The eldest daughters, 19-year-old Ella and 15-year-old Hedwig, were said to have spoken words of great comfort to their parents. Baby Agnes was buried in the family cemetery at the Kaiservilla, in the shadow of the Salzkammergut mountains.

Through her tears, Marie Valerie said she felt blessed that little Agnes had been baptized and was now in the hands of the Father, as well as with Marie Valerie's mother, the Empress.

"How comforting to think that this small grandchild has perhaps been brought to her at last in heaven!"[6]

* * *

By the time Marie Valerie gave birth to her tenth and final child, her famously glamorous mother had been dead for 13 years. With the stab of a makeshift dagger through her heart, Elisabeth had been assassinated on September 10, 1898, by an Italian anarchist in Geneva, Switzerland. Empress Elisabeth hadn't been the first choice of 25-year-old Luigi Lucheni, but she had been conveniently in the same city at the time he chose to make his anti-aristocratic views known to the world in a most violent way. Elisabeth's attendants and the employees at the Beau-Rivage hotel where she had been a guest had tried in vain to revive the fading Empress. But the blood slowly trickled from her wounded heart and could not be stopped in time to save her.

Emperor Franz Joseph had been working in his study at Schönbrunn Palace when he received a telegram from Elisabeth's attendant Irma Sztáray saying his wife had been seriously injured, then a second in rapid succession telling him that Elisabeth had died. Marie Valerie and Franz Salvator had been summoned to Schönbrunn where they received the shocking news.

Franz Joseph wept as he told his daughter what he had learned, but

6. "We felt ourselves more deeply united on the inside"

Marie Valerie noted that he never fully lost his composure, but "quickly regained the calm he had shown after Rudolf's death."

The following day, the family attended Sunday Mass, "and then I was allowed to spend this whole first day almost uninterruptedly with him, sitting next to his desk when he worked as usual, reading along with him the more detailed reports arriving from Geneva, helping him to receive the family condolence calls," she wrote in her diary.[7]

One of the first people outside of the palace's inner circle to express condolences to Marie Valerie was her former governess, Lady Mary Throckmorton. Marie Valerie responded to the Englishwoman's correspondence by rapidly filling out her own telegraph slip at Schönbrunn on the morning of September 13. Her normally composed handwriting was now large with poorly formed letters. "Heartfelt thanks for warm sympathy," she wrote, neglecting to use punctuation. She signed it simply *Valerie*, with an underscore.[8]

Over the next several days of planning the proper protocol under which to ship home the Empress's body and give her a fitting funeral, Marie Valerie recorded her father as repeating over and over, "How can you kill a woman who has never hurt anyone?"[9] Despite his outward grief, Marie Valerie wrote that her father was involved in every aspect of organizing Elisabeth's final farewell. It would include more than 80 European royals traveling in a seemingly endless string of black carriages through the streets of Vienna lined with hundreds of thousands of mourners to the traditional Habsburg burial place, the Church of the Capuchin Friars.

Exactly one week after the assassination, Empress Elisabeth's coffin was carried through the enormous archway and into the monastery's imperial vault. The family wept beside the polished oak casket bearing the Empress's coat of arms. Marie Valerie raised her head from supplication to behold a sliver of light streaming through a narrow window into the crypt where Rudolf already lay. She wrote that she heard the birds singing just outside the stone walls, a reminder of the natural world that her mother so adored. Marie Valerie then offered up a prayer for her mother's soul: "May she at last find the peace for which she so ardently longed."[10]

* * *

Shortly after the august funeral, Elisabeth's estate was settled. Both Marie Valerie and her sister, Gisela, received two-fifths of the "shockingly large fortune" that Elisabeth had amassed through the years.[11] The rest of the money went to Rudolf's daughter, Erzsi. Although the monetary inheritance was divided evenly between the sisters, Elisabeth continued to favor Marie Valerie even after death with a further bequeathment of one million guldens (approximately $12 million in today's currency) plus the exquisite Hermés Villa in the Lainzer Tiergarten. Gisela received the run-down Achilleion Palace that had stood vacant for years after the Empress grew bored and abandoned it shortly after construction on the Greek Island of Corfu.

Two months after the funeral, Marie Valerie set to work distributing some of her mother's possessions. Marie Valerie's governess, Mary Throckmorton, received a letter from the Hofburg addressed to her home at Lansdowne Road, Bournemouth. It read, "I am desired by their Imperial and Royal Highnesses the Princess Gisela of Bavaria and Archduchess Marie Valerie to forward to you the … parcel containing mementos of Her Majesty the late Empress and Queen Elisabeth."[12] Mary also received a sizable document on parchment paper conferring on her the Imperial Order of Saint Elisabeth, First Class. The award was created by Emperor Franz Joseph in memory of his wife, but named for Saint Elisabeth of Hungary, and given to women for merits in charitable or religious works. Mary was one of the first recipients of the award and was forever after address by the Palace in French as *Madame Marie de Throckmorton, dame d'honneur de la Majesté l'Imperiatrice d'Autriche*.[13]

Now considered the female head of the royal branch of the Habsburgs, Marie Valerie also started sending out death announcements and notes to some of her mother's closest confidantes. One note, folded into a black-rimmed mourning cover and stamped with a black wax seal bearing Marie Valerie's name, was addressed to the Empress's former Greek tutor, Constantin Christomanos, at the Boulevard de Sébastopol, Paris. One year after the Empress's death, Christomanos would betray his former friend and Empress by publishing details of Elisabeth's toilette and her intimate thoughts that he recorded while in her employ. Some of the Empress's most famous sayings, such as "I am a slave to my hair," can be attributed to Christomanos's published diary.[14]

Marie Valerie struggled to comfort her father by having him visit with her four children, who ranged in age from two to six, at Wallsee Palace. But the visits were awkward, and the children's natural ebullience became a worry for their mother.

"Not to know whether one should talk about our misfortune or about distracting things, to try in vain to find subjects of conversation of the latter kind, to wish the children to act natural," Marie Valerie wrote, "and

6. "We felt ourselves more deeply united on the inside"

A portrait of Marie Valerie and Franz Salvator taken around 1907. She is approximately 39 years old, while he is 41 (Library of Congress Prints and Photographs Division, George Grantham Bain Collection).

yet tremble that their shouting might irritate Papa—to see him now sink into dull unhappiness, now being nervous."[15]

Franz Joseph's assistant, Count Parr, the man who had been with the Emperor when he first received news of the Empress's death, described the domestic scene at Wallsee as unbearable.

"It is barely possible to endure the boredom, for no one dares to say a word, and so conversation at table and in the evenings dries up almost completely," he wrote.[16]

But just as she had felt it was her responsibility to try to keep her mother happy, Marie Valerie was now committed to her father's well-being. She saw him through what was to be his Golden Jubilee celebration of 50 years on the throne, which had been downgraded to more of an observance since the date was just two months after the Empress's death. Marie Valerie wrote of the Emperor standing upright, a simple and just man, "concerned only with fulfilling his difficult duties day after day, loyal and untiring, forgetting self and caring only about others."[17]

Marie Valerie became her father's official consort in the absence of her mother, and accompanied him to entertain visiting royalty, such as the Prince and Princess of Wales in 1904, and former French Empress Eugénie in 1906. She also ensured that his 80th birthday on August 18, 1910, was a joyous occasion, by overseeing the planning for more than 70 archdukes and archduchesses who arrived at the Kaiservilla in Bad Ischl for the celebrations. Marie Valerie wrote a play especially for the ceremonies titled *Homage to Alpine Flowers*, that included a ballet with two scenes.

The Emperor was undoubtedly present at Bad Ischl when Marie Valerie gave birth to her tenth and final child on June 26, 1911, and helped

48   Part I: *Verblassendes Reich*/Fading Empire, 1890–1924

Austro-Hungarian Emperor Franz Joseph I in old age (Library of Congress Prints and Photographs Division, George Grantham Bain Collection).

her through the mourning process just as she had helped him through the loss of Elisabeth. Although Franz Salvator expressed deep remorse over the death of Baby Agnes and fear over the danger to his wife's life, it was at this point in his life that he took up with the young Stephanie Richter, and fathered one last child.

7

"Antisemitism is an uncommonly diffused sickness"

—Emperor Franz Joseph

Vienna, 1911

Twenty-two-year-old Adolf Hitler made his way to the frame store of Jewish glazier Samuel Morgenstern, hoping to sell some of his watercolors for a few kronen. Adolf usually wore an old frock coat with long tails given to him by a Jewish acquaintance, and a shabby derby hat covering his hair, considered long for the day. The would-be artist had offered Morgenstern three paintings at the time of their first meeting: watercolors of Vienna's most famous landmarks, such as the Schönbrunn Palace gate, Saint Stephen's Cathedral, City Hall, and Parliament. The shopkeeper described the paintings as being in the style of Austrian architectural artist, Rudolf von Alt, and said he bought them because he found it easier to sell frames that contained actual pictures. Morgenstern "was the first person to pay a good price for the paintings,"[1] and although another frame manufacturer described the quality of Adolf's paintings as "the cheapest items we ever sold,"[2] his mediocre talent allowed Adolf to finally move out of Vienna's homeless shelters and into a clean, safe, six-story men's hostel for 2.5 kronen per week ($1.25 in today's U.S. dollars). Life was finally on the upswing for Adolf after three years of overwhelming poverty in Vienna.

* * *

As Adolf's orphan's pension had begun to run out and he continually scoffed at finding permanent employment, he had found himself homeless and hungry, later calling those days "the saddest period of my life."³ Adolf had met other desperate vagabonds at the homeless shelters he frequented and they all struggled to find menial tasks to help buy their daily bread. Adolf often ate his lunch of dry bread while sitting as a forlorn figure on a bench in Schönbrunn's public park. In the summer months, he often witnessed Emperor Franz Joseph making his daily carriage ride from Schönbrunn Palace to the Hofburg.

One acquaintance named Reinhold Hanisch viewed Adolf's moderate talents as a perfect opportunity to set up a business: Adolf would paint postcards featuring Vienna's most famous buildings, and Hanisch would hawk them to patrons at the local taverns. Eventually, the enterprising Hanisch was able to obtain orders from furniture stores and upholsterers who needed cheap artwork for their showroom floors. But Adolf preferred to study the local papers and discuss politics rather than work, and usually only buckled down when he was starving and out of options.

"I painted to make a living and studied for pleasure,"⁴ Adolf would say, leaving his business partner in a quandary.

"Often I didn't know what to do with the orders because it was impossible to make Hitler work," Hanish wrote. "In the morning he sat in the hall of the Home, and was supposed to be making drawings while I was busy canvassing the frame manufacturers and upholsterers. But then political discussion would start and generally Hitler would become the ringleader. When I came back in the evening I often had to take the T-square out of his hands, because he would be swinging it over his head, making a speech."⁵

Hanisch recalled one heated discussion about German Jewish poet Heinrich Heine that had Adolf defending the literary merits of the post–Romantic poet's work, proving that Adolf had not arrived in Vienna as an avowed antisemite—that particular hatred is something that would evolve over time. The controversy erupted over a statue to Heine that had been erected by Empress Elisabeth in the garden of her Achilleion Palace on the Greek island of Corfu. Elisabeth had worshipped Heine and had attempted to write her own poetry in his realistic and ironic style. German Emperor Wilhelm II, an ardent antisemite, had purchased the palace from Elisabeth's eldest daughter Gisela, and had promptly torn down the memorial to the Jewish poet. News of the statue's removal renewed debates about the so-called Jewish Question throughout Vienna, as well as in Adolf's men's shelter. But during one particularly lively debate, Adolf actually defended the Jewish poet as a great artist, even if Adolf were no fan of the member of the House of Habsburg who built the statue.

"[W]hen the people in the Home expressed resentment at Queen Elizabeth's erecting a monument to Heine on her estate at Corfu, Hitler argued that it was sad that Heine's fatherland did not similarly recognize his merit," Hanisch wrote.[6]

The Viennese press was full of antisemitic rhetoric at the time, not least of all due to the message of populist politician Dr. Karl Lueger of the Christian Social Party, who blamed the Jews for all of Vienna's ills. Lueger's repeated rallying cry, "Vienna is German and must remain German!"[7] struck a nerve with many Viennese in response to Emperor Franz Joseph's insistence that all of the Empire's distinct nationalities, cultures and languages were welcome—and considered equal—inside the Empire's original capital. The working class worried about the influx of non–German-speaking immigrants into the city and blamed the Emperor's tolerance for destroying the Viennese way of life. Even Marie Valerie went against her father to support German Nationalism and Lueger's position toward reclaiming the city for German-speaking people. For his part, Franz Joseph did all he could to thwart Leuger's appointment as Vienna's mayor. Repeatedly, the Emperor refused to approve Leuger's election by the people, instead sending the mayoral ballot back to the voters for one more try.

In a letter to Elisabeth before her death, Franz Joseph wrote that he received a letter from Marie Valerie, "in which [Karl] Luegar [*sic*] and his party are warmly and urgently recommended to me. Antisemitism is an uncommonly diffused sickness even among the highest circles, and their agitation is unbelievable."[8]

After four mayoral vote tallies, all of which were handily won by Leuger, the Emperor finally felt he had no other choice but to acquiesce to the people's will. Dr. Karl Leuger served as mayor of Vienna from 1897 through his death in 1910, spreading his brand of antisemitism, immigration restriction, and cultural assimilation.

When Adolf arrived in Vienna in 1908, he was originally no fan of the mayor, regarding him as a simple reactionary to problems of immigration and economic inequality.

"My common sense of justice, however, forced me to change this judgment in proportion as I had occasion to become acquainted with the man and his work," Adolf wrote. Eventually, Adolf came to regard Lueger "as the greatest German mayor of all times.... My views with regard to antisemitism thus succumbed to the passage of time, and this was my greatest transformation of all."[9]

When asked to explain how he could speak against the Jews and yet have so many Jewish friends, Lueger had famously replied, "I decide who is a Jew."[10] Adolf Hitler would one day adopt this same twisted philosophy, as in the case of Stephanie Richter, also known as Princess Stephanie von Hohenlohe, whom he would name an "Honorary Aryan" for as long as she served his purposes.

* * *

When Adolf did put aside reading and politics and actually got down to work, he often did so in the charitable *Wärmestuben*, or warming up rooms, that offered free food and shelter to Vienna's needy from winter through spring. Adolf would take his supplies and set up at a table, where he would remain insulated from the cold all day as he created his artworks. Since Adolf wasn't one to paint or draw Vienna's landmarks from life, he studied and copied from a booklet of drawings, most likely *Vienna for the Past Sixty Years*, which the city handed out in 1908 to commemorate the Revolutions of 1848 and the ascension of Franz Joseph as Austrian Emperor.

The protector of Vienna's *Wärmestuben* was Archduchess Marie Valerie, who was known to visit the charitable establishments at Christmas and other holidays. "Speeches were held, cookies and fruit were handed out, and clothing was distributed. Apart from soup and bread, sausages and beer were offered as well, plus a 'real' lunch for free."[11]

Although he partook of the goodwill offerings, Adolf resented the imperial and noble displays of charity, deriding "the snobbish, or at times tactless and obtrusive, condescension of certain women of fashion in skirts or in trousers who 'feel for the people.' In any event, these gentry sin far more than their minds, devoid of all instinct, are capable of realizing. Consequently, and much to their own amazement, the result of their social 'efforts' is always nil."[12]

* * *

While Marie Valerie was distracted with her charities and still recovering from the birth and death of Baby Agnes, Franz Salvator was attending Vienna's intellectual salons and society parties in an effort to escape the crushing melancholy that had enveloped Wallsee Palace. Stephanie Richter's carefree ways must have been a breath of fresh air to Franz Salvator, who was so used to the cold and stilted life at court. He was feeling the stagnation of middle age, complete with receding hairline and an ever-present pince-nez. After more than 20 years of marriage, he must have been taken with Stephanie's glowing enthusiasm and unbridled possibilities of youth. Here was a woman who was cultured, well-versed in the art of conversation and flattery, and had her own sense of style. Instead of following the fashion of the day, which in 1911 Vienna was all about French designer Paul Poiret's "fashion-art" of long draped dresses and culotte skirts, Stephanie chose to wear the full, knee-length skirt and fitted bodice of the traditional Austrian *dirndl*. Perhaps with all of the anti-immigrant and antisemitic talk of the day, Stephanie had decided to appeal to the German nationalism sweeping the city.

Stephanie also defied convention by purposely tanning her skin to what she felt was a healthy bronzed hue, an audacious snub at the older generations of women like Marie Valerie who shunned the sun in favor of a milky-white complexion. Stephanie was also physically very different from Marie Valerie; where Franz Salvator's wife was tall and willowy, Stefanie was petite and voluptuous, with a natural hourglass figure. She was also outgoing and engaging, where Marie Valerie was reticent and shy. Whatever it was about Stephanie, Franz Salvator was smitten, and the two began a love affair.

Instead of being discreet, however, Franz Salvator's escapades with Stephanie could be considered somewhat reckless, as if he weren't overly concerned if Marie Valerie were to hear rumors of the affair. On more than one occasion, he even hosted Stephanie at Marie Valerie's beloved Kaiservilla at Bad Ischl. It was the place where Emperor Franz Joseph loved to don his lederhosen for hunting excursions for deer, chamois, wood grouse, and wild boar. The walls of the Kaiservilla were filled with his trophies, and the Emperor's staff was no doubt present to serve Franz Salvator and his mistress when they returned from the hunt.

"It was [Franz Salvator] who took me to the emperor's own shoot near Ischl where I shot my first mountain stag," Stephanie wrote. "To describe the beauty and charm of the scenery in that heavenly spot of the world would be a futile attempt."[13] It was so heavenly, in fact, that Marie Valerie had chosen it as the site of her wedding more than 20 years earlier—a sentimental fact that didn't seem to bother Franz Salvator.

But Stephanie didn't find the Kaiservilla imperial residence to be quite as charming as the surrounding countryside.

"To me, the house at Ischl, which [Franz Joseph] loved so much, always seemed a depressing place," she wrote. Stephanie described the "monk-like simplicity" of the Emperor's lifestyle, with his plain iron bed, "the kind usually reserved for servants' quarters." She also noted the praying stool, an iron wash stand, "and a writing desk with his murdered wife's photograph with some dried flowers and a little poem she had given him the day of their engagement stuck under the glass." Stephanie wrote that

7. "Antisemitism is an uncommonly diffused sickness"

she "was never able to conquer a deep sense of melancholy on entering these walls."[14] Perhaps she could also sense Marie Valerie's presence, and Stephanie's conscience began to eat at her.

Franz Salvator also ushered Stephanie to the private zoo at Schönbrunn Palace in his imperial carriage with gilt spokes that were reserved solely for members of the monarchy. Stephanie had brought along food scraps from her kitchen to feed to some of the zoo's more than 3,000 animals, but while reaching a gloved hand through a bear's cage, she was bitten and her finger lacerated. Fearing an infection, Franz Salvator knew he had to get Stephanie to a doctor. But, although he hadn't been cautious about taking his mistress to his father-in-law's summer Palace of Schönbrunn, he did think better of taking her to the doctor in his instantly recognizable carriage. Instead, Franz Salvator dropped Stephanie off at a city tram heading toward the nearest medical facility. She would have to fend for herself this time in the name of propriety.

If Marie Valerie knew of the affair, she never spoke of it to any confidante. One person to whom she could have confided was the priest of Wallsee, Father Engelbert, who heard her confessions. But according to biographer Martha Schad, "she considered it one of the rules of life to remain alone in one's inmost being—the most difficult battle as much in happiness as in sorrow. Complete understanding should, after all be set aside for the 'One' alone." Marie Valerie offered up her prayers directly to the Almighty, believing that "one's true life should remain locked in the depths of the heart."[15]

We do know that Marie Valerie was mortified by her own father's emotional affair with a married Burgtheater actress named Katharina Schratt. The relationship was encouraged by the Emperor's wife herself, Empress Elisabeth, who had long been estranged from her husband and appreciated that Katharina kept him company while the Empress went about her world travels. Marie Valerie blamed her mother for sanctioning the relationship that blatantly flouted their Catholic marriage vows.

"Oh, why did Mama herself go so far," Marie Valerie wrote.

Frau Schratt often dined with the family at the Hofburg, and was even their guest at Bad Ischl.

"I cannot say how embarrassing such afternoons are for me, how incomprehensible that Mama finds them rather cozy," Marie Valerie wrote in her diary.[16]

Public opinion was also firmly against the unusual arrangement.

"The Emperor continues to be under the spell of an actress at the Burgtheater, Schratt, pretty and stupid, who, as is claimed, lives respectably within the Emperor's immediate family," wrote an Austrian diplomat. "The Empress, who, they say, arranged this liaison, which they call platonic but which is by no means so considered by the public, and which in any case is ridiculous—and young Archduchess Valerie. This silly business does the Emperor considerable damage in the opinion the bourgeoisie and the people have of him."[17]

Stephanie Richter, however, did not see a problem with the Emperor's liaison.

"'This old man,' I said to myself, 'will join in two or three hours Katherina Schratt,'" Stephanie wrote after her meeting with the Emperor and Franz Salvator at the Hofburg in 1914. "I could not think of anything else. Katherina Schratt was the companion of his old age, who had replaced the frosty loneliness of his palaces with the warmth of a truly bourgeois home ... Francis Joseph and Katherina Schratt was not the headline of a court scandal ... these names represent the most touching idyll, the most human chapter in the hectic history of the house of Hapsburg."[18]

Perhaps in her approval of the Emperor's affair, although it was most likely platonic, Stephanie was justifying her own affair with Franz Salvator, by giving him the warmth and humanity she felt he was missing in his decorous home.

* * *

Several years after their affair began, Stephanie became pregnant with Franz Salvator's child.

She was two months along when Franz Salvator asked his father-in-law to arrange a suitable marriage for Stephanie to a titled noble, and she gave birth to a healthy baby boy on December 5, 1914, some seven months after her marriage to Prince Friedrich Franz von Hohenlohe-Waldenburg-Schillingsfürst. Stephanie's somewhat stealthy relationship with Franz Salvator, however, would far outlast her marriage to another man.

8

"I tread the path that it is my duty to follow"

—Emperor Franz Joseph

Bad Ischl, June 28, 1914

Emperor Franz Joseph's peaceful hunting vacation at Bad Ischl was decimated by news of the assassination of his nephew and heir apparent, Franz Ferdinand, exactly four weeks earlier. Just as he had delivered news of Empress Elisabeth's assassination, the Emperor's adjutant, General Count Eduard Paar, was the one to convey the news of the murder of Franz Ferdinand and wife Sophie at the hands of a Serbian terrorist group.

"Terrible! The Almighty cannot be provoked!" Franz Joseph exclaimed. "A Higher Power has restored that order that unfortunately I was unable to maintain."[1]

The Emperor's comments belied his true dislike and mistrust of his volatile nephew, who had become heir following the deaths of Crown Prince Rudolph and the Emperor's brother, Archduke Karl Ludwig. For a time, the newspapers had buzzed about Franz Joseph reinstating the pragmatic sanction so that Marie Valerie could be named heir and successor. The sanction was created in 1713 to allow Emperor Charles VI to pass his crown to his eldest child, Maria Theresa, since he did not have a living son to succeed him. Maria Theresa became the first female Habsburg ruler, but many of her people were not prepared to accept a woman in charge of the Empire, and they fought what became known as The War of the Austrian Succession. Whether Franz Joseph ever seriously considered elevating Marie Valerie to Empress, and whether the introverted Archduchess would have accepted, we do not know.

Becoming heir apparent to the Astro-Hungarian throne had swollen Franz Ferdinand's ego to an intolerable level. He was a man without moderation, who lost many friendships due to a spiteful, petty nature, and who took his greatest pleasure by asserting his dominance over the vulnerable; by the age of 46, he had hunted down some 5,000 stags. The Emperor had disproved of the Archduke's morganatic marriage and bigotry toward many of the nationalities that made up the Austro-Hungarian Empire, and feared how his nephew would behave when he succeeded to the Habsburg throne.

Indeed, it had been stubborn pride that prompted Franz Ferdinand to travel to Sarajevo in the first place. Because his wife, Sophie Chotek, was not of royal blood—she was a Bohemian noble and a lady-in-waiting to another Habsburg wife—Franz Ferdinand's marriage had been deemed beneath him. The Emperor did not allow Sophie to attain the title of archduchess. Instead, she was styled the Duchess of Hohenberg and was forbidden from accompanying her husband in the royal carriage or the royal box at the Burgtheater. She was even forced to enter court balls as the last woman in the procession, behind all legitimate Austrian royalty. Sophie would never become Empress of Austria even when her husband ascended to the throne, and their children would be ineligible from inheriting any Habsburg dynastic rights or titles. That meant that after Franz Ferdinand's reign, the crown would pass next to his brother, Otto, and then on to Otto's son Karl.

Regardless of the court formalities, the marriage had proved a love match and was blessed with three children. Sophie was believed to have been expecting a fourth child when Franz Ferdinand insisted on taking her to Sarajevo so she would be treated with royal honors on their wedding anniversary. But the Empire's southern provinces were vehemently against Habsburg rule, desiring to break away and create an autonomous Greater Serbia. Franz Ferdinand knew it was dangerous to visit the region, but felt that since he had married a northern slavic woman, the southern slavs would view him favorably. He was terribly wrong.

As their motorcade made its way through the streets of Sarajevo, a conspirator in the crowd tossed a bomb directly at Franz Ferdinand and Sophie's open-air automobile. The Archduke deflected the bomb from hitting his wife and the device exploded in the street behind them. Flying splinters injured some of the dignitaries in the motorcade as well as spectators lining the route. While the injured were taken to the hospital, Franz Ferdinand's car continued to city hall for a brief ceremonial welcome by the mayor before the Archduke insisted on traveling to the hospital himself to visit the injured. But his car took a wrong turn along the way, leaving the couple isolated and vulnerable. As the driver stopped the car to turn

8. *"I tread the path that it is my duty to follow"*

The aged monarch, Emperor Franz Joseph, and young Archduke Otto (Library of Congress Prints and Photographs Division, George Grantham Bain Collection).

around, 19-year-old conspirator Gavrilo Princip drew his pistol and fired two shots at the Archduke and his wife. Franz Ferdinand was hit in the neck, and Sophie in the abdomen. Both were dead before they could reach help.

Once the news reached Vienna, government officials immediately began descending on the Kaiservilla to decide how to answer this affront

The assassination of Archduke Franz Ferdinand (left center) was the catalyst that pushed Emperor Franz Joseph to declare war against Serbia (Library of Congress Prints and Photographs Division, George Grantham Bain Collection).

to Austro-Hungarian authority. Marie Valerie had rushed to her father's side after hearing the news of her cousin's violent death, but the weary Emperor had told her, "For me it is a relief from a great worry."[2] Even though he was shocked at losing Franz Ferdinand to an assassin, the Emperor had known all along that his nephew's rule would have been disastrous. The Emperor was now obliged to turn his attentions directly to his 27-year-old grand-nephew Karl, who was now next in line to the throne, since Karl's father Otto had died years earlier from complications due to syphilis.

Karl and his young wife, Zita, were having lunch on the grounds of the family mansion at Reichenau at the foot of the Rax Mountains in Lower Austria, when they received a telegram directly from Franz Ferdinand's aide-de-camp informing them of the horrifying news. The implications of the murders must have hit the couple with the full force of destiny. No longer would Karl have years to learn the role of Emperor under the tutelage of Franz Ferdinand as he had planned; Karl now knew

8. "I tread the path that it is my duty to follow" 61

he would need to absorb all he could as quickly as possible from Franz Joseph, who had limited time left in which to teach him. Karl and Zita undoubtedly said a prayer for the murdered heir to the throne and his wife, as well as the now-orphaned children, before picking up the telephone to place a call to the Emperor at Ischl.

Since the old Emperor planned to remain at Ischl to confer with his ministers on how to respond to what they viewed as unacceptable Serbian aggression, Karl immediately set off for Vienna to meet the two caskets at the train station. He accompanied the military entourage back to the Hofburg, where Franz Ferdinand and Sophie were laid out beside one other, clutching crucifixes and lit by a spectral glow of hundreds of tapers.

Count Leopold Berchtold, Imperial Foreign Minister, had been pushing for war with Serbia, a country that considered Bosnia to be part of its territory even though the Austro-Hungarian Empire had annexed Bosnia six years earlier. With the full support of Germany, Berchtold sent the Austro-Hungarian ambassador to Serbia to deliver an ultimatum to the

Emperor Franz Joseph's office at the Kaiservilla. The desk on which he signed the declaration of war against Serbia is to the right with the alabaster bust of his wife, Empress Elisabeth, looking on (author's collection).

Balkan nation, and officials at the Kaiservilla held their collective breaths for 48 hours awaiting the response.

As expected, Serbia refused the provision to allow the Empire's investigators to stage an inquest on Serbian soil, believing it to be a violation of Serbian sovereignty. Emperor Franz Joseph's ministers advised him that there was no alternative but to go to war and that Germany's Wilhelm II fully supported the effort. Exactly one month after the assassinations, a reluctant Emperor, who was now 84 years old, dipped his ostrich-feather quill into the ink pot resting on his modest desk in his Kaiservilla study, and signed his name to the declaration that bore the Habsburg double-headed eagle. An alabaster bust of his late wife, Elisabeth, gazed down at the drama being played out.

"It is my duty to assign the Minister of my house and the Minister of Foreign Affairs to notify the royal Serbian government of the state of war between the monarchy and Serbia," the declaration read.[3]

The Emperor then signed a public explanation titled "To my people."

"It was my dearest wish to devote the remaining years that God may grant me to works of peace and to protect my people from the heavy sacrifices and burdens of war," it began. "Providence has decided otherwise. The machinations of a hateful opponent force me, after long years of peace, to take up arms to protect the honour of my monarchy, to safeguard its reputation and its authority.... It is with a clear conscience that I tread the path that it is my duty to follow."

Emperor Franz Joseph on horseback observing war maneuvers (Library of Congress Prints and Photographs Division, George Grantham Bain Collection).

8. *"I tread the path that it is my duty to follow"*   63

Marie Valerie and Franz Salvator around the time of the Great War (Library of Congress Prints and Photographs Division, George Grantham Bain Collection).

The Emperor then expressed his confidence in the Empire's nearly 53 million souls, the armed forces, and in the Almighty, "that He will grant me victory in the fight."[4]

There would be no annual family birthday celebration for the Emperor at Bad Ischl that August. Instead, Franz Joseph packed up and left the spa town on July 30, on a special train bound for Vienna, where he would meet up with his new heir, Archduke Karl, at Schönbrunn Palace. Franz Joseph, his life now consumed with war and worry, would never have the opportunity to return to his cherished Kaiservilla again.

Every year for as long as Marie Valerie could remember, her aunts, uncles, and cousins had gathered at the Kaiservilla to take part in the Emperor's birthday festivities that had lit up the entire spa town. Now, she would have to be content with the memories, such as those she recorded in her diary when she was 11 years old, and both her mother and brother were still alive: "On the eve of Papa's birthday there was a huge lighting display with fireworks…. Oh it was splendid! All these ships lit up on the lake; on one ship there was even music and a male choir. And then as the [His Majesty's Ship] 'Franz Joseph' came past so beautifully lit up, that was beautiful!"[5]

* * *

August 5, 1914

Delirious with thoughts of war, 25-year-old Adolf Hitler, who had been living in Germany for just over a year, marched into a Munich military recruiting station and volunteered to serve in the First Bavarian Infantry Regiment. The Bavarian Army, as well as those of Prussia, Saxony, and Wurttemberg, were under the auspices of the German military led by the German Kaiser.

News of the Austrian Emperor's declaration of war had elated those in the German-speaking world who felt it was high time to stand up to slavic leadership and other foreigners they believed were eroding German culture and autonomy. Just days before, Hitler had been among the crowd that gathered in Munich's Odeonsplatz, singing *Deutschland über Alles*, in fervent support of the war.

"Overpowered by stormy enthusiasm, I fell down on my knees and thanked Heaven from an overflowing heart for granting me the good fortune of being permitted to live at this time,"[6] he would write.

On August 16, Hitler's war dreams came true—he was officially called up to service, and reported to Munich's Recruiting Depot VI. Hitler was assigned to the Second Reserve Battalion of the Second Infantry Regiment, fitted for his uniform, and provided with the equipment he would need in order to hastily train and ship out on October 21 for the Western front, to fight in what would become known as the First Battle of Ypres in Belgium. Each man received green-grey uniforms with red stripes down the side of the pant legs, leather boots and thick belts. A shortage of proper helmets and army knapsacks meant that the men had to make do with civilian rucksacks and soft cloth hats that were meant to look from a distance like hard-topped helmets.

As it so happened, Hitler's acceptance into the Bavarian army was the result of his remarkable ability to manipulate both German and Austrian authorities.

While still in Vienna, a city he had come to despise for its poverty, multiculturalism, and fading Habsburg monarchy, Hitler turned 24 years old and finally came into his share of his father's inheritance, some 819 kronen in 1913. The money gave him the freedom to head over the border into the German fatherland, but his reasons weren't simply based on Germanic pride; Hitler was doing his best to evade the Austrian authorities.

Hitler had been so opposed to defending the House of Habsburg, the centuries-old monarchy that he said was "destined to be the misfortune of the German nation,"[7] that he had failed to register for the Austrian mil-

8. *"I tread the path that it is my duty to follow"*   65

itary as a citizen in time for his 21st birthday, as was required by Austrian law. He thought he had managed to stay under the radar and made a clean escape across the border to Germany in May 1913, but the Austrian authorities caught up with him six months later. They sent a written appeal to the Munich police: "The painter Adolf Hitler, born 1889 in Braunau am Inn, moved from Vienna to Munich on 24 May, 1913. You would greatly oblige us ... if you let us know whether the above-named has registered with you."[8] The Munich police tracked him down at the home of a tailor named Joseph Popp where he was living, and escorted Hitler to the Austrian consulate in Munich. Hitler was ordered to report immediately to his hometown of Linz to register with the Austrian military.

Hitler wrote a long, doleful letter to the authorities, where he pleaded that he did not have adequate time, let alone the money, required to travel back to Linz on such short notice.

"I beg you not to make things unnecessarily difficult for me," he groused.[9]

The Austrian authorities, somehow moved by his plea, allowed Hitler to report to Salzburg, instead, because it was closer to Munich, and ostensibly less burdensome for the struggling artist. There, the Upper Austrian Military Examination Board declared that Hitler was unfit for Austrian military and auxiliary service due to his poor physical condition, and he was allowed to return to Munich without penalty.

Whatever Hitler had done to appear too weak to serve in the Austrian army, he managed to perk up enough shortly thereafter to have been accepted into the Bavarian Army, in what became known as the List Regiment, nicknamed for the regiment's commander Colonel Julius von List. Many years later, when Hitler began to become a political thorn in the side of German authorities, a report was assembled to try to determine exactly how the Austrian national came to be allowed to fight in the Bavarian army at all. "In all probability, the question of Hitler's nationality was never even raised,"[10] the report read.

On October 20, 1914, Hitler wrote to the wife of his Munich landlord as his regiment left the German city.

Dear Frau Popp,

Please forgive me for not writing earlier. But this is the first chance I have had. As I told you, we left Munich on Saturday. We were on our feet from 6:30 a.m. until 5 p.m. And during the march we took part in a major engagement, all in pouring rain. We were quartered in Alling. I was put in the stables and I was wet through. Needless to say I could not sleep a wink. On Sunday we were on the move again from 5 a.m. to 6 p.m., all of us dog-tired, fighting action after action. At 6 p.m. we were ordered to camp in the open. The night was freezing cold and again none of us got any sleep. On Monday on the march again from 5 a.m. to 3 p.m.... Tonight, the 20th, we are going on a 4 days' train journey, probably to Belgium. I am tremendously excited.[11]

* * *

March 6, 1915

Franz Salvator's younger brother, Leopold, stood alongside the German and Turkish ambassadors in Vienna's Schwarzenbergplatz before an imposing wooden statue of a medieval German knight in full armor, with a broadsword resting between his hands. The statue had been crafted out of lightweight basswood by Viennese sculptor Josef Müllner, and seemed to peer out over the town square through a horizontal slit in his helmet. With the encouragement of the surrounding crowd, the Tuscan Archduke Leopold stepped up to the statue with a hammer and nail in hand. He chose his spot, then drove the small metal spike into the wooden knight to the sound of polite applause. Vienna's "Iron Soldier" was on its way toward becoming a knight in shining armor.

Austria's Military Widows and Orphans Fund had the idea to create the statue that would require the participation—and donations—of as many citizens as possible in order to prosper. For a small contribution, any citizen could join Archduke Leopold in showing their patriotism by purchasing a nail to help fortify the knight's armor. To receive the imperial family's blessing for the project was to ensure its success. The Emperor wholeheartedly supported the endeavor to raise money for families of fallen soldiers, and enlisted a well-known Habsburg, who was also available on that day, to hammer in the first nail.

Archduke Leopold was serving as Inspector-General of the Artillery when he was asked by the Emperor to support the charitable display in the Schwarzenbergplatz. As the older brother of Franz Salvator, Leopold was a recognizable and respected imperial figure. He lived in splendor in the 87-room Castle Wilhelminenberg near Vienna with his wife, the Infanta Blanca of Castile, and their ten children. Both Habsburg brothers shared a love of automobiles, and Leopold became one of the better-known members of the aristocratic family due to his engineering innovations. He conceived of a four-wheel drive system for military vehicles, as well as a new kind of transport truck for the troops that was produced by the Skoda factory in Bohemia.

Archduke Leopold Salvator, brother of Franz Salvator (Library of Congress Prints and Photographs Division, George Grantham Bain Collection).

Charitable giving had peaked at the beginning of the war, with the first Christmas showing particular generosity for the troops: "elaborate preparations" had been made to supply all Austro-Hungarian troops at the front with Christmas gifts. News outlets reported that the railway stations leading to Galicia and Serbia "are crowded with enormous chests, all of the same size, containing gifts for 250 men. In every chest are 250 gingerbread cakes, 75 pipes, 75 packets of tobacco, 75 patent lighters, 2,700 cigarettes, 175 cigarette holders, 250 cakes of soap, 250 picture postcards, and sprigs of fir from the Vienna forest." In all, one paper said, 4,500 cases were being sent "with twice as many smaller boxes containing liquors."[12] Yet, as the war progressed, and the imperial family were busy tending to their various wartime duties, public interest turned to personal survival with the rare average citizen having anything left over to donate to the troops.

As the most high-profile royal besides her father, Marie Valerie was unable to appear at the Schwarzenbergplatz that March day. She was consumed with rearing nine children, as well as with her duties as Patron of the Austrian Red Cross, a post that had been held by her mother, Empress Elisabeth, and for a brief time by her sister-in-law, Crown Princess Stephanie. Marie Valerie was already known as "The Angel of Wallsee" for running the "Marie Valerie Poor Hospital and Old People's Home" at the entrance to her village. Now, she took her good works a step further by opening up the elongated outer ward of her home at Wallsee Palace as a field hospital for injured soldiers. Her sister, Gisela, did the same at her home, creating a military hospital at Palais Leopold in northern Munich.

Throughout the trials of war, Marie Valerie's faith remained strong and it was important for her to act as a spiritual figurehead for the Empire's people. She, Franz Salvator, and their children joined the congregation at Vienna's gothic St. Stephen's Cathedral when Pope Pius XV called for prayers for peace across Europe. St. Stephen's was the seat of the Roman Catholic Archdiocese of Vienna and featured a nearly 450-foot spire and colorful mosaic tiled roof depicting the double-headed eagle that was the powerful symbol of the centuries-old Habsburg dynasty.

Marie Valerie was also busy keeping her father company as a much-needed diversion from the war. She and her children were now the only non-military visitors received by Emperor Franz Joseph at the Hofburg or Schönbrunn Palace, as his every waking hour was consumed with martial strategy. He was said to rise every morning at half-past three to take his morning meal in his study, then worked from five in the morning until eight o'clock at night, when he retired for the evening. His most frequent visitor was the Minister of War Alexander Freiherr von Krobatin, who brought "full details of the latest developments at the front and maps showing the changes in the position of the forces."[13]

By way of his imperial marriage, Franz Salvator was named Vice-Patron of the Red Cross, and according to the organizations statutes, "In the case of war, the Vice-Patron takes over the role of an Inspector General of the voluntary medical corps,"[14] a duty that Franz Salvator balanced with his military role as colonel of Hussar Regiment No. 15. Dressed in their bright red breeches and light blue jackets with gold braided detail, Franz Salvator's regiment made a colorful presence as their riding skills were put to the test on the Italian Front in the Tyrol.

At one point, however, Franz Salvator laid down his sword and donned his Red Cross Inspector General hat to open a military hospital in the thermal spa town of Postyen (now Piestany in Slovakia). The Archduke's visit was meticulously recorded, and 30 of the best photographs were bound in red moroccan leather for a folio that was later presented to the War Minister. The photographs show the Archduke's arrival and the official opening ceremony with soldiers in varying states of injury; some bandaged and confined to wheel chairs, many others leaning on crutches. Another shows the Archduke's retinue down by a body of water, observing soldiers taking the fresh air while the men cast a fishing line. And still more photographs, clearly meant to give the impression of well-cared-for invalids, show the men reclining while wrapped in warm towels, or bathing in the soothing mineral baths.

The University of Innsbruck recognized "His Imperial and Royal Highness the Archduke Franz Salvator, the Protector of the Red Cross, this organization which has had such a beneficial impact on the defense against war damages," by conferring on him an honorary doctorate in

8. "I tread the path that it is my duty to follow" 69

medicine. The University invited Franz Salvator to Innsbruck to receive the formal conferment, but the Archduke's High Court Master Baron von Lederer wrote back, requesting instead that the presentation be made nearly 300 miles away in Vienna. During the war, however, travel was difficult. Lederer added, "His Highness fully understands if the said event is unable to take place" and that "His Imperial and Royal Highness deigns to express that if one or another inspection trip or any other trip His Highness undertakes should afford the opportunity to come to Innsbruck, His Royal and Imperial Highness would most happily receive Your Magnificence … but this must also be left to a later date."[15] It's not known whether Franz Salvator ever accepted the degree in person, but the certificate shows that it was delivered "with the Highest Approval of His Majesty the Emperor and King Franz Josef I." Clearly, the Archduke was back in favor with the Emperor who had helped to cover up Franz Salvator's illegitimate child with Stephanie Richter, now Princess von Hohenlohe. With her marriage, Princess Stephanie "was now either related to, or acquainted with, the majority of the royal families in Europe."[16]

* * *

Immediately after her low-key wedding in London, Princess Stephanie and Prince Friedrich Franz went on honeymoon in Berlin. Despite the fact that she was pregnant, the newlyweds were planning to extend their honeymoon with an arduous journey to India for a tiger shoot with local royalty, but the trip was canceled with the July announcement that Austria was at war. The couple returned to Vienna, where she gave birth to Franz Salvator's son before Christmas.

Princess Stephanie's new husband promptly joined his military regiment on the Russian front. He also served in Switzerland, where British intelligence reported that he acted as "chief of German propaganda and director of German espionage."[17] Since the Princess had little contact with her husband for the next four years, it's not known whether she was aware of any spying activity on his part.

Rather than sitting at home with a new baby waiting for news of a husband she didn't love, Princess Stephanie took advantage of her imperial connections to join in the action. As head of the Red Cross, Franz Salvator introduced the Princess to his older sister, Archduchess Maria Theresa, who oversaw training and placement of Red Cross nurses. Princess Stephanie received her basic medical training in Vienna, was given the name 'Sister Michaela,' then received her first none-too-glamorous assignment: to roll bandages at a first aid post. She found the work tedious and boring, and according to her son Franzi, who wrote about his mother when he grew to adulthood, "Very soon she was persuading Archduke Franz Salvator to use his influence to have her sent to the front."[18] The Archduke made sure she got her wish.

Archduchess Maria Theresa, sister of Franz Salvator, who oversaw training and placement of Red Cross nurses. Princess Stephanie von Hohenlohe trained under her before heading out to the front (author's collection).

8. *"I tread the path that it is my duty to follow"*

After most likely leaving her infant son with her mother in Vienna, Princess Stephanie left for the Russian front to work in a field hospital at Lemberg, the capital of Astro-Polish Galicia, and she made sure that everyone stationed there knew of her new royal status. She had her uniforms tailor-made to flatter her figure and packed an unwieldy rubber bathtub so she could soak away the day's stresses. The Princess also included an entourage consisting of a valet and chambermaid to attend to her personal needs, which can't have made her very popular with the legitimate nurses and battle-weary military personnel. Princess Stephanie worked under the auspices of the eminent Austrian surgeon and professor Dr. Otto Zuckerkandl, whom the Princess described as "a very nervous, irritable, brilliant man."[19]

The Princess began heavily smoking Havana cigars at this time, "to dispel the unbelievably nauseating smell of human flesh which you can pick from the human carcass without any effort like cheese off a loaf. It is positively the worst smell I have ever encountered,"[20] she wrote. According to her son, Princess Stephanie would strike a match on the sole of her shoe to light the stogies, "a trick which caused great amusement among onlookers."[21]

Princess Stephanie first assisted with surgery at Lemberg, which turned out to be an amputation. She conveyed the war story to her son, Franzi, who later wrote, "she was asked to hold the gangrenous leg until it went heavy and fell into a bucket of water." She told him that she was very brave and "managed this without blinking."[22]

Stephanie would later describe a front hospital as "only spasmodically busy, immediately after an offensive or during a battle. After that the wounded are sent to the back country as soon as they can be transported to make room for others."

In all of her exposure to war patients, Princess Stephanie summed up whom she felt to be the bravest and those who were the most fainthearted. "The best patients were Tyrolians, Hungarians, [and] the Russians. Long suffering, gentle, polite. They had been used to suffering and this much more meant little to them. The worst were the Checks [sic] and the Viennese. Always whailing [sic], complaining, trying to squeeze every bit of advantage out of everyone. Never satisfied and exacting, at least such were my experiences."[23]

9

"The whole world suffered in consequence"

—Princess Stephanie von Hohenlohe

Vienna, November 21, 1916

Emperor Franz Joseph rose at his usual early hour to attend to government business and check the progress of the war. The Battle of the Somme against the British and French had ended just days before with little to show for the immense bloodshed. After five months of fighting along the 15-mile front, the Allies had pushed back the Germans only a few miles, and yet more than one million soldiers had been wounded or killed in what would go down in history as one of the costliest battles ever fought. Among the injured was German Private Adolf Hitler, who had been hit in the leg by a shell splinter.

The Emperor had been suffering for several days from a cold with an alarming cough that his doctors feared was developing into pneumonia. On November 17, an official announcement came from the Hofburg: Archduke Karl "would have charge of affairs of the realm conjointly with the Emperor."[1]

Franz Joseph had met with Karl and his wife Zita, as well as with Marie Valerie on the morning of the 21st in his study at Schönbrunn Palace, before Marie Valerie left to retrieve one of her daughters at the Vienna railway station. While his daughter was gone, Franz Joseph met with Foreign Minister Stephan Burián von Rajecz. But the Emperor's health continued to slowly decline, and soon his fever had spiked. Marie Valerie was immediately recalled to court, where she helped her ailing father to bed. After extended examinations, the doctors told her they did not expect the Emperor to last through the night.

Franz Joseph was unable to rest easy, or to fully communicate. He

9. "The whole world suffered in consequence"

continuously pointed to his throat, indicating pain, and perhaps a swelling that made it difficult to breathe.

All members of the imperial family who were in Vienna were called to the Emperor's bedside, as was Austrian Minister-President Dr. Ernest von Koerber. Solemn last rites were given, then Marie Valerie knelt by her father's head and whispered the Catholic prayer for the dying:

> Go forth, Christian soul, from this world
> in the name of God the almighty Father,
> who created you,
> in the name of Jesus Christ, Son of the living God,
> who suffered for you,
> in the name of the Holy Spirit,
> who was poured out upon you,
> go forth, faithful Christian.[2]

The Emperor was said to have become delirious, then lapsed into a coma before quietly passing away while all those around him prayed the Rosary. Katharina Schratt, the Emperor's "dear friend" and companion for 34 years, was called to the death chamber to say her goodbyes, and was said to have been received just like a family member. Marie Valerie, who never approved of her father's relationship with the actress, was said to have embraced Katharina in the time of mourning.

Although the palace had dispatched intermittent bulletins with updates of the Emperor's health, few took seriously that the "Old Gentleman of Schönbrunn," as they affectionately called him, would not recover. For many Viennese, Franz Joseph's rule was all they had ever known. When news of his death came around 11 p.m., it "had an absolutely paralysing effect on Vienna," one newspaper reported. "All amusements were at once suspended."[3]

Emperor Franz Joseph had been 86 years old and had reigned over the Austro-Hungarian Empire for a remarkable 67 years, 355 days.

* * *

Back from the war front, Princess Stephanie von Hohenlohe made her way to the Hofburg where Viennese royalty and foreign dignitaries had gathered to pay their final respects to the Emperor. Archduchess Marie Valerie and Archduke Franz Salvator were present to receive the important guests. Stephanie felt it was her right to mingle with the upper classes, since she was a Hohenlohe Princess. She was also the mistress of an important member of the Habsburg dynasty and mother of his child. But the Lord Chamberlain for the new Emperor Karl, who was the gatekeeper to the event, knew better than to let her pass. Prince Konrad Hohenlohe, although a relative of Stephanie's husband Prince Friedrich, had no love for his manipulative in-law and wasn't about to let her create a scandal on such an historically solemn day.

Legend has it that he uttered the words "Madame, you are not worthy to take a place alongside the other mourners at the bier of this great monarch. Please return home."[4] Whether or not these words were actually spoken, Princess Stephanie was relegated to watching the funeral procession with the rest of the crowd on the streets of Vienna.

The funeral procession was equally as grand as that held for the Emperor's wife, Elisabeth, 12 years earlier. Eight ebony steeds towed the ornate caisson bearing the Emperor's body through downtown Vienna, which was lined with tens of thousands of mourners, toward the iconic spire of the centuries-old St. Stephan's Cathedral. Following close behind on foot were the youthful Emperor Karl in his field gray uniform, a heavily-veiled Empress Zita all in black, and the next heir to the throne, four-year-old Archduke Otto, a contrast in white with a black tie and sash, holding tightly to his mother's hand.

Artist rendering of Emperor Karl (Library of Congress Prints and Photographs Division, George Harris & Ewing Collection).

Marie Valerie, Franz Salvator, and their children followed behind the new Emperor's family. All of the Habsburg women donned flowing black crepe gowns and waist-length veils that completely obscured their grieving faces. Once they arrived at the cathedral, they found that it "was crammed in every corner with a brilliant congregation of Kings, Crown Princes, Archdukes, diplomats, prelates, statesmen, and other personages."[5]

Princess Stephanie Hohenlohe gave her account of the historic scene while standing outside of St. Stephan's:

> After the funeral procession with all its pomp and splendour, after the mass in St. Stephan's Cathedral, Vienna's beautiful old church, the new, young Emperor Charles with his wife Empress Zita and the Crownprince [sic], little Archduke Otto came out of the cathedral while cannons were being shot off and all the bells were ringing.

9. "The whole world suffered in consequence" 75

The royal pair stood there with the blond, lovely child between them. The Emperor in Uniform, looking very young with a grave face. The Empress all in black with a long train. The Crown Prince, his golden locks hanging over his shoulders, dressed in a white suit with a lace collar and a bigg [sic] black crepe across his chest. Thus they appeared before the public, the people of Vienna and of their empire. The whole picture was so unforgettable and impressive that it took everybody's breath away. I am sure that it meant so much to all of us standing there, that each individual would willingly have given his heart, his blood, all he had, and laid it at the feet of these three young people to help them carry their new, heavy burden and make a success of it. But unfortunately for all of us it came differently and the whole world suffered in consequence.[6]

Following the funeral service, the procession traveled four blocks more to the site of the imperial crypt at the Church of the Capuchins. In keeping with the ancient Habsburg tradition, the Capuchin friars refused to open the immense double monastery doors until the imperial representative asked for admittance not for an Emperor and King, but for "a mortal, sinful man."[7] Franz Joseph's coffin was then carried inside and laid atop a raised marble platform between the Emperor's wife and son, who had preceded him in death.

* * *

Before he died, Franz Joseph had updated his will to provide for invalid soldiers, and the widows and orphans of those killed in battle. The newspapers dubbed it "Conscience Money."[8] Some 50 million marks (about $194 million in today's U.S. dollars) went directly into the fund. Marie Valerie, her sister Gisela, and Rudolf's daughter Erzi (now married to Prince Otto of Windisch-Grätz) each received around 18 million marks ($70 million).

What mattered most to Marie Valerie was her father's bequeathment of the Kaiservilla at Bad Ischl. She had once written in her diary that the thought of the villa going to anyone else was "so repugnant" that she "should like to set fire to the dear house."[9] Her mother, Empress Elisabeth, has assured her that the summer home would be hers one day, and Franz Joseph had honored her wish.

Once word of the Emperor's death reached Ischl, the local mayor and council voted to rename the central Kreuz-Plaz to "Kaiser-Franz-Josef-Platz." They also voted to fund a funeral service to be held every November 21 at the Ischl parish church of St. Nicholas, where Marie Valerie had been married.

* * *

After Franz Joseph's death, many people both inside and outside the Empire wondered what would become of the war effort. The "Old Gentleman" had been a stabilizing symbol for his subjects, many of whom now felt lost and uncertain without him. Adolf Hitler wrote years later, "In the last few years the state had been so bound up with the person of Francis Joseph that the death of this old embodiment of the Empire was felt by the broad masses to be tantamount to the death of the Empire itself."[10]

Austro-Hungarian officials tried to reassure the masses that victory and peace were still in sight. Newspapers noted the Austro-Hungarian Ambassador's optimism: "the ambassador feels that the people of the dual monarchy have been so solidified by the war that the death of their ruler, while causing deep regret, will not bring about any political changes of importance. The new monarch is said to have well defined ideas regarding peace and personally is peacefully inclined. He is described as 'a sensible man, and, therefore, in favor of peace rather than war.'"[11]

Emperor Karl, Franz Joseph's great-nephew, had been born in 1887 at Persenbeug Castle, about 50 miles from Vienna. His father was Archduke Otto von Habsburg and his mother was born a Saxon princess. In 1911, he had married Princess Zita of Bourbon Parma, and had four small children at the time of Franz Joseph's death. He was religiously pious and completely devoted to his young family.

Karl had begun his military career as an officer with troops in Bohemia and Galicia, and was immediately appointed supreme commander of the army once war was declared. However, he was ordered to stay out of direct combat, and instead served as a glorified liaison officer between the generals and Franz Joseph. Karl was not included in strategic decisions until July 1915, the time that Franz Joseph's health began to fluctuate. At this point, any real decisive power was held completely by the generals and the magisterial administrators; the old Emperor had become a mere figurehead. Karl desired to be a very different kind of Emperor, one who would bring about peace and transform the Empire into a federal union where all nationalities would be represented equally. But he had no pre-established relationship with Franz Joseph's old guard, and they did not trust the 29-year-old to help determine the future of the vast Empire. Still, in Karl's first declaration to his people as Emperor, he made it known that establishing peace was his first priority. He promised to "do everything to banish in the shortest possible time the horrors and sacrifices of war, to win back for my peoples the sorely-missed blessing of peace, insofar as this can be reconciled with the honour of our arms, the essential living requirements of my lands and their loyal allies and the defiance of our enemies."[12]

9. "The whole world suffered in consequence" 77

Photo taken about 1914 of Empress Zita with Archduke Otto (standing) and Archduchess Adelheid (Library of Congress Prints and Photographs Division, George Grantham Bain Collection).

By 1917, the Austrian army's main focus was on the Italian front, where the Alpine mountains proved as formidable a foe as the Allies. This is precisely where Princess Stephanie von Hohenlohe traveled next as a Red Cross nurse, and her experiences would affect her deeply. Since the

78 Part I: *Verblassendes Reich*/Fading Empire, 1890–1924

Emperor Karl inspecting a soldier (Library of Congress Prints and Photographs Division, George Grantham Bain Collection).

beginning of the war, 780,000 Austrian soldiers had been killed and half-a-million had been gravely injured. Poison gas was now being deployed, which brought on a whole new host of suffering.

Her assigned hospital was near Tolmezzo, and the civilian population had been so ravaged by food shortages that the people often made their way to the medical facility to offer hand-woven linen and crocheted lace in exchange for food staples like bread, salt and sugar.

9. "The whole world suffered in consequence"

"Naturally we nurses and doctors returned to our homes laden with fine things thus acquired," she wrote.

Bartering was one thing, but Princess Stephanie expressed dismay at the looting she observed once the Austrian troops overran a village.

"I am sorry to say that there were many cases where we behaved very badly when it came to appropriating things in the territory we had conquered," she wrote. "In many instances whole shops and houses were plundered empty by our soldiers, as well as by the Germans. But such robbery was not confined to the simple soldiers only. Officers went in for it too."

One Red Cross officer, Count Karl Wurmbrandt, sent trainloads of glassware and antiques back to Vienna. Stephanie herself said she acquired a bed that Napoleon had once slept in, although she said she paid cash for it to help out a starving peasant.

"I am not sure whether that makes it better or worse," she wrote.

Stephanie described how she traveled to the village of Görz (now Gorizia) at the foot of the Julian Alps on the border of Slovenia, and found that it had fallen victim to trench warfare. "In a street of average width one could see the Italian trenches on the one side walk and the

A German field bakery near Ypres in western Belgium. Adolf Hitler's List Regiment shipped off for Ypres on August 16, 1914 (Library of Congress Prints and Photographs Division, George Grantham Bain Collection).

Austrian ones on the other. And thus those poor soldiers had to live for months."

She observed that no window pane remained in the village that hadn't been shattered by heavy bombardments, and that the surrounding forest that had once been famous for its majestic beauty had been burned down to nothing but charred stumps.

The Red Cross nurses were first on the scene once soldiers had evacuated a battle. The sights and smells left behind bored into her conscience.

"I saw the most pathetic sights in those trenches. Thus the dead could only be buried with great difficulty in the stony ground of the mountains," she wrote. "Besides the rains would periodically wash the earth away. As a consequence one would see a head, or an arm, or a half disintegrated leg protruding from the ground, which was worse than seeing the whole dead body."

In some spots, she found regular graves mounded with loose dirt that had also been appropriated as makeshift gardens. "More often than not there would be tomatoes growing on top of them, planted by the hungry soldiers, with whom piety had given way to thoughts for the practical.

German soldiers reading letters in the trenches (Library of Congress Prints and Photographs Division, George Grantham Bain Collection).

There was not enough soft earth to make a grave and plant vegetables elsewhere, so the two had to be combined in one."

Adequate food, clothing, and medicine were routinely scarce in the towering Alps, and the cold was paralyzing. "And still I never heard any complaints. No one said or even so much as suggested that we might possibly lose the war."[13]

* * *

Private Adolf Hitler had never felt such a sense of purpose as he did alongside his comrades, both Jewish and Christian alike, at the western front. They called him "Adi" or "the artist," and seemed fond of him, even though they teased him for his quirkiness and tendency toward reclusiveness. One fellow soldier described him as "almost skeletal in appearance, dark eyes hooded in a sallow complexion, untrimmed moustache, sitting in a corner buried in a newspaper, occasionally taking a sip of tea, seldom joining in the banter of the group."[14]

Hitler brushed off the good-natured ribbing about his refusal to smoke, drink, or partake in a visit to a local brothel with the other men. He had never been truly part of a group before, but the shared purpose of fighting for an ideal galvanized all of the men from such disparate backgrounds. Watching their fellow soldiers die horrible deaths at the hands of the English and French also served to bond the men. At the end of the First Battle of Ypres, Hitler's regiment had been cut down to just 725 soldiers from a starting number of around 3,000.

"For all that, we beat the English," Hitler wrote his Munich landlord, Joseph Popp.[15]

Somehow, Private Hitler had survived the devastating battle, and even thrived. For his combat efforts, he was promoted to *Gefreiter*, which was akin to a "second rank" of Private, but without any authority over other soldiers. Instead of being elevated to a leadership position, Hitler was transferred to the regimental staff and made one of about eight dispatch runners whose job it was to carry messages on foot or bicycle from the command post to the front. The job was a dangerous one, and many times the runners were sent in pairs in case one was killed en route.

"I am now a staff runner," he wrote proudly to a judge he knew back in Munich. "It's slightly less dirty work but all the more dangerous. In Wyschaete alone 3 of us 8 were killed on the first day of the attack and one was badly wounded."[16]

One of Hitler's immediate superiors at the regimental headquarters was Fritz Wiedemann, who was the staff adjutant of the 16th Reserve

Infantry Regiment. Wiedemann would describe Hitler as the "paradigm of the unknown soldier carrying out his duty silently and calmly."[17] The adjutant would play an important role in the dynamics of the relationship between Hitler and Princess Stephanie von Hohenlohe in the distant future.

Hitler had a zealous loyalty to his superiors and was credited with helping to save his commander, Lieutenant Colonel Philipp Engelhardt, by shielding the exposed officer from French fire and helping to get him to safety. Just two days later, on November 17, 1914, Hitler himself narrowly escaped death. He wrote Joseph Popp that he "was saved by a near miracle,"[18] after the primitive hut occupied by Hitler, Engelhardt, and a handful of other men, was shelled to bits. Hitler had left the hut just minutes before. Engelhardt survived once again, this time with several severe shrapnel wounds. Seven of the men who had remained in the hut were killed.

"It was the most horrible thing I have ever seen in my life," Hitler wrote.[19]

By December, Hitler had been awarded the Iron Cross 2nd Class for his devotion to his regiment.

"It was the happiest day of my life," he wrote. "True, most of my comrades who had earned it just as much were dead. I beg you, dear Herr Popp, please save the newspaper in which the decoration is listed. I would like to have it as a keepsake if the Lord should spare my life."[20]

Hitler's morale remained high about the odds of winning the war, but he did complain about the torrential rains that filled the trenches the average soldiers called home, with no relief from soaked blankets and soggy bread.

"The weather is miserable; and we often spend days on end knee-deep in water and, what is more, under heavy fire," he wrote. "Let's hope that soon … the whole front will start moving forward. Things can't go on like this forever."[21]

Although he had to trudge through flooded land that had churned to viscous mud to deliver his messages, Hitler didn't spend as much time in the trenches as he would later claim; as a dispatcher, he spent nearly half of his war service at regimental headquarters near Fromelles in northern France instead of out in the elements with the other soldiers.

As the front showed little sign of budging by that first Christmas, the rest of the men in the List Regiment began to lose hope and motivation. A Catholic monk who accompanied the soldiers at the front made the observation about low morale: "As a result of their terrible days at war—

made worse by adverse weather conditions ... our troops are very dispirited."[22]

Members of Hitler's regiment returned to the trenches from a brief respite on December 26 to learn that the soldiers they were relieving had participated in a "Christmas Truce" for two days prior. The English and Bavarian foot soldiers had decided on their own without official sanction that they would lay down their weapons, leave their trenches, and meet each other in the desolate no man's land to sing Christmas carols, exchange gifts like cigarettes and chocolates, and even participate in friendly soccer matches. The List Regiment's commanders were appalled by the other regiment's breakdown in discipline and strove to prevent their own troops from following suit on Boxing Day. But they were unsuccessful. The men of Hitler's regiment erected a Christmas tree and also ventured into the cratered land between the trenches to shake the English soldiers' hands in a show of good will. Some of the English were even invited to try on German helmets. Hitler's fellow dispatch runner Heinrich Lugauer said that Hitler was sickened by the display.

"When everyone was talking about the Christmas 1914 fraternization with the Englishmen, Hitler revealed himself to be its bitter opponent. He said, 'Something like this should not even be up for discussion during wartime.'"[23] Hitler's hardline opinion mirrored that of the commanders to whom he was so devoted. The average foot soldiers had relished the good-natured break, with approximately half of the entire regiment believed to have taken part in the makeshift festivities.

After the Christmas spirit dissipated from the frigid Belgian air, however, men on both sides took aim at one another once again.

* * *

February 5, 1915

Shortly before Hitler's regiment entrenched itself near Fromelles in northern France in preparation for the Battle of the Somme, Hitler made his feelings known about his desire for a pure Germany for the first time in writing to Munich court assessor Ernst Hepp. Before the war, Hepp had purchased several of Hitler's paintings and the two had shared meals together. "I often think of Munich, and each one of us has only one wish: that he might soon get a chance to even scores with that crew, to get at them no matter what the cost, and that those of us who are lucky enough to return to the fatherland will find it a purer place, less riddled with foreign influences, so that the daily sacrifices and sufferings of hundreds of thousands of us and the torrent of blood that keeps flowing here day after day against an international world of enemies, will not only help to smash Germany's foes outside but that our inner internationalism, too, will collapse. This would be worth much more than any gain in territory. Austria will fare as I have always said she will."[24]

In other words, Austria would collapse due to its multinationalism, but a pure Germany would thrive and become the dominant power in Europe.

Just a few months after sending this letter, for reasons unknown, Hitler no longer received any mail or care packages at the front, and no longer spoke of family or friends back home. Perhaps he, himself, had stopped writing, since it was at this point in the war that he said he struggled between thoughts of self-preservation and the admonitions of duty. Duty won out, and all that mattered to him from that point onward was victory on the battlefield. "The more this [inner] voice admonished one to caution, the louder and more insistent its lures, the sharper resistance grew until at last, after a long inner struggle, consciousness of duty emerged victorious. By the winter of 1915–16, this struggle had for me been decided. At last my will was undisputed master. If in the first days I went over the top with rejoicing and laughter, I was now calm and determined. And this was enduring. Now Fate could bring on the ultimate tests without my nerves shattering or my reason failing."[25]

Instead of writing letters, Hitler now spent his free time sitting alone to draw and read philosophy. His comrades would later describe him as a lonely man, and historians have pointed out that photos taken of his regiment at the time always show Hitler sitting or standing at the periphery, like an afterthought. There was one thing left, however, that Hitler cared about in addition to his duty; a small, white terrier dog that had managed to cross safely from the British trenches, across no man's land, to Hitler's side. Hitler named the dog Foxl, meaning "little fox," and delighted in teaching the obedient animal tricks. Foxl seemed to be the only creature left to receive any deep emotional attachment from Private Hitler.

Hitler was frantic when he couldn't find Foxl as his regiment prepared to move on to its next location. Some 25 years later he would say, "The swine who took him from me doesn't know what he did to me."[26]

* * *

October 5, 1916

Although Hitler wasn't overly fond of interpersonal relationships, he clearly loved his regiment—an entity that had finally given his vagabond hand-to-mouth life a greater purpose. Historians believe he may even have declined military promotions in order to remain with his unit. So, it's no exaggeration that Hitler's worst fear came true four days into the Battle of the Somme when a grenade exploded near his dugout causing a minor leg injury that required him to be sent home to Germany. Hitler was terrified that he would never see his regiment—his ersatz family—again. While other soldiers were pretending to be injured or were even self-mutilating so they could get away from the ferocious fighting on the Somme, Private Hitler was begging to stay.

"It's not so bad, Herr Lieutenant Colonel, eh?" he told Staff Adjutant Fritz Wiedemann. "I can stay with you, stay with the regiment."[27] But Hitler and several other men were carried away to an army hospital about 60 miles away in Hermies before being put on a train back to Germany.

While he was convalescing, more than 50 percent of Hitler's company were killed or injured in the fighting. The List Regiment was withdrawn from the front just 12 days after arriving. Being forced to evacuate the Somme early may have saved Hitler's life.

Hitler spent just under two months recuperating in an army hospital near Berlin, and was there when news of Austrian Emperor Franz Joseph's death spread throughout the German-speaking world. Hitler did not record his thoughts on the momentous passing of the leader he had so despised, yet whom he had credited for starting the war that Hitler felt was long overdue.

"Those who today shower the Viennese government with reproaches on the form and content of the [war] ultimatum it issued, do it an injustice," he would write years later. "No other power in the world could have acted differently in the same situation and the same position."[28]

10

"There was danger in the air"

—Princess Stephanie von Hohenlohe

Princess Stephanie von Hohenlohe returned home to Vienna on leave from her Red Cross duties, where she began to notice that the living conditions in the city were abysmal.

"I saw a poor, tired and terribly emaciated cab horse fall dead in the street from malnutrition.... This opened my eyes for the first time, and I suddenly began to notice incidents like these: people standing for hours in front of the 'konsumverein' [consumer association] with their ration cards, a woman picking up old rotten cabbage leaves and having to fight for them," she wrote.[1]

Even members of the aristocracy, with their immense staff of chauffeurs, grooms, stable boys, valets, cooks, maids, gardeners, gatekeepers, laundresses, and the rest, had nowhere to turn for food. There was no sugar, butter, eggs, or bread to be served up on fine porcelain, since it was all required at the front by the German and Austrian armies. Instead, turnips were diced, boiled, mashed, or made into round cakes for nearly every meal. At Franz Salvator's Wallsee Castle and Leopold Salvator's Castle Wilhelminenberg, the servants and the large families shared what little food, clothing, and coal for warmth that they could gather.

When Princess Stephanie expressed her concern to her friends that the war did not seem to be going in their favor, she was scolded for being a defeatist.

"How can you expect the people to do their duty when others like you are putting doubt in their minds," a friend who worked in the foreign office asked her.

Before heading back to the front, Princess Stephanie recalled seeing an Italian airplane flying over Vienna. The sight left her shaken.

"I felt that we could not possibly win the war," she wrote.[2]

10. "There was danger in the air"

* * *

Adolf Hitler decried the low morale he encountered in Germany while recovering from his wounds. He had not been back in the fatherland since the beginning of the war two years earlier, and he, too, saw the starvation brought on by the Allied blockade. As many as 700,000 Germany died from malnutrition and related illnesses during the war. Still, Hitler saw no reason why the people were not rallying. "Anger, discontent, complaints met one's ears wherever one went ... the general spirit was deplorable ... devotion to duty was considered a sign of weakness or bigotry."[3]

The hungry people were desperate to assign blame, and turned against the Jews, whom they charged as being war profiteers who were deliberately withholding provisions. Antisemitic vitriol was rampant in Munich and Berlin, the two cities where Hitler spent his recuperation period.

Hitler was itching to get back to the battlefield and wrote to Fritz Wiedemann that he was "battle ready" and "longed to return to my old regiment and old comrades."[4] On March 5, 1917, Hitler got his wish, only to find that desertion and insubordination were running rampant among the troops. For Hitler, to whom duty was paramount, disobeying a direct order was beyond unthinkable. Thrilled to be back with his military family, Hitler kept his head down and resumed his job as a message runner. One month later, with the United States seething at the unprovoked German U-boat attacks that were claiming American lives, President Woodrow Wilson formally declared war against Germany.

While the German generals were contemplating the all-too-obvious fact that the war was lost, Hitler was awarded the Iron Cross, First Class, on August 4, 1918, for braving heavy fire to deliver a crucial communication to the front. It was a remarkable honor for a mere private, whom many believed had declined talk of promotion in order to remain with the regiment to which he felt so attached. Hitler had been nominated for the honor by a Jewish officer, Lieutenant Hugo Gutmann.

* * *

Princess Stephanie undoubtedly experienced similar antisemitism from the starving, striking citizens of Vienna, and it may have come as somewhat of a relief to leave the city. However, when she returned to the front on the Piave River in northern Italy, minus her chambermaid and butler, the atmosphere was foreboding.

"[C]onditions had deteriorated very much," she would write. "There was very little to eat for the people in the hospitals and the troops themselves. The after effect of the second attempted but unsuccessful offensive was bad ... there was discontent everywhere.... Although no one knew anything it was felt somehow that there was danger in the air."

Despite the hardships on the Piave, Franz Salvator's nephews Leopold and Rainer, both soldiers, survived the intense fighting.

Princess Stephanie's stay at the Italian front did not last long. She received a telegram from a friend "in a high official position" warning her to leave immediately "for a place, any place, with good railway communications. I knew what that meant. It was a warning that Austria Hungary had reached the breaking point and that he wanted me to be able to get away as quickly as possible when that moment came. It was shattering news. After all our efforts, everything was going to be lost after all."

The Princess asked her Red Cross superior if she could take leave since the hospital was relatively quiet. In fact, by the end of the summer 1918, some 230,000 soldiers had deserted the Empire's army. Princess Stephanie packed up, then left for Trieste and on to Vienna, a trip that took her three days. "It was a difficult journey. There were no direct trains. In fact hardly any trains at all, especially for women.... My husband, mother and child were all somewhere or other and with the war nearing its end, my work done, I had to set about finding and looking after them."[5]

Once she located her mother and nearly four-year-old son, Franzi, they packed up and moved to a resort on the Adriatic where they waited out the inevitable end of the war.

* * *

November 11, 1918

Emperor Karl sat in the Blue Chinese Salon of Schönbrunn Palace where he was presented with a document that would effectively end 640 years of the old way of Habsburg rule. Although he had a host of ideas for reforming the government and monarchy, his immediate desire was to stop the bloodshed immediately; the war was lost and he could not in good conscience allow the battlefield slaughter to continue. Karl read the document over carefully before signing: "Filled with an unalterable love for all my peoples I do not wish to make my person a hindrance to their free development. I accept in advance the decision that is taken by German-Austria concerning its future form of state. The people has taken charge of government through its representatives. I relinquish every participation in the affairs of state. At the same time I release the Government of Austria from its office."[6] By "relinquishing every participation in the affairs of state," Karl was not formally abdicating; he had decided instead to vacate Vienna for now and would return when the time was right to implement his reforms and forge a new future for the Habsburgs and for Austria.

Many years later, Princess Stephanie von Hohenlohe would tell her son Franzi a story: a friend of hers had been given a message to deliver to Emperor Karl shortly after he stepped down as the head of the government, but was surprised to find no guards patrolling Schönbrunn's grounds.

"Knowing where the private apartments were situated, he went on until he came to a door where a sentry was leaning against a door, fast asleep. He had not been relieved of duty for twenty-four hours. From inside the apartments came the voices of children."[7] When the man knocked, Karl himself answered, just as any ordinary man would do. The imperial mantle had quite obviously been lifted from his shoulders.

Shortly thereafter, Emperor Karl and his family bade a final farewell to their last remaining supporters, and made their way down to nondescript automobiles that were waiting in the palace courtyard. Surreptitiously, the motorcade left Schönbrunn through a side gate and out to an uncertain future.

As for the government in Vienna, a Provisional Assembly was now in place that proclaimed a new Republic of German Austria. The government claimed the German-speaking territories in the western portion of the former Empire, and claimed the right to an *Anschluss*, or a merger, with Germany.

But the Allies, consisting of Britain, France, Italy, Russia and the United States, weren't condoning such a consolidation of power in the German-speaking world. It forbade the *Anschluss*, and allotted the German-speaking areas of Bohemia, Moravia, and Silesia to the newly-formed Czechoslovakia. Adolf Hitler would have much to say about the territorial division in the decades to come.

* * *

November 12, 1918

Adolf Hitler was in a military hospital psychiatric ward when he learned of the Central Powers' surrender. During the second battle of the

Marne, known to history as the war's last German offensive, Hitler and two other dispatch runners had been exposed to a British mustard gas attack. "Toward morning I, too, was seized with pain which grew worse with every quarter hour, and at seven in the morning I stumbled and tottered back with burning eyes; taking with me my last report of the War. A few hours later, my eyes had turned into glowing coals; it had grown dark around me."[8]

Once Hitler arrived at the hospital, doctors determined that he had been exposed to such a small quantity of gas that he should be back on his feet in no time. When this didn't happen, they determined that his blindness was not a physical problem, but a mental one. The diagnosis: "psychopathy with symptoms of hysteria."[9]

While still struggling with whatever disorder was keeping him from the battlefield, the List Regiment was notified on November 11 that the war was officially coming to an end. Hitler found out a day later from the hospital chaplain.

"I was on the road to improvement when the monstrous thing happened," he wrote.[10] "When the old gentleman tried to go on, and began to tell us that we must now end the long War, yes, that now that it was lost and we were throwing ourselves upon the mercy of the victors, our fatherland would for the future be exposed to dire oppression, that the armistice should be accepted with confidence in the magnanimity of our previous enemies—I could stand it no longer.... Again everything went black before my eyes; I tottered and groped my way back to the dormitory, threw myself on my bunk, and dug my burning head into my blanket and pillow."[11]

Hitler called the surrender "the greatest villainy of the century."[12]

11

"We hope that God's mercy will give us better times"

—Marie Valerie

With the war officially lost and Emperor Karl searching for safe quarter, the rest of the Habsburgs now had a monumental decision to make: renounce their aristocratic titles, which were now illegal within the former Empire, and remain in their homes—or be expelled and have their property confiscated. At least one news report erroneously published that Marie Valerie and her family chose to flee Austria. "The Archduchess Marie Valerie, daughter of the late Emperor Franz Josef, is at present in Switzerland living incognita, according to messages published at Zurich, but her exact whereabouts are unknown. It is stated that the Archduchess was compelled to abandon her estate in Moravia owing to the hostile attitude of the populations."[1]

The truth was, Marie Valerie and Franz Salvator decided it was more important to renounce their titles of Archduchess and Archduke in order to remain in their Austrian home with their nine children. They would become citizens of the Austrian Republic with no more imperial privileges and would be henceforth known officially as Frau and Herr Habsburg. Marie Valerie may have even looked hopefully on the new German-centric Austrian government, in keeping with her German nationalistic bent. Opting to relinquish their titles and live in the new republic, however, was viewed by some Habsburgs as a betrayal of the "priceless heritage and high honor earned by the ancestors, so as to curry favor with an upstart and untried regime."[2]

A letter written by Marie Valerie from Wallsee in December 1919 gives a hint as to how she was coping with her new life as an average citizen, albeit one who still lived in a castle. The former Archduchess had received news of the death of her beloved English governess, Mary Throckmorton, at the age of 87, from Mary's sister. Marie Valerie wrote back:

Dear Madam,

    The sad news your kind letter brings me grieves me deeply and I hurry to express you my innermost and most heartfelt sympathy. Your dear sister embodied for me remembrances of my earliest childhood, and her so long & true affection & interest in all that concerned me and mine always touched me deeply & will live on in my heart in loving gratitude. I unite my prayers with yours, dear Madam, that the soul of your dear sister may enjoy ineffable & everlasting bliss, and I will also have holy masses offered in this intention. I am so happy to hear her death was peaceful & without suffering. It must be a great consolation to you to have surrounded her with such loving care till the end!

    Thank you also for you interest in our cares. We have comparatively good news from our sick daughter Gertrude. I am going to pass a few weeks with her in Switzerland soon. The doctors give us every hope for her recovery. The rest of our family is well, I am thankful to say, and we hope that God's mercy will give us better times. We continue to live quietly in our old home in the country, where life is easier than in town.

    I remain in true sympathy, dear Madam.

Your's [*sic*] very sincerely
Marie Valerie[3]

    The new Austrian government allowed Marie Valerie to retain ownership of the Kaiservilla, and the family continued to spend the summers in the spa town; Marie Valerie's older sister, Gisela, must also have renounced her Habsburg titles because she was permitted to visit with Marie Valerie in Bad Ischl as a guest. Gisela, and her husband, Prince Leopold of Bavaria, renounced their German royal titles and remained in their home at Palais Leopold in northern Munich, in what was now the Weimar Republic.

    One newspaper reported on Marie Valerie's summer life at the Kaiservilla: "The couple have a large family, nine children, and they troop about the tiny village in the plainest of gowns and with no semblance of the etiquette which once hedged even those of distant kinship to the Hapsburgs [*sic*]. Marie Valerie never was attached to the routine of court and she submits to the new dispensation very gracefully. She mingles in the village activities and several times a summer she throws open the lovely grounds of the Kaiservilla for the pleasure of the countryside."[4]

    In intermittently opening the Kaiservilla to the public, Marie Valerie was continuing a tradition begun by her father, Emperor Franz Joseph. Visitors were granted permission to tour the grounds through the Villa Director, but only when the Emperor was not in residence.

    In the immediate aftermath of the war, Marie Valerie immersed herself in her household's financial matters. Still using her obsolete letterhead with a crown insignia above her initials "MV," she exchanged letters often

11. "We hope that God's mercy will give us better times"

with Baron Lederer, who was the Lord High Steward to her husband, Franz Salvator. Each adult Austrian Archduke had his own High Steward to help manage the imperial household, and Baron Lederer continued to offer his services even after the monarchy was disbanded. Money was clearly an issue now that there were no longer regular disbursements from the familial coffers. Marie Valerie clearly had a good deal of capital in the bank that Baron Lederer helped manage and dispense in the form of a trust. However, the funds were now subject to taxes, which worried Marie Valerie.

"Thank you very much for putting all the financial matters and respective payments in order, but I am now almost having qualms about my increased monthly allowance as this originates again from this enormous 'war gains tax,'" she wrote Lederer on April 23, 1920.[5]

In the same letter, she asked him to order silverware for Wallsee Castle, but questioned herself, wondering if the purchase would be affordable. "I think it's best for now to order only 6 forks or, if the price is too high, even just 4 or 3? Please make the order! The price should not be more than 400 kroner—500 at the most" (about $80 to $100 in 1920s U.S. dollars, or about $1,000 today).[6]

Despite her financial concerns, Marie Valerie continued her philanthropic work.

"I consent to the charitable fund that has grown so well being used as a donation for the Wieden children's hospital," she wrote Lederer on May 3, 1920.[7]

Marie Valerie also seemed to be in the midst of some legal wranglings with her older sister, Gisela, possibly over the inheritance left by Emperor Franz Joseph when he died four years earlier.

"What factors comprise this 'asset value at the time of the inheritance,' which everything seems to revolve around?" she asked Lederer. "You are right in assuming, dear Baron Lederer, that the thought that we could perhaps be in the wrong troubles me! (Even if I don't believe in the 40 million factored out of it by Georg!)"[8]

Georg was Gisela's eldest son who was 40 years old at the time, and clearly advising his mother on the matter.

Just over a week later, Marie Valerie went into great detail regarding the legal tensions with her sister. Marie Valerie spoke of not yet completing her "testament," or written testimony for the courts. She underlined certain words for emphasis.

> On the 31st of March I wrote to my sister that I think it decidedly unjust to seize the testament and presented this as a matter of *conscience*. Then Georg got involved in his letter of [April 24], and, still in the context of the matter of conscience I

brought up, Gisela came back to the topic in her letter of [May 6].... But since I only spoke about taking a stance of good conscience, as mentioned, from a legal perspective, the matter has not yet even been raised at our end. To do this seems very appropriate to me. I want to keep it almost as an offer of equity towards my sister. I should at least like to write to her ... "my legal situation is so absolutely clear and certain that it cannot be contested effectively and that you will obtain no result other than great legal costs." Please let me know if I may write that in the next letter? ... I think it would be good to include to make them aware that they will achieve absolutely nothing, and will only cause *damage*. I am greatly saddened, dear Baron Lederer, by your words that it will certainly go to trial, *as I wish to do everything to avoid this*. I fear [the attorney] takes the view that the sooner it goes to trial, the better that is for us, but I do *not* share this view.[9]

But the news was not all legal and financial, as when Marie Valerie wrote of her second-eldest daughter's successful childbirth. "You will have received my telegram with the happy news of Hedwig's delivery and will certainly rejoice with us," she wrote of the birth of her grandchild. "Praise the Lord everything is going very well."[10]

Throughout her letters to Baron Lederer, Marie Valerie spoke often of conferring with her husband, Franz Salvator, on the important household matters. Although she most likely knew of his continuing relationship with Princess Stephanie von Hohenlohe and his monetary support of their illegitimate son, Franzi, both Marie Valerie and Franz Salvator continued to work together as a marital team regarding their own children, grandchildren, and household management.

* * *

Franz Salvator's brother, Leopold Salvator, was one of the Habsburgs who opted to retain his title and flee Austria. Fortunately, he had somewhere to go; his wife was the Infanta Blanca of Spain and they would take their ten children to her ancestral homeland. Leopold's second youngest son, named Franz Joseph after the old Emperor, was away at Jesuit boarding school when he recalled one of the family's attendants, named Stepanek, meeting him at the Vienna train station and explaining what was happening.

"There's trouble at Wilhelmineberg," Stepanek told him. "There's a mob marching on your father's castle. Her Highness and your brothers and sisters are scattered in different hiding places all over town."[11]

When young Franz Joseph asked about his brothers Leopold and Rainer who were fighting on the Piave River in northern Italy, Stepanek answered, "There's no more fighting on the Piave. Your brothers have come back, with buttons and insignia torn from their uniforms. There's not an officer left with epaulettes on his shoulders. This is the Revolution! No man in soldier's garb can show his face."[12]

Franz Joseph was hidden away at Stepanek's family apartment until the young Archduke could be reunited with his scattered family.

Leopold Salvator and the Infanta donned disguises, packed doctored passports, and took the younger children, while the older boys were left to fend for themselves, "keeping in hiding until the prearranged signal summoned them all to a secret point of departure. They left Wilhelmineberg during the night, climbing over the gates while the watchman drowsed on his beat."[13]

Since the republic's provisional government had cut off all imperial income and had begun seizing assets, the Infanta Blanca decided to sew the family jewels into a sash that she wore under her coat. The jewels included an emerald necklace and a piece known as the "Marie Antoinette Brooch" that she intended to break up and sell off piecemeal as the need for money arose. Another diamond-studded piece called the "Diadem of Hortense," that had been presented by Napoleon to Empress Josephine's daughter, was too difficult to conceal and was left with Stepanek to safeguard.

Leopold Salvator's family finally met up at a predetermined train station where they divided themselves into various boxcars on a train bound for Trieste, some 370 miles southwest of Vienna. It was evident to the refugees, who included Italian and South American diplomats, that this train had been used recently by the Red Cross to transport wounded soldiers since the bunks will still sodden with blood. The travelers pooled what little food they had, sharing pieces of black bread, sardines and pickled meats. They also took turns searching for kindling to keep the small wood stoves burning.

Instead of the normal seven hours to Trieste, this journey took nearly nine days due to all the roadblocks and security stops. Leopold Salvator's family, still in disguise, next boarded a train for Genoa, then took a Spanish freighter to Barcelona. Now onboard the ship, the dozen family members split into smaller groups just in time for an announcement to be made by a military commission: "An Austrian archduke, his wife and ten children have escaped," the spokesman announced. "He is a high enemy officer and as such accountable to the tribunal determining war guilt. We have orders to search the boat."[14]

Fortunately the disguises and false passports did their job, and the freighter set out to sea. But Spain did not automatically offer the family a respite from dangerous politics; as the ship approached the Barcelona harbor, the Infanta Blanca, whose brother was the Carlist pretender to the Spanish throne, wrote a wireless dispatch to her Spanish family's avowed enemy King Alfonso XIII, humbly begging for sanctuary. King Alfonso took pity on his wayward cousin and agreed to admit her to her ancestral home, as long as she promised not to engage in any Carlist plots to reclaim the throne. She agreed at once.

Leopold Salvator, the Infanta Blanca, and their brood were now safe to live as ordinary Spaniards, and set about finding suitable lodgings and employment.

The wayward Emperor Karl also negotiated with Spain as an exile destination for his family, but Karl was acting on the premise that the arrangements would only be temporary. He had already attempted once to cross from Empress Zita's family's home in Switzerland back into Hungary in 1921 to reclaim that country's throne. Karl had been crowned King of Hungary shortly after inheriting the title Emperor of Austria in 1916, but the Communists, under the bloody rule of Béla Kun, had taken over Budapest at the end of the war. Commander-in-Chief of the Austro-Hungarian Navy Admiral Nicholas Horthy marched into the Hungarian capital in 1919 with the force of the military behind him to overthrow the government of the Hungarian Soviet Republic. Horthy helped re-establish the Kingdom of Hungary and led as its regent with the understanding that he would hand over the reins to Karl as king once again when the time was right. But Horthy felt that it was still too soon for a Habsburg restoration and would not guarantee Karl the full support of the people or the backing of the army.

While Karl retreated to consider his future options, he received a note from the Spanish government: "His Majesty's Government consents to receive the Emperor Karl in Spain.... At the same time, however ... the Spanish Government accepts no responsibility whatever for the Emperor's movements after his arrival in Spain."[15]

Spain, like the rest of Europe, instinctively knew that Karl would not rest until he was restored to the Hungarian throne, even if the Austrian throne was a lost cause. Karl considered himself anointed by God as the Hungarian peoples' rightful ruler and felt it was his duty to look after those he had sworn to serve. In the end, the risk may have been too great for Spain, and the exile deal was never completed. Karl headed back to Switzerland where he and Zita together plotted their return to Budapest.

* * *

Once she reunited with her husband, Princess Stephanie von Hohenlohe learned that her dual Austro-Hungarian citizenship had disappeared along with the Empire, and even though she had been born in Vienna, she was suddenly a Hungarian citizen. Prince Friedrich had been forced to make a decision on his—and his wife's—citizenship now that the Empire had been dissolved. The Prince chose Hungary, perhaps because his mother had been from the noble Hungarian House of Esterházy and he felt that he would be able to trade on the family name in order to find employment. In addition, noble titles wouldn't be officially abolished in Hungary for decades to come, so he could remain Prince Hohenlohe. Princess Stephanie and her son, Franzi, were issued Hungarian passports, but she opted to remain in Vienna, rather than cross the border into the communistic Hungarian Soviet Republic, which, as it turned out, would only last for one brutal year before being replaced by a regency. Vienna would also keep her much closer to Franzi's true father, Franz Salvator, whom she knew would continue to look after them.

Soon, Prince Friedrich demanded a separation from the commoner wife he had married under delicate circumstances at the start of the war. He had done his duty by giving baby Franzi his aristocratic surname. Now, with little left to connect the couple, Prince Friedrich filed for divorce, which was formalized in Budapest on July 29, 1920. Stephanie was pleased to be free from a husband she didn't love and the completely unfamiliar Hungarian lifestyle she had no desire to adopt, but she refused to drop the title "Princess" from her name. It was an appellation she had no right to keep, but the Prince wasn't in a mood to argue. Just six months later, he married a Hungarian countess who became the legitimate Princess Hohenlohe-Waldenburg-Schillingsfürst. Stephanie would simply shorten her name to "Princess Stephanie von Hohenlohe," and the name itself would continue to open many parlor doors.

12

"One could only envy her"

—Archduchess Gisela

Princess Stephanie threw herself into the 1920s with all the reckless hedonism the new decade afforded. Her war experiences faded from memory and she spent her time traveling to Paris, the south of France, and other glamorous European cities. When she was back home in Vienna, the Princess cultivated an important friendship with Dr. Ignaz Seipel, a vehement antisemitic member of the Christian Social Party who served as Austrian Chancellor for the first time from 1922 to 1924. He arranged for her to have police protection during the dangerous post-war period in Vienna, and even obtained for her a private box at the opera.

Princess Stephanie was well aware of the food shortages, workers' strikes, and devalued currency that were threatening to crush the once magnificent metropolis. She now asked herself, "What could we, and what especially can I, as a woman, do about all this? Nothing, except entertain the tired diplomats and ministers in whose overburdened laps these responsibilities lie. They always like to chat with a woman after a hard day signing treaties," she wrote.[1]

In keeping with this philosophy, Princess Stephanie became an escort to wealthy, powerful men who frequented Vienna's Hotel Sacher, sipping flutes of champagne, and comforting the careworn leaders who were charged with rehabilitating Central Europe. Her own apartment became a salon for the rich and powerful to congregate. Princess Stephanie mingled with and flattered foreign journalists and international businessmen who showered her with gifts and even marriage proposals. She became friends with the Duke and Duchess of Windsor, David Lloyd George, Georges Clemenceau, Margot Asquith, and a host of other notables. One person in particular would have a great influence on her future: Sir Henri Deterding, chairman of the board of Royal Dutch Shell, who also held a

British knighthood. Deterding was an early admirer and financier of a young and "promising" German politician named Adolf Hitler.[2]

* * *

Castle Wallsee, September 6, 1924

Marie Valerie, always a quiet force for charity, had begun to decelerate her activities in recent months. Soon, her increasingly sporadic trips into the village of Wallsee-Sindelburg with baskets full of food for the poor finally ceased altogether. It was truly the end of the imperial era; Marie Valerie, daughter of the steady, reliable Austria-Hungarian Emperor Franz Joseph and the flighty, ethereal Empress Elisabeth, who grew up in stately splendor and continued to serve her people even after the horrific war had led to the disbandment of the Empire, was dying.

Marie Valerie hadn't been feeling well for a time and may have noticed some unusual swellings on her body, but she put her health in

Wallsee Castle, where Marie Valerie and Franz Salvator raised their family after 1897. She opened parts of the castle as a military hospital during the Great War and became known as "The Angel of Wallsee" for her charity work (LOOK Die Bildagentur der Fotografen GmbH/Alamy).

God's hands through incessant prayer. Finally, when she could no longer deny her symptoms and pain, Marie Valerie called for her doctor who diagnosed her with cancer of the lymph nodes. He gently told her that it was too late for radiation treatment to be successful, and advised her to put her affairs in order. She was just 56.

On a warm fall day, Marie Valerie lay gravely ill in her bedchamber at Castle Wallsee surrounded by Franz Salvator, her children and grandchildren. Her youngest daughter, Mathilde, had just turned 18 the month before this tearful gathering.

Whatever her legal issues had been with Gisela, the two sisters had made amends before Marie Valerie's doctor administered a substantial dose of painkillers to ease her excruciating pain.

"I saw Valerie on August 11 in soundness of mind, fully cognizant of her condition and looking towards her end with such devout faithfulness, even joy, that I believe an unexpected recovery would have been a disappointment for her," Gisela wrote to her sister-in-law. "She was quite at peace that God would work all things together for the best for her husband and children that she was not in the least concerned. One could only envy her."[3]

After Franz Salvator and the children kissed her cheek for the last time, Marie Valerie was carefully dressed and laid out in her coffin for a private funeral service. Some 40,000 people from the surrounding town then followed behind the Angel of Wallsee to her final resting place at Wallsee-Sindelburg Cemetery. During the procession the passenger steamship *Marie Valerie* sailed in front of the castle several times on the Danube with its flag flown at half-mast and the crew standing at attention in tribute to their fallen Archduchess.

The parish church dispensed black-bordered mourning cards featuring Marie Valerie's photo so parishioners could pray for her eternal soul. The cards defied the new Austrian government by referring to her with the outlawed title of "Archduchess."

"My Jesus' mercy! Sweet heart of Mary, be my salvation!" read the words surrounding Marie Valerie's likeness.

> In the pious memory of and prayer for
> Her Royal and Imperial Serene Highness
> Archduchess Marie Valerie
> born in Ofen, 22nd of April 1868,
> died in Wallsee, 6th of September 1924.

"Ofen" is the German name for Buda, Hungary, the place her mother, Empress Elisabeth, had loved so much and had fervently wanted Marie

12. "One could only envy her"

Valerie to love as well. But despite her mother's efforts, Marie Valerie felt an irresistible pull toward her Germanic roots. Although she was never overtly political, her heart lay with the German nationals in Vienna.

Parishioners were encouraged to read Romans 8:28 ("And we know that all things work together for good to them that love God, to them who are the called according to his purpose") and Proverbs 31:20 ("She stretcheth out her hand to the poor; yea, she reacheth forth her hands to the needy").

The mourning card ends with the words "Most Holy Heart of Jesus, I believe in your love for me."

Parishioners were then informed that they would receive "300 days of indulgences each time" they recited prayers for Marie Valerie.[4] In the Roman Catholic Church, "an indulgence is a way to reduce the amount of punishment one has to undergo for sins."[5] The faithful were promised that these spiritual privileges could be used to repair their own relationships with the Almighty.

Several days later, a foundering Franz Salvator, feeling completely disoriented without the wife on whom he had depended for 34 years, wrote to Gisela's husband.

> Dear brother-in-law!
>
> Many thanks for your sharing in our sorrow. What we have lost cannot be expressed in words and it is only now when daily life gradually begins to resume its normal pace that one becomes aware of what is missing in the house! Some very difficult times are now ahead of me, I must now bear the full responsibility for many matters, particularly ones regarding the children, alone.[6]

* * *

As Marie Valerie was laid to rest in Austria, Adolf Hitler was finishing up a 13-month prison sentence for his attempted overthrow of the German and Bavarian governments, which became known as the Beer Hall Putsch. Far from destroying his nascent political career, however, the time he spent at Landsberg Prison allowed him to solidify his revolutionary message by giving him time to dictate his Nazi manifesto, *Mein Kampf*, while assigned to his rather comfortable cell surrounded by his fellow putschists. While in prison, they were permitted to wear their own clothes instead of prison uniforms and could keep most of their own personal items. They weren't required to work—in fact, prison trustees did all the chores, including making the prisoners' beds and cleaning their cells. Hitler received stacks of mail and gifts from admirers each day and gained a considerable amount of weight from the sweets and pastries they sent along.

"Hitler's punishment is the sort handed out for a gentleman's indiscretion—a holiday distinguished by some legalese," wrote journalist Carl von Ossietzky.[7]

Hitler would say that without his time spent at Landsberg, he would never had slowed down and focused enough to compose *Mein Kampf*. "It had been stupid of the government, he claimed, to imprison him: 'They would have been better off letting me speak and speak again and never find my peace of mind.'"[8]

Following the Great War, as Hitler neared 30 years old, he had returned to Munich and opted to remain in the army, which, unlike his spotty artistic career, offered a guaranteed salary, shelter, and regular meals. Eventually, he was recruited to become an army spy to keep an eye on any hint of Marxism among the troops. As part of his training, Hitler was obliged to attend an anti–Bolshevik course in history and politics at the University of Munich, where he fell under the spell of an antisemitic lecturer who blamed the Jews for creating "capital slavery"[9] within Germany. Hitler began lecturing and debating other students on the materials after class, and in August 1919, awakened a dormant aptitude as a powerful public orator. "I could speak!"[10] he said of discovering this new-found talent. Army leaders soon caught on and tapped Hitler to lecture the troops on such topics as "Who Bears the Guilt for the World War?"[11] In keeping with the general feelings sweeping Munich at the time, the answer was always, the Jews.

The troops were mesmerized by his style of speaking and gave him the highest praise in their after-course evaluations.

A drawing of Hitler made about 1923 when he became famous for staging the Beer Hall Putsch that left 20 people dead. Instead of ruining him, his conviction for high treason put him on a path to ultimate power (Library of Congress Prints and Photographs Division, George Grantham Bain Collection).

12. "One could only envy her"

"Herr Hitler is, if I may say so, a born popular speaker."

"His fanaticism and popular style ... commands the attention and cooperation of the audience."

"Once, when a long lecture wasn't finished on time, he asked [us] if he should stop or if [we] agree to hear the rest of his talk after hours. Everyone immediately agreed."[12]

At this point in 1919, Hitler either so fervently believed in the culpability of the Jews for the German peoples' woes or he became an expert at pandering to popular opinion through the army's propaganda, since he had always aimed to please those in high command. Hitler was soon viewed as such a passionate expert on the Jewish debate that his lecturer asked him to respond to another student's written question for clarification on what place existed for the Jews in German society. What followed was Hitler's one thousand-word letter of September 16, 1919, his first recorded written statement about the "Jewish Question." "He wrote that antisemitism should be based not on emotion, but on 'facts,' the first of which was that Jewry was a race, not a religion. Emotive antisemitism would produce pogroms, he continued; antisemitism based on 'reason' must, on the other hand, lead to the systematic removal of the rights of Jews. 'Its final aim,' he concluded, 'must unshakeably be the removal of the Jews altogether.'"[13]

Hitler had apparently wiped from his mind the Jews who had helped him throughout his life: Dr. Eduard Bloch, to whom he had been so grateful for caring for his sick mother as she lay dying; his Jewish friends in the Vienna men's shelters who listened to his incessant political ramblings; the Jewish Viennese merchants who purchased his artwork to keep him from starving; and Jewish Lieutenant Hugo Gutmann who recommended him for the Iron Cross, First Class, during the Great War; among many unnamed others. In his mind, they were all now lumped into one undesirable category that needed to be systematically eliminated.

One of Hitler's army spying assignments took him to a small meeting of the right-wing German Workers' Party. Hitler got so taken up in the political talk when someone mentioned Bavarian secession from the German federation that he forgot his role as spy and began to vociferously defend the idea of a unified Greater Germany. The party leaders realized what an asset he would be to the cause, and Hitler was soon convinced to become a party member, with its emphasis on denouncing the Jews, destroying what it called "Big Capital" and uniting workers with the middle class. The group soon amended its name to the National Socialist German Worker's Party—*Nationalsozialistische Deutsche Arbeiterpartei*—or Nazi for short.

With his penchant for fiery rhetoric, Hitler became the group's propagandist, whipping up a crowd of 2,000 people at Munich's Hofbräuhaus beer hall in February 1920. Right-wing supporters cheered while the few Left-wingers present heckled his fascist doctrines. Nazis and Socialists clashed on the streets after the event, much to Hitler's delight. "It makes no difference whether they laugh at us or revile us. The main thing is that they mention us," he said.[14]

Eventually, Hitler became the main draw at Nazi gatherings, as thousands of people showed up wherever he was spewing vitriol toward the Jews, the Marxists, and Germany's current government, the Weimar Republic, a parliamentary democracy. After threatening to quit unless he became the sole party leader "with dictatorial powers,"[15] Hitler seized control of the Nazi Party and developed a unique ability to appeal to Germany's working-class, small-scale merchants, and wealthy conservatives alike.

Hitler began to brand the Nazi Party with its own symbol of the Aryan cause in stark black, white and red: the Nazi swastika flag. He started a party newspaper, the *Völkischer Beobachter* (National Observer), designed uniforms to give the party an official and intimidating presence, and began recruiting hard-nosed thugs to serve as brass knuckle-wearing Storm Troopers for "security." War flying hero Hermann Göring joined the Nazi Party and was quickly put in charge of bringing the rogue Storm Troopers under control. Other early followers of Hitler included war airman, Rudolf Hess, who served as Hitler's personal assistant, as well as Ernst Hanfstaengl, a Harvard-educated German-American businessman, who introduced Hitler to important members of high society.

Ever since Benito Mussolini and his Fascisti Party toppled the Italian government in October 1922, Hitler, now called "Führer" by his party members, began planning his own revolutionary national uprising. His original plan was to stage a 379-mile march from Munich to Berlin, where he planned to take power. The German economic crisis was at an all-time high and the desperate people were demanding a change. "By September [1923], the million mark note was practically worthless," wrote German journalist Sebastian Haffner. "The billion became the new standard unit, and by the end of October it was the trillion."[16]

Hitler had managed to increase the Nazi Party enrollment to 55,000 solely by energizing crowds wherever he spoke, and had made a powerful ally in General Erich Ludendorff, a hero of the Great War who promoted the "stab-in-the-back" theory that Jewish Marxists and Bolsheviks were to blame for betraying the German army. Both Hitler and Ludendorff desired an authoritarian fascist government in Berlin, and they were willing to shed blood to get it. Hermann Göring was already making plans to prepare lists of people in each town and district to be eliminated as soon as the putsch was in motion. "At least one of them will have to be shot immediately after the proclamation [of the putsch] to set an example," he told his Storm Troopers.[17]

* * *

Munich, November 8, 1923

As 2,000 Nazis marched to the center of Munich, Hitler and three bodyguards made their way into the large Bürgerbräukeller beer hall, where the head of the Bavarian government was speaking to a huge crowd of citizens. Hitler forced his way to the stage, then climbed up on a chair and fired his pistol into the ceiling, shouting, "Silence!"[18]

Once the stunned crowd of 3,000 were focused on the pale, diminutive man in the dark suit, he took the stage and began his rant: "National revolution is under way," he shouted. "The hall is under the control of 600 heavily armed men. No one is allowed to leave. If things don't immediately quieten down, I will have a machine gun posted on the gallery. The Bavarian government has been deposed. The Reich government has been deposed. A provisional government has been formed."[19]

Hitler then escorted three of the Bavarian politicians from the stage to discuss the handover of power. Hitler intermittently negotiated with and threatened the men, saying he had four bullets in his gun and was not afraid to use them to end all of their lives, including his own, if necessary. Fortunately for the politicians, General Ludendorff showed up and was able to calm the negotiations until an agreement was reached.

Hitler returned to the hall where he addressed the appalled crowd and remarkably managed to win them over to his nationalistic fervor. "In the coming weeks and months, I intend to fulfill the promise I made myself five years ago to the day as a blind cripple in an army hospital never to rest or relax until the criminals of November 1918 are brought to the ground! Until a Germany of power and greatness, of freedom and majesty, has been resurrected on the ruins of Germany in its pathetic present-day state! Amen."[20]

The crowd was said to have been so moved that they could barely sing along to the German national anthem that had spontaneously started up.

Unfortunately for Hitler, as he left the beer hall to carry out the next phase of his plan, Ludendorff took the Bavarian politicians at their word that they were on the revolutionaries' side and let them go free. The three men immediately went to the authorities and broadcast a radio message stating that they rejected the Hitler putsch and that police had been instructed to arrest all of the revolutionary leaders. Göring's Storm Troopers didn't get the message that they were on the losing side, and began terrorizing and arresting Jewish citizens in Munich and smashing up the offices of the left-wing *Münchener Post* newspaper.

In the early hours of November 9, Hitler and Ludendorff finally realized that they had been betrayed and that the police would soon be after them. They decided to organize their 2,000 men to march through the center of Munich at noon, and at first, crowds gathered to cheer them on. But fighting quickly broke out between Hitler's men and the police, and then a gunshot rang out. Both sides exchanged fire until the smoke cleared to reveal at least 14 putschists and four police bleeding to death in Munich's central square. A draft constitution found on one of the dead putschists included a plan for creating concentration camps for Jews once the proposed revolution was completed.

Hitler managed to escape with just a dislocated shoulder, thanks to his bodyguard, Ulrich Graf, who shielded the Nazi leader and took several bullets for him. Göring was shot and seriously wounded, but Ludendorff remained unscathed.

Two days after the failed putsch, Hitler was arrested and thrown into Landsberg prison. He was exhausted, unnerved, and began a hunger strike in a feeble attempt to end his life.

"He sat there before me in his chair like a lump of misery, badly shaven, exhausted, and listened to my simple words with a tired smile and complete indifference," recalled one of the prison guards.[21]

Eventually, the prison psychologist and his lawyer talked Hitler back from the brink and got him ready to stand trial for high treason. Now fully recovered and back on message, Hitler would use the trial to grandstand and deliver his edict of "bring[ing] the [German] people back from slavery"[22] to an international audience, courtesy of a packed press corps.

Hitler put on quite a show in the courtroom, raving and gesticulating wildly at one point for nearly three hours, and although he was found guilty of high treason and sentenced to five years imprisonment, he was deemed eligible for parole in just six months. Rather than condemning Hitler and his nine co-defendants for their crimes against the state, the judge praised the men as "having acted in a purely patriotic spirit, led by the most noble, selfless will."[23] The men were essentially lionized for causing the deaths of four policemen and strong-arming Jewish citizens on the streets of Munich while threatening to overtake the country's government in Berlin. The whole legal farce would ensure that Hitler reached folk-hero status by the time he left Landsberg Prison on December 20, 1924.

PART II

Stehendes Reich/Rising Empire, 1927–1939

13

"She first came to our notice in 1928"

—MI5 file regarding Stephanie von Hohenlohe

Monte Carlo, Winter 1927

Princess Stephanie von Hohenlohe left her Paris apartment at 45 Avenue George V with its nine servants and collection of shaggy Skye Terrier dogs, and hurried off to the gambling palaces of Monte Carlo. She had adopted the style of the Roaring 20s, with bobbed hair and a chic Marcel wave, winged eyeliner, and red lipstick that defined the Cupid's bow.

Stephanie's son by Franz Salvator, Franzi, now 13, was away at boarding school, and she was free to travel the continent at a moment's notice. This season, however, Stephanie was expected at the Monte Carlo Sporting Club by an English friend who promised to introduce the Princess to a very important British press baron, Lord Rothermere. Stephanie knew he could help her realize a major political intrigue that would elevate her beyond a mere society hostess to an actual power player in post-war Europe: obtaining British support to improve the lot of the Kingdom of Hungary, now ruled by a regent.

Lord Rothermere had been born Harold Sidney Harmsworth in London in 1868. He and his brother Alfred created a newspaper empire that included *The Daily Mail*, *The Daily Mirror*, *The Evening News*, and *The Sunday Dispatch*. The brothers' papers took a new approach to journalism that was criticized for being too sensationalistic and for appealing to a base audience, but it made them a fortune with an enormous following. Harmsworth was dubbed a baronet in 1910 and was elevated to the peerage in 1914 as Baron Rothermere of Hempstead in the County of Kent. Following the world war, in which he served as air minister, he was created the 1st Viscount Rothermere. In 1922, his brother died, leaving Rothermere sole heir to the newspaper conglomerate. As such, he had great power to influence politics, and was looking for a way to help mold post-war Europe. Rothermere was described at the time as "sifting through the trends of the age looking for clues about the future."[1]

He simply hadn't yet found his cause, until he met Princess Stephanie von Hohenlohe at the baccarat table on the French Riviera.

Perhaps he was intrigued by the sight of an upper-crust woman smoking a Havana cigar in public, or he was simply being polite to the mutual friend who introduced them, but Lord Rothermere sat and spoke with Stephanie until she was able to turn the conversation exactly where she wanted it to go: toward Central European politics.

Harold Sidney Harmsworth, 1st Viscount Rothermere, hired Princess Stephanie as a secret contact with Hungary's Admiral Horthy and Germany's Adolf Hitler. Eventually, the Viscount and the Princess would turn on one another (Library of Congress Prints and Photographs Division, George Grantham Bain Collection).

According to Stephanie's son, who later wrote about the encounter, Rothermere told Stephanie that he had been feeling uneasy because there was currently no interesting news to report to help him sell papers. He allegedly said, "Good news has never yet sold a newspaper. People want crime, earthquakes, scandals and divorces."[2]

At which point, Stephanie gently suggested that there was a great tragedy playing out in post-war Europe that had yet to be discovered by any news reporter and which was guaranteed to sell papers—the plight of the Hungarian people, who had been torn from each other as if in a major divorce caused by the horribly unjust Treaty of Trianon.

Stephanie undoubtedly knew nothing of the Treaty of Trianon until it was presented to her by major political players in the Hungarian government. Throughout the 1920s, the Princess had made hundreds of contacts through her Aunt Clotilde's popular cosmopolitan salon in Berlin, and at some point, she met Admiral Horthy, the *de facto* regent of the Kingdom of Hungary. After the brief Communistic terror of Béla Kun when Horthy marched into Budapest and was named regent, Horthy had publicly proclaimed that he was doing all he could to restore deposed Austrian Emperor Karl to the throne. In reality, however, Horthy had no intention of giving up his new-found power.

A report from the British High Commission in Budapest reported that "the Hungarian Government had recently become so alarmed at the success of certain Karlist plots in the Hungarian Army that they had had to deprive some of a further removal of undesirable junior officers."[3] If Horthy had truly wanted the Habsburg ruler restored to the throne, he would have stocked the army with supporters, not depleted them.

After the failed March 1921 "Easter bid" to regain the Hungarian throne, Karl had continued conspiring until it was decided in October 1921 that Karl and Zita, who was pregnant with the couple's eighth child, would fly incognito by light plane into Hungary and seize the palace from Horthy in Budapest. The plan nearly worked, had it not been for Great Britain's outright opposition to the restoration. Once it became known that Karl had landed in Hungary and was receiving support from every town through which his train passed on the way to Budapest, the British accused Karl of inciting a civil war and encouraged Horthy to repel any attempt at a restoration. In the end, Horthy's army won out, and after two tense days of standoff, Karl's train retreated out of the Budapest station for good.

Monarchists considered Horthy to be the worst sort of traitor for refusing to willingly hand the throne back to Karl, and Karl clearly felt divinely justified for trying. He hinted that he would never stop his efforts.

"I have done my duty, as I came here do to," he told Hungary's primate, Cardinal Csernoch. "As crowned King, I not only have a right, I also have a duty. I must uphold the right, and the dignity of the Crown. For me, this is not something light. With the last breath of my life I must take the path of duty. Whatever I regret, Our Lord and Savior had led me."[4]

Karl, Zita, and their seven children reached their final exile on the heavily-guarded Portuguese island of Madeira one month later. Karl would die just four months after that, at the age of 34, from respiratory failure due to pneumonia. On May 31, 1922, Zita gave birth to a baby girl, whom she named after Marie Valerie's mother, Empress Elisabeth. Zita would continue to fight for the restoration of the monarchy through her eldest son, Otto, who would be targeted by Adolf Hitler in the next decade.

13. "She first came to our notice in 1928"

*   *   *

Horthy believed that the British were Hungary's best hope in helping to unravel the Treaty of Trianon, which was the equivalent of the Treaty of Versailles to Germany. With the stroke of a pen, Hungary, a country with a population of 20,000,000 and an area of 125,000 square miles was reduced to just 8,000,000 people and a land mass of just 36,000 square miles.[5] Through social networking, Horthy knew that Princess Stephanie had the press contacts needed to bring Hungary's plight to the world's attention. And Stephanie, for her part, wasn't satisfied talking with mere reporters; she would prove her value as a budding political operative by going straight to the top of the British press pyramid.

At the baccarat table that evening, Lord Rothermere was so intrigued by Princess Stephanie's story of Hungary's plight that he invited her to lunch the next day to hear more. Stephanie regaled him with a tale of a once proud nation that had lost two-thirds of its territory under the treaty that had been signed by the Hungarian delegation under protest in 1920. Hundreds of thousands of Hungarians, who spoke only their native Magyar, suddenly found themselves citizens of foreign-speaking lands of Romania, Czechoslovakia, or Yugoslavia. Once considered the breadbasket of the Austro-Hungarian Empire, Hungary's mills were now mostly dormant and rail cargo for exports was at a standstill. Economically, Hungary was in bad shape, and its people both inside and outside of the country were suffering.

Princess Stephanie had sold Admiral Horthy's cause admirably, and Lord Rothermere was compelled to publish a 2,612-word article for *The Daily Mail* on June 21, 1927, titled "Hungary's Place in the Sun." The article appeared under his byline, although there was speculation as to whether Princess Stephanie had a hand in its composition.

"I decided, therefore, to publish in The Daily Mail an article putting the case for revision of the Treaty of Trianon fairly and objectively before the British public," he wrote to explain his interest in the cause. "It was evident to me that the existing situation in Hungary could not continue indefinitely. So much suffering, so much despair, so deep and rankling a sense of oppression constituted a mass of bitterness in the centre of Europe which, if allowed to continue, would inevitably find its ultimate expression in violent action."[6]

Rothermere had come to fear what many Europeans did also; that the harsh terms of the post-world war Versailles, Trianon, and Saint-Germain-en-Laye Peace Treaties would lead to a new European war in the near future. But with Princess Stephanie's urging, he focused his attentions squarely on Hungary.

The day before the article was published, *The Daily Mail* editors sent a telegram to Princess Stephanie's Paris apartment: "We have received instruction from Vis count [sic] Rothermere to notify you that an article boosting Hungary according to your desires is appearing tomorrow."[7]

On June 20, 1927, with a dateline of Budapest, Lord Rothermere's article began: "Eastern Europe is strewn with Alsace-Lorraines. By severing from France the twin provinces of that name, the Treaty of Frankfort in 1871 made another European war inevitable. The same blunder has been committed on a larger scale in the Peace Treaties which divided up the old Austro-Hungarian Empire. They have created dissatisfied racial minorities in half a dozen parts of Central Europe, any one of which may be the starting-point of another conflagration." Rothermere called the frontiers of the new Central European States "arbitrary and uneconomic" and in italics stressed, *"We ought to root up all the dry grass and dead timber of the Treaty of Trianon before some chance spark sets fire to it. Once the conflagration has started it will be too late."* Rothermere credited Hungary with fighting back Bolshevism on its own and proposed that the nation should once again appoint a king if that were the peoples' wish, since he believed a monarchy was the only way to truly suppress Communism. He then laid out his proposal for righting the Allies' injustice perpetrated against the nation. "I suggest that the time has come for the Allied Powers who signed that arbitrarily drafted instrument the Treaty of Trianon to reconsider the frontiers it laid down, in the light of the experience of the past seven years. When an arrangement does not work well after a trial of seven years, there is a strong probability that it is inherently unsound.... I should like to see our Foreign Office follow the lead which Italy has given to the Powers of Western Europe in holding out a helping hand to Hungary. Hungary is the natural ally of Britain and France. She has a right to a place in the sun."[8]

The article was an immediate success in Hungary and Rothermere was credited with opening the eyes of the British public to the predicament of Hungary's people and the fragility of Central Europe's political situation. Rothermere wrote a second pro–Hungary editorial in August of that same year, and *The Daily Mail* offices began receiving up to 2,000 reader letters of support per day. Rothermere was taken aback by the success of Stephanie's original idea. He wrote to her in April 1928: "I had no conception that a recital of Hungary's sufferings and wrongs would arouse such world-wide sympathy. Now from all parts of the world I am in receipt of such a flood of telegrams, letters and postcards that the work entailed in connection with the propaganda is rapidly absorbing all my energies."[9] Rothermere was forced to hire two Hungarian-speaking secretaries to handle all of the unexpected mail.

Princess Stephanie was now regularly traveling between London and Budapest, delivering messages between Lord Rothermere and Admiral Horthy regarding the restoration of a Hungarian monarchy. Admiral Horthy couldn't have been happy about this suggestion since he had worked so hard to prevent the return of King Karl while clutching power for himself. But he owed Rothermere a debt of gratitude for having shone a light on Hungary's troubles and most likely humored him with the idea.

Now that she had proven herself a valuable international asset whom Admiral Horthy called "the great Hungarian stateswoman,"[10] Princess Stephanie was starting to gain the unwanted attention of British intelligence for her frequent travels. Rumors were swirling that she was the one orchestrating the Hungarian machinations and that Lord Rothermere was her puppet.

Rothermere eventually felt forced to defend himself: "It was entirely of my own initiative that I came forward as an independent advocate of justice for Hungary. My intervention had not been instigated or solicited in any way by the Hungarian Government or by anyone acting on its behalf,"[11] he wrote.

Rothermere's advocacy was so successful that became known as "The Little Father of Hungary," and in due time, Hungarian streets, parks, and memorials were named after him. In 1928, he decided that a foreigner would be the best choice for Hungary's new monarch, and not surprisingly to everyone around him, Rothermere's name was put forward as candidate for king.

The Viscount acted as if he were thrown off guard when his Hungarian friends who "were obviously doing me the greatest honor in their power" nominated him "for one of the most ancient and historic crowns in Europe."

"The discovery that, without my knowledge, I had become the choice of a new Hungarian Monarchist Party placed me in a most embarrassing position," he wrote with a strained modesty.[12]

Once he realized it just wasn't realistic for him to leave his businesses to move to Hungary and lead people of a culture and language he didn't understand, Rothermere put forth his more flexible son, 30-year-old Esmond Harmsworth, as candidate for king. Esmond had traveled to the University of Szeged in southern Hungary to receive an honorary doctorate in his father's stead for service to the Hungarian cause, and was received with all of the fanfare due an international dignitary. Rothermere saw this as a positive sign that Esmond could be a viable alternative to wear the Crown of Saint Stephen.

Princess Stephanie must have been secretly put off by Rothermere's assertion that an outsider should become king, and indeed, he did eventually change his stance, writing, "it was self-evident that, if Hungary was ever again to have a king, her selection should be restricted to members of that nation."[13] Stephanie was undoubtedly waiting for the right moment to lobby for her own son, Franzi, to sit on the throne. Not through his Habsburg paternity; Archduke Franz Salvator would never publicly claim the boy as his own. But the parent with which Franzi shared a surname, Prince Franz von Hohenlohe-Waldenburg-Schillingsfürst, came from the royal Hungarian line of Esterházy that reached back to the Middle Ages. Even though Stephanie knew that Franzi wasn't a true Esterházy blood relative, no one else did at the time. Even if no one ever doubted Franzi's true paternity, Stephanie must have known that the Hungarian nobles would delve into the peerage on her side of the family and would learn that she was of Jewish ancestry. Antisemitism was as rampant in Budapest as it was in Vienna and Berlin at the time, so there was no chance that her son would ever be accepted as monarch.

As Stephanie was mulling over her own son's future, Rothermere changed his mind yet again. This time he declared: "Now was the moment, and only now, to solidify the social and political structure of the mid-European nations by restoring their exiled monarchs to their thrones. A return of the Hapsburgs [sic] and the Hohenzollerns to their God-given functions would pacify the world and revive its prosperity," he told Stephanie.[14] Rothermere would now send her on a mission to approach Empress Zita and Germany's deposed Kaiser Wilhelm II with a proposal of royal reinstatement.

Empress Zita undoubtedly knew of Princess Stephanie's questionable reputation within Viennese society in general and the Habsburg family in particular, and had no intention of receiving Rothermere's diplomatic go-between. Instead of granting Stephanie an audience herself, Zita arranged for her lady-in-waiting, Countess Viktoria Mensdorff, to meet the Princess at a hotel in Brussels, Belgium, where Stephanie presented Lord Rothermere's letter regarding the restoration of the Hungarian monarchy. Archduke Otto, true heir to the Hungarian throne, later wrote, "The Rothermere affair rose up like a soufflé in in the summer of 1932. We never got fully to the bottom of it but our feeling was that it was really

13. "She first came to our notice in 1928"

somehow linked to Archduke Albrecht and his ambitions to secure the Hungarian throne for himself."[15] The Habsburg successor, obviously in the midst of a family squabble, ignored Rothermere's advances, choosing to pursue his own path back to the throne.

Stephanie was met with equal suspicion by the German ex-Kaiser who had been exiled in the Netherlands after the war. The meeting had been arranged by Crown Prince Wilhelm, who had been allowed to retain his palace in Berlin. Stephanie had known the Crown Prince for years and always flirted shamelessly when they were together. The Crown Prince appreciated Rothermere's offer to restore the Hohenzollern family to the German throne, but had been a member of the Nazi Party since 1930 and believed Adolf Hitler would be the true savior of the German people. The ex-Kaiser was also a Hitler supporter, and proved to be extremely wary of Rothermere's proposal.

"The Kaiser receives me himself," Stephanie wrote. "He is friendly, but not enthusiastic about the scheme. Rothermere's brother, Lord Northcliffe, had [during the the Great War] coined the phrase 'Hang the Kaiser!' The Kaiser was naturally suspicious about entangling himself with a member of Northcliffe's family."[16]

Regardless of her recent failures, Stephanie was now being paid handsomely by Lord Rothermere for her work. A financial adviser had counseled Stephanie to negotiate a contract with Rothermere under which he would employ her as a "society columnist" for his newspaper. However, her unpublished memoirs shed greater light on the arrangement. "All my life I had been gaily unemployed, provided with an utterly unearned yet highly welcome income. It was fortunate that in the circumstances of 1932 I proved to be employable. With high hopes I embarked upon my romantic career *in secret diplomacy* and I was inwardly proud of the transition from a dreaming amateur *in politics* into a well-paid professional."

In her unpublished memoirs, the words "in secret diplomacy" and "in politics" were heavily scratched out with pencil.[17]

Under the contract, Stephanie's annual retainer was set at £5,000 (about $244,000 in today's U.S. dollars). For every assignment she completed, she would receive an additional £2,000 ($61,000).

Although her Hungarian connections initially alerted Great Britain's security agency MI5 to Princess Stephanie's diplomatic activities, it was her affiliation with upstart politicians in the National Socialist German Workers' Party that really got their attention.

"She first came to our notice in 1928 when she came to this country and succeeded in worming her way into society circles in London," stated one file entry. "Princess Hohenlohe has ... acted as a link between Nazi leaders in Germany and Society circles over here."[18]

* * *

One of the Germans with whom Stephanie became acquainted at this time was Otto Abetz, a former member of the Hitler Youth, an organization that dated back to 1922. Although he would not formally join the Nazi Party until 1937, Abetz spent the late 1920s and early 30s in France, where he claimed to be working for better relations between the two countries. Stephanie was still living in Paris when she met him, although the French government was becoming increasingly agitated by her presence. France was in league with Czechoslovakia, Yugoslavia and Romania—a group known as "The Little Entente"—that was firmly against Stephanie's plans to dismantle the Treaty of Trianon and give Hungary back its former lands. In addition, the French "strongly suspected" Stephanie "of being a German agent."[19]

Finally, in 1932, Stephanie packed up and moved in a hurry into London's Dorchester Hotel. According to an official FBI report on her espionage activities, she may have been officially expelled: "Princess Hohenlohe is reported on good authority to have been exiled from France in 1932 because of espionage activities, at which time she proceeded to London where she cultivated her old friendships and soon offered her services to the Nazi chieftains who realized the tremendous value of her connections to the Third Reich."[20]

After she fled France, the Parisian authorities searched her flat and found she had left behind some very important files. It seems that the Germans had wanted her to work her magic with Lord Rothermere the way she had with Hungary, by bringing attention to the injustice of the Treaty of Versailles. The German government had promised her a staggering £300,000 ($15 million in today's U.S. dollars) if she succeeded in helping to reacquire lands taken from Germany after the war. It's almost unfathomable how the German government would have paid the sum, considering the ruinous post-war economy and the billions in reparations they already owed.

While Germany's Weimar Republic was promising to pay Princess Stephanie handsomely to manipulate Lord Rothermere to its ends, Rothermere was paying Stephanie to ingratiate herself with Hitler's rival Nazi Party, which was now in position for a final and legitimate power grab. The Nazis would soon be the largest elected party in the Reichstag, paving the way for Hitler to be appointed Chancellor. Stephanie was playing both sides of the diplomatic field, making sure never to tip her hand.

13. "She first came to our notice in 1928"

In order to gain an audience with Hitler himself, Stephanie decided to get as close as she could with the Führer's personal adjutant, Captain Fritz Wiedemann, who had been Hitler's superior during the war. One person who came to know Wiedemann well was Martha Dodd, daughter of U.S. Ambassador to Germany William Edward Dodd. Martha wrote that Wiedemann "was supposed to be one of the most powerful men behind Hitler's throne and to enjoy the absolute trust of Hitler." She arrived in Berlin in 1933 and had a front-row seat for Hitler's rise to power, which she supported at first, until the murderous "Night of the Long Knives" purge opened her eyes to the brutality of the Nazi regime. Martha had an affair with the married Wiedemann and described the adjutant as "the 'strong man' in Hitler's closest circle. Tall, dark, muscular, he certainly had great physical brawn and the appearance of bravery.... Wiedemann's heavy face, with beetling eyebrows, friendly eyes and an extremely low forehead was rather attractive. But I got the impression of an uncultivated primitive mind, with the shrewdness and cunning of an animal and completely without delicacy or subtlety."[21]

Hitler had hired Wiedemann as his personal adjutant after Hitler had been chancellor for nearly a year. Following the war, Wiedemann had retreated to southwestern Bavaria to farm the land. But he proved to be a better soldier than farmer, and after losing a good deal of money, Wiedemann asked some army friends to approach Germany's chancellor to see if Hitler remembered his old army captain and could help him get back into the military. Hitler had a soft spot for his war comrades and appointed Wiedemann his personal adjutant in Berlin. Most likely with the help of German Crown Prince Wilhelm, Stephanie became acquainted with Wiedemann and began laying the groundwork to meet the Führer in person and deliver a message of support from Lord Rothermere.

At the same time, the world was starting to take note of the brutal tactics of the Nazis against their political opponents, as well as their sworn enemies, the Jews. But Lord Rothermere was so fearful of Communism, that he chose to look the other way and to wholeheartedly back Fascism instead. On July 10, 1933, he wrote in the *Daily Mail*:

> I urge all British young men and women to study closely the progress of the Nazi regime in Germany. They must not be misled by the misrepresentations of its opponents. The most spiteful distracters of the Nazis are to be found in precisely the same sections of the British public and press as are most vehement in their praises of the Soviet regime in Russia.
>
> They have started a clamorous campaign of denunciation against what they call "Nazi atrocities" which, as anyone who visits Germany quickly discovers for himself, consists merely of a few isolated acts of violence such as are inevitable among

a nation half as big again as ours, but which have been generalized, multiplied and exaggerated to give the impression that Nazi rule is a bloodthirsty tyranny.[22]

While Rothermere was belittling the "few isolated acts of violence," hundreds of political prisoners and ordinary Jewish citizens were already being shuffled through the iron gates of the newly-established concentration camp at Dachau. It would become known as a "school of violence" for the *Schutzstaffel*, or SS guards.[23]

Journalist Bella Fromm, who was a diplomatic correspondent in Berlin following the rise of the Nazis, was appalled that a foreign press baron like Lord Rothermere would support such a brutal regime without truly understanding the consequences. Fromm was an upper-class Jewish woman working for the Jewish-owned publishing house the Ullstein Press, and was feeling the squeeze of more and more restrictions against her profession and her people as Hitler gained strength. On the same day that Lord Rothermere's editorial was published, she wrote in her diary:

> The disintegration spreads. All camps and classes change color to brown. Even the *Stahlhelm* [the Imperial German Army] has gone over to the Nazis. The disintegration has penetrated beyond the frontiers of our country. People like Lord Rothermere champion their cause….
>
> What a pity the noble lord has had no opportunity to sample some of the benefits brought to our country, in one of the concentration camps![24]

As the situation degraded further, Fromm would become familiar with Princess Stephanie and her role in promoting Hitler's agenda.

14

"Hitler is going to rule Germany"

—Lord Rothermere

December 1933

A black Mercedes idled outside Berlin's elegant Adlon Hotel to transport Princess Stephanie just a few yards down *Unter den Linden* Boulevard to the Reich Chancellery. She had made sure to dress conservatively and to forego wearing lipstick, learning in advance that Hitler couldn't stand the sight of women in what he considered to be garish cosmetics. She would make it a point to charm him and to follow his lead. Although she would guide the conversation, she had to let him feel as though he were in control.

As always, Stephanie had done her research and knew that Hitler did not make it a habit to involve women in politics. He had a very traditional view as women as mother figures and not as decision makers. He had said, "In my view, a female who gets involved in politics is an abomination. In military matters, it's completely intolerable! No woman should have even the smallest position in any local Party branch. In 1924 some political women turned up at my door … they wanted to become members of the Reichstag.… I told them, 99 per cent of the matters debated are men's business, which they can have no opinion on!"[1]

Hitler had made an exception for Princess Stephanie, however, because she had been well-recommended by Wiedemann, as well as by Crown Prince Wilhelm, and she was acting on behalf of Lord Rothermere, whose help Hitler needed to spread Nazi propaganda throughout Great Britain.

Stephanie had made it her lifetime's study of how to appeal to powerful men in order to get what she wanted, but she was now stepping into very dangerous territory. She was a full-blooded Jewish woman about to negotiate with the man who was making it his life's work to purify his country of her people. If Stephanie hadn't read the highly popular *Mein Kampf*, which clearly laid out Hitler's naked ambitions to reunite all German-speaking people while eradicating the Jews, she would most certainly have heard about the official anti–Jewish Nazi oppressions that took place immediately after Hitler took power in January 1933. These included nationwide boycotts of Jewish businesses, a law that excluded Jews from all civil service positions, the disbarment of non–Aryan lawyers, and a law to limit Jewish students from attending public schools. If these events were too subtle for her, there were the spectacular book burnings at universities across Germany the previous May to rid the country of such subversive authors as Ernest Hemingway, Helen Keller, and Erich Maria Remarque. Also burned by the Nazis were works by German Jewish poet Heinrich Heine, a favorite of Empress Elisabeth, and the author whom Hitler had actually defended in his youth in a Viennese men's homeless shelter. One of Heine's most famous quotes was from the 1821 play *Almansor*: "*Dort, wo man Bücher verbrennt, verbrennt man am Ende auch Menschen*" ("Where they burn books, they will also ultimately burn people").[2]

Perhaps as a Hungarian citizen or a Princess or a diplomat she felt untouchable. Or perhaps she had long ago buried any visceral connection to her heritage.

* * *

When the Princess gracefully entered the Reich Chancellery's reception gallery, Hitler was politely waiting to take her gloved hand for a welcoming kiss. Stephanie sized him up immediately. At only 5'9" tall, he was not at all imposing, and she found him to look quite sickly with his thin hair, pale complexion and pink spots on his cheeks. "The general impression, but one which you only get on seeing him at close range, is that of a very keen and simple man…. A suburban teacher, or better some small employee," she wrote.[3]

American Martha Dodd had a similar impression on meeting him around the same time. "He seemed modest, middle class, rather dull and self-conscious—yet with this strange tenderness and appealing helplessness."[4]

Both women commented on the unique quality of his ice-blue eyes. "His eyes, which are a pleasant pale blue, could be called beautiful if they were not slightly protruding," Stephanie wrote.[5]

"Certainly the eyes were his only distinctive feature," wrote Dodd. "They could contain fury and fanaticism and cruelty; they could be mystic and tearful and challenging.... Only in the mad burning eyes could one see the terrible future of Germany."[6]

Once Hitler fixed those eyes on Stephanie, they remained on her for the entire interview. As they sat down to tea and he began to speak, she said she found "his diction and enunciation [were] unnatural and stilted, doubtless as a result of his effort to conceal the accent and dialect typical for Austrians of poor breeding and low estate."[7] Instead of putting on her usual princess airs, she reached back to her girlhood experiences in middle-class Vienna and modified her own speech and behavior to meet him at his level.

"I am one of the few persons with whom he held normal conversations," she wrote. "By that I mean one where both parties speak in turn. A conversation of two human beings. Usually though, this is not the case: either he makes a speech and one has to listen, or else he sits there with a dead serious face, never opening his mouth."[8]

The two were now completely comfortable with one another and Stephanie sealed the new friendship with flattery: she told Hitler that Lord Rothermere had declared after the March Reichstag elections, "Remember this day. Hitler is going to rule Germany. The man will make history and I predict that he will change the face of Europe."[9] Hitler was, of course, delighted and smitten with his new friend.

Stephanie presented Hitler with a letter from Lord Rothermere, plus a translation of a pro–German article Rothermere had published, before a deeply impressed Hitler held the Princess's hand, looked deep into her eyes, kissed her affectionately, and finally took his leave. Such outward signs of sentiment between the two would come to raise eyebrows among the Führer's staff, although Joseph Goebbels, Hitler's propaganda chief, seemed to understand the attraction.

"A strongly erotic woman," is how Goebbels described Princess Stephanie von Hohenlohe in his diary.[10]

* * *

Lord Rothermere couldn't have been happier when he learned of Stephanie's success, and he gladly handed over the promised £2,000 bonus. Hitler had sent along a reply, dated December 7, 1933, and Rothermere was encouraged to read about the Chancellor's desire for peace, even though Hitler had recently withdrawn Germany from the League of Nations.

Dear Lord Rothermere,

You were kind enough to convey to me through Princess Hohenlohe a series of proposals, for which I wish to express my sincere thanks.

In addition, I would like to voice the feelings of countless Germans, who regard me as their spokesman, with regard to the shrewd and well-directed journalist support of the policy which we all hope will lead to the ultimate liberation of Europe. Princess Hohenlohe gave me the translation of the splendid article that Your Lordship has written: I have already taken the liberty recently of referring to the article. What I particularly welcome in the article is that it points out the value of an Anglo-French defence alliance. I am convinced that Anglo-French friendship can be very helpful in maintaining a genuine peace. Germany itself has no aggressive intentions whatever towards France; determined as we may be to defend ourselves against attack, we certainly do not harbour the slightest intention of provoking a war. As veterans of the Great War—I myself was at the Front for four-and-a-half years, facing British and French troops—we all have a very personal experience of the horror of European war. While having no sympathy with cowards and deserters, we frankly accept our duty towards God and our country to prevent with all the means at our disposal the repetition of such a catastrophe. However, this can only be achieved for Europe if the treatment of that critical problem, whose existence cannot be denied, can be removed from the climate of hatred in which victor and vanquished confront each other, and placed on a basis where nations and states can negotiate with each other on equal footing.

Granting such equality of status to Germany implies no threat to the security of France....

It should not be overlooked that I am offering the friendship of a nation of 66 million, which has much of value in other respects too. And just as I see no reason for a war in the west, no more do I see any for a war in the east.

Our efforts to bring about an understanding between Germany and Poland spring from the same desire to eschew the use of force and to approach the tasks we face pragmatically and without emotion....

If I have been frank in presenting these thoughts to Your Lordship, I have done so in order to express my appreciation of the high journalistic position held by Your Lordship in the British press.

I thank you once again for the support that you have shown for a genuine policy for peace in Europe.

Yours sincerely,
Adolf Hitler[11]

He may have been writing words of peace to Lord Rothermere, but Hitler was already devising plans to unite the German people in Czechoslovakia, Poland, and his beloved Austria.

* * *

Rothermere sent Stephanie immediately back Berlin with a symbolic gift for Hitler: a photograph of the Viscount in a solid gold Cartier frame worth more than $60,000 in today's currency. When the Führer turned the frame over, he found Rothermere's *Daily Mail* editorial from September 24, 1930, with the headlines "A NATION REBORN" and "NEW CHAPTER IN EUROPEAN HISTORY."

Stephanie translated the article for Hitler, reading, "The sweeping success of the German National Socialist Party—in other words, the Fascist Party, at the general election of September 14, will, it is my strong conviction, prove to be an enduring landmark of this time. It will stand out as the beginning of a new epoch in the relations between the German nation and the rest of the world."[12]

If there had been any doubt left, the solid-gold gift convinced Hitler of Rothermere's full support. Hitler was now counting on the press baron's articles to convince the British public that a strong and appeased Germany would be the way to future European peace.

* * *

Stephanie had been such a success with the Führer that she would want for nothing whenever she was in Germany on one of Rothermere's missions. Hitler began referring to her as his "dear princess" and authorized Fritz Wiedemann to establish a lavish fund to pay for all of her hotel, restaurant, telephone, and travel bills. Wiedemann was also encouraged to purchase expensive clothing and other gifts for Stephanie—whatever it would take to continue promoting positive Anglo-German relations and to keep Rothermere writing positive articles about how Hitler alone offered the path to peace in Europe. What Hitler hadn't authorized was for the Princess and his married adjutant to become lovers. Hitler was enamored with Stephanie, but he seemed to enjoy admiring her without actually becoming involved, just as he had with his teenaged fantasy sweetheart Stefanie Isak back in Linz.

Although Stephanie von Hohenlohe spoke flattery to Hitler's face, she found him physically repulsive; the exact opposite of the tall, dashing Fritz Wiedemann. Of the Führer, she wrote in detail:

> The ugliest things about him are his nose, his moustache, his mouth and his feet. His nose is too large. Not at the bridge, but from nostril to nostril. The bit between the nostrils is a very ugly shape, so that one is forced to stare at it and wonder what it is. His moustache really does look like Chaplin's and is narrower than his mouth, which is small anyway. It is much narrower than the base of his nose, and draws attention to the whole thing even more....
>
> When Hitler talks, you hardly see his teeth, but when you do, neither their colour nor their shape are at all attractive, and his front teeth are edged with a thin gold strip. His mouth is small, far too small for a man, and when he opens it, especially when he gets worked up, it is extremely unappetising. It becomes distorted into an ugly little hole....[13]

Wisely, Stephanie kept her opinions to her journal, and finally received the prize she had been working toward. In March 1934, Hitler handed his dear Princess a letter, inviting Lord Rothermere to visit him in Berlin. Calling the Viscount his "kindred spirit," Hitler said he was unable to travel to England, "partly due to my position today and partly due to other difficulties, it is impossible for me to leave the orders of the Reich. However, I have already told the good lady who brought Your Lordship's letter and memento, how delighted I would be, on your possible visit to Germany, to describe in detail my view on the European questions that interest you."[14]

Stephanie from Vienna had singlehandedly brokered a power meeting between one of the most influential press barons in the world and Germany's soon-to-be omnipotent dictator.

15

"One blood demands one Reich"

—Adolf Hitler

Franz Salvator, now in his 60s and nearly completely bald, his mustache turned white by time, balanced a cigar between the fore- and middle fingers of his left hand as he stared into the camera lens. He looked to be slightly uncomfortable with having his photo taken, as if his conversation with his female companions were being interrupted. Beside him stood society hostess Lady Melchett, and next to her, a middle-aged Princess Stephanie von Hohenlohe, dressed in the traditional dirndl she always wore when she was back home in Austria.

The former Archduke and the Princess continued to see each other throughout the years, perhaps to rekindle their love affair, but undoubtedly to talk of their son, Franzi, who was now studying at Oxford. A writer for the *Sunday Express* newspaper, owned by Lord Beaverbrook, a contemporary of Rothermere's, wrote a first-person account of his interaction with Franzi while at university.

> "When I knew him he was tall and slim, with a heavy sallow face and black eyebrows almost meeting in the centre. When he first went to Oxford his hair was dark." One term he came back from a holiday on the Continent almost a platinum blond. Asked why it had changed he laughed and said, "It must be the sun!"
>
> Like his mother, Franzi was known for his love of entertaining.
>
> He became an active member of almost every undergraduate club, organized treasure hunts, dances and theatricals, rowed for his college, and was invited to everyundergraduate party.
>
> His own parties were famous far beyond the university. Guests came from the country and from London. He drank nothing stronger than tomato juice, took care never to get into difficulties with the university authorities, and though he had many women friends, was never involved in the slightest scandal.
>
> He had two of the largest and most expensive rooms in the new wing of Magdalen College. Later he moved into "digs" where he surrounded his bed with portraits of

film stars, princes, sons and daughters of British politicians, high officers in the services, and members of titled families.

Apparently, Franzi never spoke of his provenance, either Austrian or Hungarian, and his classmates could only guess at his true nationality. "Undergraduates believed him to be an Austrian for he often wore Austrian dress, a green Homburg hat trimmed with silk cords and a gay sports jacket. In vacations he organised undergraduate visits to Austria and Germany." A photo of Franzi taken about this time in Austria showed him wearing traditional lederhosen, knee socks, fitted jacket and tie.

As Hitler came to power in Germany, the *Sunday Express* writer said that Franzi's classmates began to become suspicious of his German connections.

A few who suspected that his social activities were a cloak for political manoeuvres were laughed at, but after a time there were persistent rumours about his associations with Nazi leaders. People asked where he got the money for entertaining and why he was so anxious to make friends in every undergraduate circle.

Portrait of Franz Joseph von Hohenlohe, called Franzi, taken in 1936 when he was 22 years old. His full German name was Prince Franz Josef Rudolf Hans Weriand Max Stefan Anton von Hohenlohe-Waldenburg-Schillingsfürst (National Portrait Gallery, London Photographs Collection, Given by Bassano & Vandyk Studios).

Undergraduates recalled his conversations and remarked on the number of questions he asked, first on general topics, then about politics, and finally on military and diplomatic affairs. His studies gave him an excuse for remaining in England, for as a member of the university he could do many things which would otherwise have aroused suspicion.[1]

Records show that Franzi was friendly with several of his mother's Nazi sources, and as he finished up his studies at Oxford, he wrote a letter to Fritz Wiedemann, asking for his advice in obtaining a position with the German Diplomatic Service. Wiedemann was apparently convalescing from knee surgery at the time Franzi wrote his letter.

"I would like to take this opportunity, while you are laid up and perhaps have a little less to do, to put a request to you," Franzi wrote.

> Would you be kind enough to answer a few questions that I have wanted to ask you for a long time?
>
> First of all, what preparations, examinations or formalities are necessary for the German diplomatic service?
>
> Are foreign qualifications such as the French "Baccalauréat" or the British "Diploma of Responsions" and "Degree off Bechelor of Arts" recognised for a career as a German diplomat? I would also very much like to know, if an entrance examination is obligatory, whether one can take this before doing military and labour service.
>
> I would be hugely obliged to you dear *Herr Hauptmann*, if you could answer these questions as soon as possible. My address is 51 High Street, Oxford.
>
> But I must not bother or detain you any longer.
>
> I am most grateful to you in advance and remain, with very best wishes for a speedy recovery.
>
> Your sincerely devoted
> Franz Joseph Hohenlohe[2]

Wiedemann replied with his thoughts on the best course of action and advised Franzi to use his name as a reference when filling out the papers regarding his Aryan ancestry.

Even though Marie Valerie had been gone for ten years, Franz Salvator had not asked Stephanie to marry him. Or perhaps he had and she had declined. According to Franzi, Stephanie had received a multitude of marriage proposals over the years from rich and powerful men, and had turned them all down. Although she accepted their money and gifts, she enjoyed being independent, as well as working at her new-found career as a paid "diplomat."

Whether or not Franz Salvator ever considered spending the rest of his days with Stephanie, he did finally remarry in April of 1934 to Melanie Freiin von Risenfels. Although she was from a noble family born at Seisenegg Palace in Viehdorf, Austria, in 1898, the marriage would have been considered morganatic under the rules of the old Austro-Hungarian Empire. But none of that mattered anymore. Austria was in turmoil now that the National Socialists were demanding unification with the German Reich. It was a dream come true for Hitler, who had written at the opening of *Mein Kampf* that "German-Austria must return to the great German mother country.... One blood demands one Reich."[3]

* * *

The Austrian Nazis had been making such a clamor about uniting the country with Germany, that Austrian Chancellor Engelbert Dollfuss effectively banned the Nazi Party, dissolved parliament and set up his own dictatorship under what he called "Austro-fascism." Dollfuss turned to Italy's dictator Benito Mussolini for protection, and Mussolini guaranteed Dollfuss the Austrian independence he desired. The relationship led to the "Rome Protocols" in February 1934, which meant economic cooperation for Italy, Austria and Hungary. Hitler hurried to Venice in June to meet with Mussolini for what was to be his first trip abroad as the new German Chancellor. Mussolini was not impressed with Germany's Führer, calling him "more mule-headed than intelligent."[4] No agreements were reached over Austria's future and Hitler headed back to Berlin where he was planning a political purge that would shock the nation and become known as "The Night of the Long Knives."

From June 30 to July 2, a politically paranoid Hitler had members of his own Brownshirt paramilitary group executed, including SA leader and supposed close friend Ernst Röhm, whom Hitler suspected of treason. Murder squads spread out throughout the country to take out men suspected of supporting a rumored Röhm putsch attempt. Röhm himself was presented with a pistol and given the opportunity to honorably shoot himself. When he had not taken the initiative after ten minutes, the SA leader was shot dead by the SS. Hitler's "cleansing action"[5] in Germany was finally over with up to 200 of his own party members dead.

When Bella Fromm learned that two of her friends—former Chancellor Kurt von Schleicher and his wife—had been among those murdered, she was devastated and was warned to watch out for her own safety.

"Kurt and Elisabeth von Schleicher's assassination was such shattering news to me that I sat there, my head spinning, the ground falling away from under my feet,"[6] she wrote. Fromm fled to the countryside to await the end of the slaughter.

In Vienna, however, the killing was just beginning. On July 25, some six weeks after Hitler had met with Mussolini to discuss the future of Austria, the Viennese Nazis staged their own coup to take over the government. A group of SS troops stormed the Federal Chancellery in central Vienna and shot down the 42-year-old Dollfuss. The putschists then took over the Austrian Broadcasting Service, but were thwarted by the Austrian army and Former Justice Minister Kurt von Schuschnigg, who quickly formed a new government and restored order. When the smoke cleared, some 200 Austrians were dead. Schuschnigg would go on to become Chancellor of the Federal State of Austria and would do his best to thwart any future German attempts at incorporating Austria into the Reich.

Hitler had been in Bavaria enjoying the Wagner Festival when word broke of the attempted Austrian coup. He had undoubtedly given the plan his approval, as confirmed by Propaganda Minister Joseph Goebbel's diary entry: "Committed a boundless stupidity. Got involved in domestic Austrian affairs. Border closed. Anyone crossing it will be arrested. No other choice." Officially, the German government released a statement that "no German office had any connection with these events,"[7] but not a soul believed them. Mussolini was already on the march, having moved two army divisions to the Austrian border.

Average Germans, knowing full-well their government had been involved, were reluctant to discuss the matter in public.

"When I received the shocking news about the Dollfuss assassination, I went at once to the Austrian Ministry to express my condolence," wrote Bella Fromm. "Councilor of Legation Rudolf Saemann was touched: 'You are a courageous person to come here. So far, you are the only one in private German circles who has had the courage.'"[8]

Hitler flew into hysterics after learning that his attempt to reclaim his homeland had gone up in flames. He called it a "second Sarajevo," and feared that Italy would declare war against the Reich at any moment. Hitler immediately phoned German Vice Chancellor Franz von Papen and named him Ambassador to Vienna in a bid to normalize relations with the Austrians and try to placate the Italians. Diplomacy was the only thing that would get him out of this dangerous and embarrassing situation.

Hitler would also have to get back to concentrating on diplomacy with the English and have Princess Stephanie actually schedule the agreed-upon meeting with Lord Rothermere. But first, fortune would once again favor Adolf Hitler.

Just one week later on August 1, Hitler visited 86-year-old German President Paul von Hindenburg and saw for himself that the lung cancer ravaging the old man would soon claim its victim. Hitler said his farewells to the man who had elevated him to chancellor and hurried back to Berlin to have his cabinet pass the Law on the Head of State of the German Reich. Before Hindenburg was even dead, Hitler made sure that he alone would become Führer and Reich chancellor, with complete dictatorial powers. As soon as Hindenburg's death was announced on August 2, the armed forces, or *Wehrmacht*, were forced to swear an oath of complete loyalty to Adolf Hitler: "I swear by God this holy oath that I will show absolute obedience to the Führer of the German Reich and People, Adolf Hitler, the commander-in-chief of the Wehrmacht, and that as a brave soldier I will be willing to sacrifice my life at any time for this oath."[9]

As a hero of the Great War, Hindenburg's death marked the end of an era for many Germans. He was also seen as the last hope for keeping the reins on Hitler and Nazi excesses. Now he was gone, and Hitler was in complete control.

"Goebbels' voice announced the death over the radio," Bella Fromm wrote on August 2.

> Flags were lowered to half-mast. An almost impenetrable silence followed. I reflected on the enormity of Germany's disaster and on the role that unfortunate old man had played in it.
>
> It was Memorial Day, a day of somber reflection anyway. A day on which to think of the heroes who gave their lives for a cause that is no longer considered sacred. The Jews were not allowed to hoist flags in honor of the fallen, though thousands of Jews mourned their own kind who never returned from that holocaust. All these men paid for an idea with their lives. For an ideal of freedom that has been stripped from those of us who remain.[10]

On August 19, the German people overwhelmingly voted to approve Hitler's consolidation of power and legitimized his dictatorship.

One of the first measures the Führer took was to get rid of subversives he felt were undermining his regime. These included foreign journalists like respected American correspondent Dorothy Thompson, who had written an unflattering article published in *Cosmopolitan* in 1932 about Hitler as being irrelevant to the future of world politics.

"When I walked into Adolph Hitler's salon in the Kaiserhof hotel, I was convinced that I was meeting the future dictator of Germany," she wrote. "In something like fifty seconds I was quite sure that I was not. It took just about that time to measure the startling insignificance of this man who has set the world agog."

Thompson came to know Princess Stephanie von Hohenlohe in London, and although Stephanie kept her unflattering opinion of Hitler's physical appearance to her journal, Thompson shared hers in the article. "He is formless, almost faceless, a man whose countenance is a caricature, a man whose framework seems cartilaginous, without bones. He is inconsequent and voluble, ill-poised, insecure. He is the very prototype of the Little Man. A lock of lank hair falls over an insignificant and slightly retreating forehead.... The nose is large, but badly shaped and without character. His movements are awkward, almost undignified and most unmartial.... The eyes alone are notable. Dark gray and hyperthyroid—they have the peculiar shine which often distinguishes geniuses, alcoholics, and hysterics."

Thompson wrote that the interview had been difficult to conduct "because one cannot carry on a conversation with Adolph Hitler." "He speaks always as though he were addressing a mass meeting. In personal intercourse he is shy, almost embarrassed. In every question, he seeks for a theme that will set him off. Then his eyes focus in some far corner of the room; a hysterical note creeps into his voice, which rises sometimes almost to a scream. He gives the impression of a man in a trance. He bangs the table."

When she asked him, essentially, if he would form a dictatorship should he come into power, Hitler admitted that he would: "I will get into power legally," he told her. "I will abolish this parliament and the Weimar constitution afterward. I will found an authority-state, from the lowest cell to the highest instance; everywhere there will be responsibility and authority above, discipline and obedience below."

Thompson had been bemused by this seemingly insignificant demagogue who was suggesting that the German people would vote away their rights. But that's exactly what happened on August 19. Thompson was panic-stricken that she had misread the situation so badly. She tried to make up for it by writing articles exposing the Nazis' inhumanity.

"It must be said, it must be re-iterated," she wrote, "that there has been and still is a widespread terror, which extends throughout the whole of Germany."[11]

Thompson kept it up until the Gestapo knocked on her door at Berlin's Adlon Hotel, and gave her just hours to vacate the country. As the first foreign correspondent expelled from Nazi Germany, she made front-page news around the world.

Bella Fromm discussed the incident with U.S. Ambassador William Dodd and wrote about it on August 28:

> Went to see Dodd at the embassy. We talked about Dorothy Thompson's expulsion. She had been given twenty-four hours to get out. "You should go away too," he told me.
>
> "Excellency, a single individual is of no importance. It is still possible to do good work here," I said.
>
> He told me that [Deputy Führer Rudolf] Hess has promulgated further measures against church and Jews. "As his decrees are secret orders, it is, of course, difficult to put a finger on any of his outrageous tricks."
>
> Dodd is fully aware of the impending catastrophe. He promised to keep my name carefully out of any counter measures. "We are both trying hard to help mankind," he said when he saw me out.[12]

* * *

Berlin, December 1934

Lord Rothermere, his son Esmond Harmsworth, and Princess Stephanie were finally able to arrive together in Berlin for the long-awaited meeting with Hitler, although much had changed since their correspondence had begun one year earlier. Hitler was now the legal, all-powerful dictator of Germany, who had bungled one attempt to incorporate Austria into the Reich by force. He would now have to double-down on his diplomatic overtures toward England if he were to continue to convince Lord Rothermere to write favorable pieces about the Reich. He must continue to convince the Viscount that dismantling the Treaty of Versailles was the only way to assure future peace in Europe. Fortunately for Hitler, neither Rothermere, nor Princess Stephanie seemed the least bit concerned about the autocracy, the infringement on basic human rights, and the silencing of the German free press and political opponents that had overtaken Germany. In fact, Rothermere was said to have been "absolutely delighted" with the royal reception he felt he receive on arriving in Berlin.[13]

To cover the event for the *Daily Mail*, Rothermere also brought along his special correspondent, George Ward Price. Price had followed the rise of National Socialism in Bavaria since the early 1920s. One week before Hitler's Munich Beer Hall Putsch, Price published the following unflattering article about Hitler in Rothermere's paper:

> How far the civil-war insanity has gone in Germany is indicated by the conclusion of a partnership between Ludendorff and Hitler.
>
> Five years ago, at the end of the war, no German brain could have conceived the possibility of these two men even meeting—except in the same way as an Admiral of the Fleet meets a Maltese bum-boat man—Ludendorff, the Kaiser's right-hand man, and Hitler, the ex-housepainter, who in the war, was an officer's batman, and as likely as not, stood to attention to be kicked by a drunken German subaltern.
>
> Hitler is of Austrian origin, which does not prevent his being more violently pro-German than the Germans themselves. "Down with the Treaty of Versailles, the Peace of Shame," is his cry. "Hang all Jews! Expel all foreigners!"
>
> No one in England has ever heard of Hitler until eighteen months ago. Then he began to make sudden incursions into the crowded cafes and beer-halls of Munich. There he delivered impromptu speeches, not without eloquence of the "tupenny-coloured" kind, about the iniquities of the Allies, and the "servile spirit" of the Government of Berlin. He went on to organize yet another of the multiple corps of irregulars that are as common in Germany as goose-clubs in England. So he built up a following, until the mighty Ludendorff, who used to keep even the Kaiser waiting, was constrained to take him into partnership.
>
> And now, in double harness, the old cavalry-charger and this wild mustang from the back of beyond go prancing forward together to the conquest of Germany. As Samuel Pepys used to say, "What shall come of it, God knows."[14]

As the years passed, however, Price began to take Hitler seriously, and gave the Nazi leader one of the first international platforms by which to reach readers outside of Germany.

"As a journalist, I made many contacts with Hitler during the subsequent years when he was building up his power," Price wrote. "Since I reported his statements accurately, leaving British newspaper-readers to form their own opinion of their worth, I had many opportunities of observing him under different sets of circumstances. He appreciated having a foreign auditor for the long harangues in which he tried to justify himself and his policy. He told [Hermann] Göring, who repeated it to me, that I was the only foreign journalist who reported him without prejudice."[15]

The *Daily Mail* party joined the Führer's entourage of 23 prominent guests, including Hermann Göring, Joseph Goebbels, and Foreign Minister Joachim von Ribbentrop at Hitler's official residence in Berlin. It was his first major dinner party for foreign guests since he had assumed power, and the undereducated army corporal from Linz was trying hard to impress. His private apartment above the Reich Chancellery was decorated with carefully chosen baroque art, and every table and sideboard was covered with fresh flowers.

Lord Rothermere proffered a return dinner invitation to be held on December 20 at the elegant Adlon Hotel. Princess Stephanie would hostess, and it would be the most important dinner party of her life; no detail must be overlooked.

Twenty-five people were invited, including Dr. Goebbels and his wife, Magda; Foreign Minister Baron von Neurath and his wife; Göring and actress Emmy Sonnermann, whom he would later marry; Ribbentrop and his wife Annelies; and British banker E.W.C. Tennant, a principal founder of the Anglo-German Fellowship. Additional members of German government were present, plus a smattering of German opera singers for variety.

Princess Stephanie had followed French protocol to seat the very important guests: the host, Rothermere, sat at the center, and the guest of honor, Hitler, sat to his right. Stephanie, as hostess, sat opposite Rothermere and beside Joachim von Ribbentrop.

For Hitler, December 20 was an auspicious occasion: it was the ten-year anniversary of his release from Landsberg Prison for the Munich Beer Hall Putsch; essentially, it was the anniversary of the event that put him on the map as a politician. As the guests took their places at the table, Hitler began one of his ceaseless soliloquies about the events of the past decade, while Stephanie tried to keep up interpreting for the English guests.

When Stephanie's carefully chosen main course of roast chicken was served to all but Hitler, who ate a vegetarian meal, the Führer was still droning on, this time about Anglo-German relations. Lord Rothermere was starting to squirm in his seat, waiting for the right opportunity to make a toast, but the moment didn't seem to be presenting itself.

When Hitler finally paused for breath, Rothermere made his move, grabbing his wine glass as he stood. The relieved guests did the same, but someone bumped into a vase of meticulously placed flowers, which exploded into thousands of shards when it hit the hardwood floor. Without missing a beat, Hitler's SS bodyguards, who feared an assassination attempt, burst into the room with loaded guns and ushered the Führer out of the hotel, with the other high-level Nazis in hot pursuit.

Princess Stephanie, Lord Rothermere, and the rest of the guests were left flabbergasted by exactly what had transpired. All was made right in the coming months, however, as Hitler and Rothermere were once again exchanging letters by April 1935, and Rothermere informed Hitler that the majority of the English were on his side. The Viscount wrote, "The recent correspondence in the Daily Mail in regard to the claims of your government for changes in the Treaty of Versailles show that seven out of every 10 of the persons writing letters were in favour of Germany's claims being entirely acceded to."[16]

16

"Sincere thanks for the great understanding"

—Adolf Hitler

As the overtly friendly meetings with Stephanie von Hohenlohe continued, Hitler's inner circle was alarmed that their leader was so freely confiding in a woman they suspected of being Jewish, and knew for a fact was not the submissive German housewife archetype they were used to. Princess Stephanie didn't look a thing like the Aryan ideal that Hitler espoused, so why was he being fooled by her? As Austrian-Jewish theater director Max Reinhardt would one day say, "Her outward appearance made it clear for all the world to see."[1] Ernst "Putzi" Hanfstaengl, head of the Nazi's foreign press bureau, called Stephanie a "professional blackmailer and full-blooded Jewess."[2] He urged Hitler to cut ties with the princess, lest she betray him and the German government he had built.

Before Stephanie, Putzi had been Hitler's expert on the English-speaking world. Born in Munich to a wealthy family and educated in the United States at Harvard University, Putzi moved back to Germany for good in 1922, and first heard Hitler speak at a Munich beer hall. Putzi became close friends with the budding politician, introduced him to important society figures, and helped finance the publication of *Mein Kampf* after Hitler's release from prison. Hitler had told Putzi to keep an eye on the English-speaking press: "You know England and America," Hitler had told him. "Watch what they say about us. Also, make sure that they hear what we are doing; perhaps they will wake up to the importance of what we are trying to accomplish."[3]

Putzi did so and more; he struck up a deal with American newspaper magnate William Randolph Hearst whereby Hitler would write articles for Hearst publications and receive commissions. In a bid to make even more money, Putzi brought in offers from additional newspapers, but

Hitler started to become annoyed with Putzi's wheeling and dealing. Princess Stephanie and Lord Rothermere offered an alternate outlet for Hitler, and Putzi didn't like it one bit.

Hitler brushed off Putzi's and everyone else's concerns. According to a report by the U.S. Office of Strategic Services, the precursor to the CIA, "Hanfstaengl says that Hitler refused to believe [that she was Jewish] and promised he would have her family investigated. Later when the subject came up again, Hitler said that the investigation showed that everything concerning her family was 'in order.' Hanfstaengl becomes very emotional when speaking of the Princess and was obviously jealous of her relationship with Hitler, whatever that might have been."[4]

Hitler undoubtedly never had the Princess investigated, lest he learn something he really didn't want to know. As if to prove his point, Hitler sent Stephanie a personal invitation to the Nuremberg Nazi Party Rally on September 15, 1935, at which the Nazis announced their new race laws. Far from being horrified, Stephanie wrote that she was dazzled by the "tribal excitement of Nuremberg," which she called "a shrine of Nazidom" and "an orgy of dedication" to the Nazi ideology.[5]

The Nuremberg Laws, which had been drawn up just days before by Hitler's "Jewish expert" in the Reich Interior Ministry, excluded German Jews from Reich citizenship and made it a crime for Jews to marry or have sexual relations with persons of "German or related blood." The laws also defined a "Jew" as someone with three or four Jewish grandparents, regardless of whether they had converted to other religions.[6]

On the day of the announcement, Bella Fromm wrote, "Had tea at the Uruguayan Minister's, Virgilio Sampognaro. He is a lovable gentleman, cultured and charming. The broadcast of Hitler's hymn of hate shook both of us badly. [Baron von] Brandenstein foretold the coming of the Nuremberg laws three years ago, it flashed through my mind. Secretary of State [Bernhard] von Bülow, whom I met at the hotel entrance, greeted me. 'One feels ashamed to be a German,' he said."[7]

Another woman present at the Nuremberg Rally was Unity Valkyrie Mitford, an English socialite and Hitler fanatic. Mitford was an avowed antisemite who was seethingly jealous of Hitler's close relationship with Princess Stephanie. Mitford was said to have made her feelings known loudly to the Führer: "Here you are, an anti–Semite, and yet you have a Jewish woman, Princess Hohenlohe, around you all the time."[8] Hitler ignored Mitford's gibes.

Stephanie's other main adversary in the Reich was Foreign Minister Joachim von Ribbentrop. Stephanie wrote that Ribbentrop "considered

16. "Sincere thanks for the great understanding" 139

himself the one and only political authority on England in the Third Reich, and anyone who did not agree with him that the English were hopelessly decadent, that they would never stand up to fight against the Germans, and that their world empire has reached its zero hour, was a personal enemy of his."[9]

Although none of the other high-ranking Nazis had ever been to England or could speak any English, Ribbentrop was the exception to the rule. Born in Prussia, Ribbentrop spent time in London and Canada as a boy and went on to work as a journalist in the United States then back to Canada as a wine importer. He returned to Germany and fought in the world war, then married into a wealthy German family in 1920.

Martha Dodd described Ribbentrop as a snob and an extremist with "no intellectual ability whatsoever." "With an inordinate ambition and a pomposity and self-esteem rarely seen so openly proclaimed among Nazis, he bears the mark of acquired wealth upon him and the brand of a man lost in confusion, seeking his way through the Nazi way of life in conceit and self-consciousness."

She told of his frosty reception as German Ambassador to London. "His behaviour in London was so conspicuously gauche that I have heard many enemies of Nazi Germany declare the only prayer they had was that Ribbentrop be allowed to stay in London as the Nazi representative. Of course, his worst and most publicized blunder occurred when he was presented to the King—whereupon he Heiled Hitler! The English felt such contempt for him, from all reports in Berlin and in London, they scarcely acknowledged him socially. He was regarded as a nouveau riche and a fanatic, and both qualities are notoriously frowned up on by the stiff, reserved, and supposedly aristocratic English."[10]

Ribbentrop had met Stephanie in London and became intrigued with this mysterious woman who stood between himself and the Führer. He started asking about her and researching her background and activities.

"Thus, in his eyes, I became an arch-fiend, a subversive meddler, a pestilential intruder," Stephanie wrote.[11]

One thing Ribbentrop did find out was that Stephanie and Fritz Wiedemann were having a clandestine affair. Ribbentrop had no love for Hitler's adjutant, especially when he learned that Stephanie was angling to get Wiedemann promoted to Reich Foreign Minister, a position for which Ribbentrop himself was vying. He went to great lengths to snub Stephanie, as was the case before the opening of the new German embassy in London. Wiedemann had to phone the Führer for his intercession before Stephanie was finally invited to the party. Hitler also required

Ribbentrop to apologize directly to the Princess, which deepened Ribbentrop's resentment.

Bella Fromm became aware of Princess Stephanie during a trip to London and learned of her connection to Ribbentrop. Fromm dug into Stephanie's background and wrote in her diary, "Another satellite of Ribbentrop in London is the Austrian-born Jewess, Steffie Richter, now Princess Hohenlohe-Schillingsfuerst by marriage. She and her family are born informers. Steffie managed, as far back as 1923, to be expelled from France for that reason."[12]

* * *

Stephanie next delivered an expensive tapestry to Hitler that Rothermere wrote was for "Adolf Hitler the artist and not the great leader."[13] Hitler instructed Wiedemann to write a thank you note to Stephanie and to apologize for not yet sending a return gift of a framed picture. When signing off, Wiedemann did not hide his affection for the Princess.

> Your Highness
>
> The Führer instructed me to tell you how extremely sorry he is that he has not been able to prepare the picture nor to write the letter for Lord Rothermere on account of his being so over burdened with work.
>
> As soon as he finds time and peace—which as he hopes will be with in the next days he will write to Lord Rothermere, and express his thanks for the wonderful tapestry which you have brought to him.
>
> Would it be possible your highness that you would personally take delivery of that letter and would you please let me know where you can be reached?
>
> With the kindness and sincerest regards of the Führer which I am instructed to transmit to you.
>
> I kiss your hand as your very devoted Wiedemann[14]

The gift earned both Stephanie and Rothermere an invitation to Hitler's mountain retreat at Obersalzberg to discuss a variety of issues. In January 1937, they boarded Hitler's private railway train at the Austrian border and rode it to Berchtesgaden in Upper Bavaria. The train cars featured wood panelling with velvet carpeting, hot and cold running water, and telephones for communicating with passengers in the other carriages. If the train was impressive, the Berghof itself was magnificent, with its stunning mountain views, Italian paintings and French tapestries. The bathrooms contained gold-plated fixtures and Italian marble basins.

Rothermere and Stephanie joined Joseph Goebbels and his wife, Magda, as overnight guests, an honor afforded to very few foreigners. Since Hitler was not known as an early riser, they gathered the next morning in a cosy

16. "Sincere thanks for the great understanding" 141

sitting-room heated by a ceramic-tiled stove for breakfast at 11 a.m., with the Princess given the seat of honor to the Führer's right. Stephanie acted as interpreter for Rothermere. Goebbels wrote in his diary, "Rothermere pays me great compliments.... Enquires in detail about German press policy. Strongly anti–Jewish. The princess is very pushy."[15]

After breakfast, Hitler, Rothermere, and Hitler's personal interpreter, Dr. Paul Schmidt, took a walk to discuss the business at hand. For Hitler, walks were always downhill with a car waiting at the bottom to drive him back up so he wouldn't have to over-exert himself.

The two men talked about a possible German-British alliance to prevent another war between the two countries. They also discussed the threat of communism, as well as the "Jewish Question." Hitler accused Winston Churchill of backing the anti–Nazi campaign in England "on behalf of his Jewish paymasters."[16] Rothermere promised to continue offering the support of his newspapers.

The stylish Princess Stephanie von Hohenlohe, 1937 (author's collection).

In the evening, the party watched the war film *Stosstrupp* (Shock-Troops) *1917*, which everyone found quite moving. Hitler proclaimed to the group that he was enthralled with Stephanie and even stroked her hair and pinched her cheek. Stephanie loved the attention, but noted, "Eva Braun in the house."[17]

Eva Braun had been Hitler's mistress since about 1932 when she was 25 and he was 43, but it was her plight to live mostly in the shadows. Hitler was obsessed with fostering an image of a chaste warrior who only had time for the Reich. He took great pains not to appear with her as a couple in public, and his hard line took a toll on her emotional health. Eva attempted suicide in 1932 by shooting herself in the chest, a desperate act that got Hitler's attention for a time. She began keeping a diary in 1935, shortly before her second suicide attempt, where she recorded her isolation and loneliness. Eva was well-aware of other women in Hitler's life, including Unity Mitford, whom she called by her middle name, Valkyrie.

May 28, 1935

I have just sent him a decisive letter. I wonder if he will sit up and take notice? Well, we shall see. If I don't receive a reply by 10 o'clock tonight I shall swallow 25 pills and gently fall asleep.

Is this the passionate love he has so often sworn me, when he won't send me one kind word for 3 months? True his head is full of political problems but hasn't there been a respite? And what happened last year? Didn't he have lots of bother with Röhm and Italy, and still he found time for me.

I know I can't really judge whether the present situation is not much more trying for him, but it's not asking too much to expect to leave word with the Hoffmanns [Hitler's photographer] or with someone else. I am afraid something else is behind it all. I am not to blame. Certainly not. Perhaps another woman, though not that girl Valkyrie, she would be quite impossible, but there are so many others. What other reason could there be? I can't think of any.

May 29

Dear Lord, I am afraid he won't answer today. If only someone would help me, everything is so terrible and hopeless. Perhaps my letter reached him at the wrong moment. Perhaps I oughtn't to have written at all. Whatever happens, uncertainty is more unbearable than a sudden end. Dear Lord, help me, let me speak to him this day, tomorrow will be too late. I have decided on 35 pills, this time I want to make "dead certain." If only he would ring me.[18]

The diary ends abruptly here. Fortunately, Eva's sister found her unconscious and called a doctor who saved her life. Eva continued to live secretly with Hitler with hopes that he would one day make her his wife.

During Stephanie's excursion to the Berghof in 1937, Eva was carefully tucked away, unable to fraternize with the guests, and yet everyone knew she was there—like a ghost that no one acknowledged.

* * *

After the Berghof visit, Hitler showered Stephanie with mementos of their flirtatious yet restrained relationship. He sent her a silver-framed photograph of the overnight guests with the inscription, "In memory of a visit to Berchtesgaden." He also sent her a bouquet of roses and a sheep-dog puppy that she named Wolf, after Hitler's own Alsatian. Stephanie wrote him a gushing letter of thanks once she returned to London.

My very dear Reich Chancellor,

Our goodbyes were so hurried and surrounded by so many people, that I hardly had time to thank you properly for your hospitality.

You are a charming host—not to mention your beautiful and excellently run home in that magnificent setting—which all leave me with a wonderful and lasting impression. It is no empty phrase when I say, Herr Reich Chancellor, that I enjoyed every minute of my stay with you....

16. "Sincere thanks for the great understanding"

Your gift of the dog has given me great pleasure, not only because I love dogs—but also because, to me, dogs symbolise loyalty and friendship—which in this instance pleases me all the more.

What a shame that you are no ordinary mortal, to whom one can say—I hope we meet again soon…!

Once again, many thanks for the two wonderful days.

In sincere friendship
Stephanie Hohenlohe[19]

As Hitler and Stephanie were exchanging gifts and letters that read like school crushes, Stephanie's true object of affection was Fritz Weidemann, with whom she was spending more and more time. Both were 45 years old, and although Stephanie was a free woman, Weidemann had been married for 18 years and had three children. That didn't stop him, however, from pursuing beautiful and interesting women like American Martha Dodd, and others who crossed his path. Something about Stephanie intrigued him more than others, enough to jeopardize his relationship with the Führer, so the two kept their relationship as quiet as possible. As an indirect token of her affection, Stephanie convinced Rothermere to give her the money to purchase a gold cigarette case at Cartier and have it engraved with Wiedemann's name. Around the same time, Stephanie delivered an expensive jade bowl to Hitler, who wrote that he would display it proudly at the Obersalzberg as a token of Rothermere's efforts toward Anglo-German relations. "Your leading articles published within the last few weeks, which I have read with great interest, contain everything that corresponds to my own thoughts as well," Hitler wrote. "I know, my dear Lord Rothermere, that

Hitler's adjutant Fritz Wiedemann with Princess Stephanie in the background, 1937 (author's collection).

the new Germany has no more sincere and warm-hearted friend in England than you."[20]

While Hitler was focusing on international relations, his SS henchmen were working to suppress Nazi opposition within Germany. On July 15, 1937, they opened the Buchenwald concentration camp near Weimar. The camp was meant initially for male prisoners only and featured an electrified barbed-wire fence, watchtowers, and SS guards with itchy trigger fingers and automatic machine guns. Many of the early prisoners were political dissidents. Jews would follow shortly.

Hitler had one more special gift for Stephanie at the close of 1937: the Honorary Cross of the German Red Cross for her tireless activities on behalf of the German Reich. Wiedemann travelled to the Ritz in Paris where she was staying to personally decorate her with the medal. Hitler also wrote her a letter thanking her for Christmas presents and referring to some trouble she experienced for her support of the Nazi cause.

> Berlin, 28 December 1937
> Currently in Obersalzberg
>
> Esteemed Princess!
>
> I wish to give you the most heartfelt thanks for the books on American high rise builds and bridges which you had delivered to me as a Christmas present. You know how much I am interested in architecture and related subjects and from that you may judge what enormous pleasure your gift afforded me.
>
> I have also heard reports of how upstanding and kind-hearted you have been in the last few years in advocating for the new Germany and its basic needs among your circles. I well know that some unpleasantries for you have arisen from this and for that reason I wish to give you, esteemed Princess, sincere thanks for the great understanding you have shown to our people as a whole and to my work in particular.
>
> I add this thanks my best wishes for the new year and remain with devoted greetings
>
> Adolf Hitler[21]

Princess Stephanie's advocation for the new Germany among the British was about to pay off for Hitler. The Führer had decided once and for all to settle the "Austrian Question," and he met with soon-to-be British foreign minister Lord Halifax to declare that "a closer connection between Austria and the Reich had to be created under all circumstances."[22] Halifax responded that the British government would discuss the issue as long as the Germans promised not to resort to violence, as in the previous attempt to annex Austria. Hitler's interpreter Paul Schmidt commented on how the Führer's confidence had shifted from just two years ago. "His triumphal tone of voice alone would have signaled to a neutral observer that the times had changed. The Hitler of 1937 no longer carefully felt his way forward like the Hitler of 1935. He was clearly convinced of his own strength and others' weakness."[23]

Hitler now firmly believed that England would not suppress his plans to enfold Austria into the German Reich.

17

"Austria will be ours"
—Joseph Goebbels

February 1938

Hitler summoned Austrian Chancellor Kurt Schuschnigg to the Berghof at Obersalzbberg in order to push the importance of German policies within the leader of the alpine nation. Ever since Chancellor Dollfuss' assassination, Schuschnigg had worked to ensure Austrian autonomy, but that was soon to come crashing down around him. Hitler openly berated Schuchnigg, accusing the Austrian Chancellor of betraying his German overlords.

"My task was preordained," Hitler told the Austrian chancellor in his most intimidating tone. "I have taken the most difficult path any German has ever had to take, and I have achieved more in German history than any German was ever destined to achieve."

Hitler blamed Austria for having provided no positive contribution to German history, saying that every important national idea had been sabotaged by the Habsburgs and the Catholic Church. Hitler then threatened to send in troops if Schuschnigg did not fall in line. "Surely you do not think you could put up even half an hour's resistance? Who knows? Maybe I'll be in Vienna tomorrow morning like a spring storm. Then you'll see!"[1]

Hitler then told Schuschnigg that Mussolini agreed with German policies regarding Austria, which was patently false. Göring had presented the idea of an *Anschluss*, or "joining," with Austria about a year earlier to the Duce, declaring, "the Anschluss must and will come—nothing can stop it." But the interpreter present at the meeting recorded that Mussolini "energetically shook his head," to signal no.[2]

Foreign Minister von Ribbentrop then appeared with a list of German demands that would all but crush Austrian autonomy if implemented:

allow Hitler's supporters in Austria to operate freely; appoint Austrian Nazi politician Arthur Seyss-Inquart as interior minister; impose a general amnesty or suspended sentences for imprisoned Austrian Nazis; and allow for Third Reich oversight of Austrian foreign, economic and military policies. Fearing Hitler's threat of military intervention and seeing no other way out of the situation, Schuschnigg signed a pledge to address the demands within three days, then headed back to Vienna in defeat and reconfigured his government to meet Hitler's requirements.

Schuschnigg would later reveal that even Otto von Hapsburg, son of Empress Zita and the late Emperor Karl, had written from his home in Belgium and offered to serve as Chancellor if it would save Austria from the Nazis. But Schuschnigg must have decided that such an attempt at a restoration would be futile and that Hitler would stop at nothing to hunt down Otto and arrest or kill him.

Goebbels wrote, "[Hitler] put Schuschnigg under pressure. Threatened with cannons. And Paris and London would not come to his rescue. Then Schuschnigg caved in completely. A little man."[3]

Hitler's move toward the *Anschluss* seemed to be no secret to Nazi observers like Bella Fromm. In early February, she wrote, "It looks as though they're getting ready for *Anschluss*, and it seems to be in the process of being engineered by the fat Hermann [Göring]. They are sweeping aside everyone who refuses uncompromising approval."[4]

Schuschnigg tried one last trick to thwart Hitler's *Anschluss*; he would let the Austrian people vote on whether they wanted to amalgamate with Germany. Schuschnigg called a plebiscite, since Hitler had publicly stated that a majority of Austrians would support joining the Reich if they were allowed to vote. Hitler was incensed that Schuschnigg was calling his bluff and was convinced that the only way to accomplish his goals was to move German troops into Austria.

On March 10, Goebbels wrote, "The die has been cast. We're going in on Saturday [12 March]. Immediately proceed on all the way to Vienna … the Führer himself will travel to Austria. Göring and I are to remain in Berlin. In eight days, Austria will be ours."[5]

However, the Führer was concerned about how Mussolini would react, since Germany was not prepared to go to war with the Italian nation. Hitler sent a letter to the Duce in the care of Prince Philip of Hesse, informing him of the plans for *Anschluss*. In the letter, Hitler informed Mussolini that Austria was planning to restore the Habsburg monarchy and that Schuschmigg was attempting to hold a "so-called plebiscite."

Hitler wrote, "In my responsibility as Führer and Chancellor of the

German Reich and likewise as a son of this soil, I can no longer remain passive in the face of these developments."[6]

Mussolini's reply was better than Hitler could have hoped for.

"Mussolini said that Austria would be immaterial to him," the Prince of Hesse told Hitler by telephone.

Hitler replied, "I shall never forget him for this, no matter what happens. If he should ever need any help or be in any danger, he can be convinced that I shall stick to him whatever may happen, even if the whole world gangs up on him."[7]

Now that Italy was nullified and England and France were preoccupied with their own internal affairs, Hitler was free to have his way with Austria.

* * *

Around 10 a.m. on March 11, Germany issued an ultimatum to the Austrian government: postpone the popular referendum by 5 p.m., and have Schuschnigg resign while naming Nazi puppet Arthur Seyss-Inquart his successor. Schuschnigg agreed to postpone the vote but refused to resign right away. After conferring with his ministers, however, Schuschnigg came to the conclusion that he had little choice but to acquiesce. Around 8 p.m. the Austrian chancellor staged a radio address to the Austrian people explaining that he would resign in order to prevent violence from befalling the country. Seyss-Inquart was named chancellor around midnight.

On March 12 at 5:30 a.m., German troops marched into Austria anyway, but instead of meeting any resistance, they were surprised to be welcomed by the people. Goebbels read the Führer's proclamation at noon over the radio that the German army had been "summoned by the new National Socialist government in Vienna" to "guarantee that within a short span of time the Austrian people will be given the opportunity in a genuine popular referendum to determine its future and shape its destiny."[8]

Shortly thereafter, Hitler's motorcade was on its way to his former hometown of Linz. Rothermere's special correspondent for *The Daily Mail*, G. Ward Price, hurried to the city on the Austro-German border where he wrote that he found the entire population of about 60,000 people awaiting Hitler's arrival in the town square.

"Here, indeed, history was being made before one's eyes," Ward Price wrote.

> I managed to get admission to the balcony of the town hall from which Hitler was sure to address the citizens. After a further wait of some hours, by which time darkness was setting in, he arrived, greeted by deafening applause.

> As he looked on the Austrian population below began to chant the slogan of the Nazi Party: "Ein Reich! Ein Volk! Ein Führer!" [One State! One nation! One leader!] Hitler's face took on a look of ecstasy as he heard this manifestation of devotion to himself and his regime....[9]

One of the observers was 66-year-old Dr. Eduard Bloch who had treated young Adolf and his cancer-stricken mother.

"The weak boy whom I had treated so often and had not seen for thirty years stood in a car," Bloch recalled. "He smiled, waved and gave the Nazi salute to the people who crowded the street. Then for a moment he glanced up at my window. I doubt that he saw me but he must have had a moment of reflection. Here was the home of the noble Jew who had diagnosed his mother's fatal cancer.... It was a brief moment."[10]

Amidst the cheering and chaos Ward Price was able to ask Hitler if he expected to be received with the same enthusiasm in Vienna. "I will show you tomorrow," was the reply. "You can join the motor-cavalcade that will bring me to Vienna, and you will be able to see for yourself what the people of Austria feel about me."[11]

That evening, the entourage lodged at the Weinzinger Hotel by the Danube. Hitler called for his state secretary to draw up legal documents that would be known as the Law on the Reunification of Austria with the German Reich. The first article asserted simply: "Austria is a territory of the German Reich."[12] Henceforth, Austria, or Österreich, meaning "eastern realm," would be known as Ostmark, or the "eastern march" of the Reich.

Hitler also took the time to visit his parents' graves at Leonding before moving on to Vienna. SS chief Heinrich Himmler had asked for an extra day to secure the city—by the end of his cleansing efforts, Himmler would have arrested some 79,000 "unreliables" within Austria's capital.

The next day, Ward Price wrote that the 150-mile drive to Vienna produced "the most excited demonstration of enthusiasm" that he had ever witnessed. Workmen lined the walls of their factories, nuns came out from their convents to wave Hitler on, and army cadets from a military academy made an arch for Hitler's motorcade with their drawn swords. All along the way, people tossed flowers at the entourage.

Hitler's convoy of black Mercedes entered Vienna from the direction of Schönbrunn Palace, the former imperial summer residence where Marie Valerie had spent days playing with her sister, brother, and her mother's impressive collection of pets before the world war tore the Empire apart. Ward Price described the procession as driving at a slow pace down the long, straight thoroughfare known as the Mariahilferstrasse toward the

Hotel Imperial where Hitler would spend the night. The Viennese lined each side of the road ten deep, and he said the crowds were so loud that the bands playing along the route could not be heard. Scores of Viennese paraded through the streets waving Nazi flags.

Hitler triumphantly enters Vienna on March 13, 1938, next to the Lord Mayor during the Anschluss. Behind him are Rudolf Hess and Josef Goebbels (author's collection).

"If ever a nation showed delight in being annexed it was the people of Austria on that March afternoon in 1938," Ward Price wrote. On March 15, Hitler made his way to the Hofburg Palace, where thousands of people were gathered in the Heldenplatz.

> The heading given by the London *Times* to the news of the Anschluss was "Rape of Austria." That afternoon Hitler addressed a vast crowd in the big parade-ground of the Burg, which had been the palace of the Habsburg dynasty. By chance I met him as he came down the stone staircase from delivering this oration. His face glittered with tears. "Is that a 'rape'?" he asked scornfully, waving a hand at the tight-packed, cheering multitude below.[13]

Nazi supporters in Germany hailed Hitler as a hero for seizing the opportunity to unite the German speaking peoples of Austria and Germany without bloodshed. Those who were not Nazi supporters were dismayed at how easily it all happened, and without any foreign opposition. Bella Fromm wrote, "The blow against Austria, although expected, had a paralyzing effect on all of us. Hitler had hurried 'to the support of the poor brother nation in its hour of internal difficulty.' It was well-prepared. The Austrian Nazis fomented disorder. The Austrian Nazis appealed for help. The German Nazis marched in."[14]

Yet, it was far from peaceful in Austria for those who weren't Aryan. Jewish men and women were forced to clean gutters and scrub former Austrian Chancellor Schuschnigg signs from the sidewalk to the jeers of Nazi guards and circling crowds. Others were conscripted to clean public toilets and those of the SS barracks. While his SS looted wealthy Jews of their valuables, Heinrich Himmler was overseeing construction of the Mauthausen Concentration Camp on the Danube in Upper Austria. It would become the site of the largest number of officially listed executions in its existence—35,318.

As for former Chancellor Schuschnigg, he was kept under house arrest until May, when he was taken to Gestapo headquarters in Vienna and incarcerated for another 17 months under deplorable conditions. He would eventually end up in misery at Dachau.

* * *

Princess Stephanie would be rewarded handsomely for her role in helping to bring about the *Anschluss* through positive relations with the British. On June 8 she received an unexpected cable from Fritz Wiedemann at the hotel where she was staying in Paris.

"Recommend you come to Berlin urgently as Chief wants to speak you this week,"[15] it read.

Stephanie was back in Berlin on June 10, where she made her way through the grandiose doors of the Reich Chancellery and into Hitler's cavernous office. Unbeknownst to anyone but Hitler at the time, he was about to lay all doubts to rest about Stephanie's background or loyalties by making her an official bride of the National Socialist Workers' Party. At some point during an unprecedented four-hour meeting, Hitler solemnly pinned the Nazi Party's Gold Medal of Honour to Stephanie's bodice. The gold medal, which boasted a swastika on the front and Hitler's own signature on the back, was awarded to very few long-standing Nazi Party members "who have rendered outstanding service to the National Socialist movement and to the achievement of its goals."[16] The ceremony now rendered Princess Stephanie von Hohenlohe-Waldenburg-Schillingsfürst, who was once a Jewish girl from Vienna, an honorary Aryan and full member of the Nazi Party.

Hitler's inner-circle was gobsmacked at the favoritism shown to this woman whom they clearly viewed as a nefarious Jewish interloper who would ultimately cause problems for the Führer. Hermann Göring swore he knew about the meeting ahead of time, telling Stephanie, "I know everything. It's my job to know everything." She responded, "But do you actually know everything we talked about in all that time, *Herr Feldmarschall?*"[17]

Stephanie would speak of the "peculiar relationship" between Hitler and Göring to the U.S. Office of Strategic Services in the not-so-distant future. She told the intelligence agency that Hitler spoke to her at great length about Göring's "undying loyalty and devotion." Stephanie said that as Hitler spoke, tears welled up in his eyes. "'What would I ever do without [Göring],' [Hitler] said, shuddering at the very thought and then added, 'He had to promise me not to drive his car too wildly a long while ago and now I made him give up flying. It would be too dreadful to think…' there he broke off and shook his head as if to cast off a terrible vision which he could not endure."

"Some time later the Princess has occasion to tell Goering in private some of the compliments that Hitler has showered upon him," the OSS wrote in its report.

> Goering was thrilled to the core. The Field Marshall's radiance and delight showed that such words from such lips meant more to him than even uniforms and jewels. He reciprocated wildly. It was a veritable explosion of loyalty, devotion and hero-worship. Hitler was undoubtedly the greatest German who ever lived. The Bavarian braggart and brute disappeared and a proud little boy came to the surface.
>
> The Princess is of the opinion that there are probably no other two men in the world who appreciate each other more ardently and sincerely and then added that although they are so vociferous as individuals they are probably tongue-tied when they try to say to each other what they think of each other.[18]

17. "Austria will be ours" 153

Stephanie recorded the jealousy surrounding her special treatment, convinced that "every one of their clique yearned to have the Führer or at least his ear, exclusively to himself."

When Stephanie wrote about her lengthy meeting with Hitler, she referred to the Reich Chancellor by his first name, implying that she called him "Adolf" when they were in private. "Every visit of mine to the Reich Chancellery seemed to them an impudent encroachment on their sacred privileges, and every hour that Adolf wasted upon me was an hour which he might have spent to so much greater advantage in their devoted company."[19]

The *Anschluss* would also grant Stephanie the opportunity to live like a real Habsburg princess in a way that Franz Salvator could never have offered her. The Nazis confiscated a magnificent rococo palace near Salzburg, Schloss Leopoldskron, from Jewish theater director Max Reinhardt, which was his stage name. He had been born Maximilian Goldmann in Baden in 1873, and went on to become an actor, director, and playwright who developed an important German-language acting school. Through

Jewish theater director Max Reinhardt's Leopoldskron Palace near Salzburg was confiscated by the Nazis after the Anschluss and given to Princess Stephanie so she could entertain in style (author's collection).

the intercession of Fritz Wiedemann, Reinhardt's manor was "gifted" to Stephanie as her own personal residence. The *London Evening Standard* made the announcement on July 21, 1938: "Princess Hohenlohe Waldenburg-Schillingsfürst, who is believed to have arranged Captain Wiedemann's meeting with Lord Halifax, and who acted as Wiedemann's hostess in London, plans to acquire Schloss Leopoldskron near Salzburg, as a holiday home. The mansion was requisitioned after the annexation of Austria."[20]

Bella Fromm was more forthcoming in her characterization. "Breaking up the Wiedemann marriage was a mere bagatelle in comparison with the work of the Stephanie-Wiedemann team on behalf of the National Socialists. It was just tough on Frau Wiedemann that she was wounded and inconsolable. For these exceptional services Stephanie was rewarded by Hitler with Schloss Leopoldskron near Salzburg, once the home of that world-famous genius of the theater, Max Reinhardt."[21]

But it was more than just a magnificent home; the Nazis expected Stephanie to utilize the location as a political salon where she could entertain international VIP's visiting the annual Salzburg music and drama festival. Britain's MI5 kept an eye on the activities, writing a memo: "In July [1938] she rented Castle Leopoldskron near Salzburg, and was said to have entertained prominent Nazis there and to have introduced them to English friends," and "Schloss Leopoldskron is only an hour's drive from Hitler's home and she is frequently summoned by the Führer who appreciates her intelligence and good advice. She is perhaps the only woman who can exercise any influence on him."[22] A warrant was issued to open all letters and telegrams addressed to the Princess so MI5 could continue to monitor her Nazi correspondence.

It's uncertain whether Stephanie actually paid any rent to live in the palace, but Fritz Wiedemann was authorized to pay the enormous costs associated with upkeep on the building that had been commissioned in 1736 by the Catholic Prince-Archbishop of Salzburg. When Max Reinhardt acquired the property in 1918, he made it his life's work to restore the structure, so he could use it to stage some of his theater productions. A good deal of the "upkeep" probably included electrical work for Nazi surveillance so Hitler's henchmen could listen in on Stephanie's guests, who would include princes, counts, ambassadors, bankers, prelates, professors, singers and actors, according to her son. Bella Fromm referred to this strategy as a "system of high society espionage."[23]

Stephanie had grand plans to host large receptions in the palace and ordered several upgrades of her own. She wanted an oversized electric cooker, plus a large refrigerator and modern electrical appliances in the kitchen. In order to make everything run properly, an electrical transformer had to be installed on the grounds. Stephanie also had a tennis court built and required regular maintenance of the lavish gardens. To round out the small staff currently on hand, Stephanie's son wrote that from London, she brought "her lady's maid.... A cook, two scullery maids, two footmen, three maids and some laundresses were hired locally—just sufficient to run the spacious castle.... Leopoldskron was furnished, though sketchily. Steph added her own linen and silver, put in central heating, a half-dozen more bathrooms and furnished the bedroom annex in her flawless taste."[24] Hitler considered it money well spent, since the palace was confiscated state property and his esteemed Princess was its mistress.

Stephanie did take pity on Max Reinhardt and his wife, actress Helene Thimig, who was incensed with the whole arrangement. Thimig wrote, "What a macabre joke: Reinhardt's creation—now a palace for the Nazis! And this Aryanised palace has been placed under the management of the Jewish Princess von Hohenlohe!"[25] Out of the goodness of her heart, Stephanie saw to it to pack up the Reinhardt's things, including furniture, a collection of theatrical costumes, books, and artwork. According to Stephanie's son, the belongings made up 16 piano-sized crates that were shipped off to Hollywood, where the Reihnardts had fled, "at Steph's expense."

Apparently, Stephanie was offended that she never received a thank-you note from either Reinhard, nor his wife, for the Princess' magnanimous gesture. Reinhardt was quoted a year later as saying, "Yes, the stuff arrived. But what are sixteen crates when one has lost a Leopoldskron?"[26]

Now that Austria was firmly in Germany's grasp, Stephanie and Wiedemann turned their attentions toward delivering Czechoslovakia's German-speaking region, the Sudetenland, to the Führer.

18

"One of these days there will be a big scandal"

—Jan Masaryk, Czech Ambassador in London

In July 1938, Fritz Wiedemann's plane touched down at Croydon Airport for a secret meeting with British Foreign Secretary Lord Haliax to discuss Hitler's desire to retake the Sudetenland of Czechoslovakia. Stephanie met Wiedemann at the airport and greeted him with a lover's embrace before slipping into a car and driving off to Stephanie's home in Mayfair. But the couple's journey was not the clandestine one they had planned; they were being followed by a journalist named Willi Frischauer, who had believed for some time that the Princess was deep in league with the Nazis.

Frischauer was a Viennese-Jewish journalist who was forced to flee Austria after the *Anschluss* and he now worked for Britain's *Daily Herald*. He received a tip from an airport source that Wiedemann was on his way to London and made sure he was there when Hitler's adjutant landed. Frischauer was on the couple's tail the next day when they drove to Halifax's house at Eaton Square on July 18 for the secret summit on the Sudetenland that included Permanent Under-Secretary for Foreign Affairs Alexander Cadogan.

Hitler had laid down his position to Wiedemann, and although no notes were taken at the meeting, Wiedemann ostensibly delivered Hitler's words directly to the British Foreign Secretary: "Why do the Czechs not give the Sudeten Germans their autonomy? England has given it to Ireland, France had a vote on the Saar, why are the Czechs not doing this as well? The Sudeten question has to be solved anyway. If the Czechs don't give in, the question has to be solved one day by force, he [Hitler] was determined to do this. England has clearly declared itself to be on the side of the Czechs. The Czechs are sabotaging a sensible solution."[1]

Wiedemann reported later to German Foreign Minister von Ribben-

18. "One of these days there will be a big scandal"   157

trop, "I then told [Halifax] exactly what the Führer had instructed me to say. Halifax asked me repeatedly whether it would be possible to get an assurance from Germany that force against Czechoslovakia was not planned. I told him outright: 'You will not get such an assurance.'" Wiedemann then reported Halifax's reply, which, if true, showed a remarkable desire to see Nazi Germany prevail: "I, as English Foreign Secretary, aim to get so far in my lifetime that one day the Führer will be seen entering Buckingham Palace at the side of the King of England [amid] the acclamations of the English people."[2]

As Wiedemann headed to the airport the next day to fly back to Berlin, he saw Frischauer's headline announcing the "secret" meeting with Halifax: "HITLER'S AIDE IN LONDON—SEES FOREIGN SECRETARY."[3] The international press picked up the story, and both the German and British governments scrambled to issue benign statements about simply advancing Anglo-German relations, rather than the true purpose of carving up Czechoslovakia. The Czech ambassador in London, Jan Masaryk, who suspected what Hitler was really up to, was outraged. He wrote: "If there is any decency left in this world, then one of these days there will be a big scandal when it is revealed what part was played in Wiedemann's visit by Steffi Hohenlohe, née Richter. This world-renowned secret agent, spy and confidence trickster, who is wholly Jewish, today provides the focus of Hitler's propaganda in London. Wiedemann has been living with her. On her table stands a photograph of Hitler, signed 'To my dear Princess Hohenlohe—Adolf Hitler' and next to it a photograph of Horthy, dedicated to 'a great stateswoman.'"[4]

Hitler gave both Wiedemann and Stephanie the cold shoulder following what the Führer considered the failed London mission due to the embarrassment it caused the Reich. As Foreign Minister, Ribbentrop was furious with the pair for operating a secret foreign intrigue without his knowledge. The couple decided to lay low until the situation played out.

Bella Fromm wrote, "The people at the Czech Legation are frightened and discouraged. How far will Hitler go to get his Sudeten Germans? Most of Europe is in suspense."[5]

Hitler was tiring of diplomacy and consulted his generals about sending strong armored divisions into Czechoslovakia to settle the matter once and for all. He was surprised when they did not jump at his suggestion, and he complained about "fear and cowardice in the army."[6] At about the same time, Hitler received a remarkable request from British Prime Minister Neville Chamberlain to meet to discuss the Czech crisis. The 70-year-old Chamberlain flew on an airplane for the first time in his life and arrived at the Berghof for a summit with the Reich Chancellor. Chamberlain was as unimpressed with Hitler's appearance as Stephanie had been on first meeting him.

"He looks entirely undistinguished," Chamberlain wrote. "You would never notice him in a crowd and would take him for the house painter he once was."[7]

Hitler immediately got down to business.

"If you agree that the principle of self-determination is the basis of the Sudeten question," he told the British Prime Minister, "we can then talk about how this principle can be put into practice."[8] Chamberlain responded that he would need to discuss the matter with his cabinet. He proposed another meeting, and in the mean time, Hitler promised he would not use force in Czechoslovakia. However, Propaganda Minister Goebbels made sure the Sudeten German agitators made it all but impossible for the Czech government to keep the peace in the region.

After returning to London, Chamberlain and his cabinet agreed that the only way to prevent war was to appease Hitler by returning the Sudetenland to the Reich. He received France's buy-in, and together, the two governments sent letters to the Czech government demanding that it cede all territories with a German population totalling more than 50 percent. Prague felt it had no choice but to acquiesce.

Chamberlain touched down in Cologne for his second meeting with Hitler on September 22, 1938. He expected the talks to go smoothly, since Hitler would be getting everything he had asked for at the previous meeting. Unfortunately, Hitler was unhappy with the new borders presented to him and he declared that he could not accept the deal. The negotiations dragged on, with Hitler refusing to concede and the Czechs beginning to mobilize their armed forces. According to Goebbels, "The whole situation is so tense it's coming apart at the seams."[9]

Nearly a week passed without a solution. When a motorized army division headed down Wilhelmstrasse toward the Czech border, a few hundred Germans stood quietly, as if in silent protest to the possibility of another war. Hitler appeared on the Chancellery balcony to observe the convoy, but quickly retreated when there was no cheering. He had gotten the message, and sent a letter to Chamberlain to see if one more chance at diplomacy might win out in the end. Chamberlain suggested a conference in Munich with the leaders of France and Italy—the Czechs were left out of their own peace negotiations. On September 30, an ill-tempered Hitler signed the Munich Agreement, allowing for the peaceful annexation of the Sudetenland without the extra territories Hitler had wanted. Bella

Fromm wrote, "Hitler, Mussolini, Chamberlain and Daladier sign the Munich pact, giving Germany Sudetenland. Once again war is 'avoided.'"[10]

Fritz Wiedemann used the occasion to credit Stephanie with helping to reunite the Sudetenland with the Reich. He wrote to Lord Rothermere, "It was her [Princess Stephanie's] preparation of the ground that made the Munich Agreement possible."[11]

Stephanie also used the occasion to get back into Hitler's good graces. She wrote him a congratulatory note from Berlin's Adlon Hotel. "There are moments in life that are so great—I mean, where one feels so deeply that it is almost impossible to find the right words to express one's feelings.—Herr Reich Chancellor, please believe me that I have shared with you the experience and emotion of every phase of the events of these last weeks. What none of your subjects in their wildest dreams dared hope for—you have made come true. That must be the finest thing a head of state can give to himself and to his people. I congratulate you with all my heart."[12]

Bella Fromm was not around to experience the aftermath of Hitler's victory, however. She had made the decision in May to vacate Germany as quickly as she could. By September 6, she was on a train bound for Paris, where she would board a ship to New York. But even as her train pulled out of Germany, she would not be spared a last humiliation. At about 2 a.m., two uniformed guards burst into her sleeper car, demanding her emigrant's passport and insisting on searching every corner of the compartment.

"They turned everything inside out," she wrote. "They took the soles from my bedroom slippers. They squeezed the toothpaste from the tube."

The guards accused her of trying to smuggle valuables out of the country, despite her protests that her jewelry had been the property of her family for generations. They threatened her with being sent back to Germany if she refused to sign a statement: "I am a Jewish thief and have tried to rob Germany by taking German wealth out of the country. I hereby confess that the jewels found on me do not belong to me and that in trying to take them out I was eager to inflict injury on Germany. Furthermore I promise never to try to reenter Germany."

"I signed," Fromm wrote. "I had to get out of this country. This was a country to get out of if you had to do it naked. Half an hour later, the train crossed the border. I was in safety. My heart was pounding, and I began to cry. Tears of liberation. I was uneasy up until the time the train stopped at the Gare du Nord. The statement, together with my jewels, had gone into the pockets of my tormenters."[13]

Fromm was one of the lucky ones. She just missed being part of the greatest torment the Nazis had yet to rain down upon the German Jews.

Methodically, over the years, Joseph Goebbels had made sure that life for Jews under the Nazi regime had become increasingly intolerant, so as to force willful emigration like Fromm's. But those who defiantly stayed behind were pushed to the extreme until the situation was ready to explode by early November 1938. On November 7, a 17-year-old Polish Jew named Herschel Grynszpan, whose family had been deported from the Reich and was living in misery in a refugee camp, shot the German Third Legation Secretary Ernst vom Rath while in Paris. Goebbels turned outrage over the shooting into a rallying cry against all German Jews, especially once vom Rath finally died from his wounds on November 9. The German official's death coincided with the fifteenth anniversary of Hitler's Beer Hall Putsch of 1923, and the Nazis were spoiling for a fight. Goebbels made sure the Nazi press encouraged rabid violence, the burning of synagogues, and the destruction of as much Jewish property as possible. The Propaganda Minister recorded in his diary, "In Hessen big antisemitic demonstrations. The synagogues are burnt down. If only the anger of the people could now be let loose!"[14] Soon the violence spread, with reports of vandalism and worse in Kassel, Dessau, and Munich.

Goebbels gave a speech that evening announcing the death of vom Rath and encouraging what he called "demonstrations" against the Jews throughout Germany. He recorded the conversation he had with Hitler in Munich. "I go to the party reception in the Old Town Hall. Huge amount going on. I explain the matter to the Führer. He decides: let the demonstrations continue. Pull back the police. The Jews should for once get to feel the anger of the people. That's right. I immediately give corresponding directives to police and party. Then I speak for a short time in that vein to the party leadership. Storms of applause. All tear straight off to the telephone. Now the people will act."[15]

Police across the country were instructed to arrest as many male Jews as possible and the fire-brigade were told to extinguish only the flames that threatened nearby Aryan-owned buildings. Goebbels recalled the sound of shattering glass from shop windows being smashed. "The dear Jews will think about it in future before they shoot down German diplomats like that," he wrote. "And that was the meaning of the exercise."[16]

When *Kristallnacht*, or Night of Broken Glass, was over, some 100 synagogues in Germany had been demolished, several hundred others had been burned, and at least 8,000 Jewish-owned shops had been destroyed. At least 100 Jews had been murdered, and 30,000 male Jews

18. "One of these days there will be a big scandal" 161

had been arrested and sent to concentration camps at Dachau, Buchenwald, and Sachsenhausen.

The Austrian Jews fared no better. Major synagogues were burned, Jewish-owned storefronts were demolished and concert halls were turned into temporary prisons. Police were instructed to arrest as many male Jews as possible, especially the wealthy, and women were desecrated and humiliated. Once the damage had been done, some 680 suicides were reported in Vienna.

Princess Stephanie's aunt Olga was one of those arrested in Austria during the Jewish pogroms. She would eventually be taken to the Theresienstadt concentration camp in Czechoslovakia, where she would perish in 1942.

* * *

Stephanie's blown cover with Fritz Wiedemann at the Croydon Airport had been an embarrassment for all involved, and Lord Rothermere no longer cared to be associated with someone he now called "a very indiscreet woman."[17] He wrote her a conciliatory letter, putting an end to their business relationship. "My mission to create a better feeling between Britain and Germany has largely succeeded. Mine was a lone voice in the wilderness four years ago but now it is generally accepted by almost every political party in this country that good relations between Britain and Germany are essential for the peace of the world. You have helped much to achieve this better understanding. I do not wish to be considered an international busybody!"[18]

Stephanie attempted to convince the Viscount that he still needed the intelligence she could bring him from the Reich, writing, "What is happening in Germany now is momentous."

> They are passing through their greatest crisis. Changes are taking place there which are of decisive importance for the future of Europe. All the conservatives are being kicked out and only the extremists have or are taking their places.
> What you read in the papers is all bunk because only very few know what really is going on. It is all camouflage which Hitler himself has set up to hide the truth. I will tell you all about it in detail when I see you.
> You will have to be very careful in the future. As a matter of fact, I cannot see how you will be able to support Hitler any longer under these new conditions and at the same time serve the best interests of your own country.[19]

But Rothermere was not swayed and the Princess was incensed that her longtime source of income was evaporating before her eyes. She contemplating suing the Viscount for breach of contract and set Wiedemann to work photographing all of the letters Rothermere had written to Hitler over the years. Stephanie also most likely drafted a letter that Wiedemann signed and sent off to the Viscount. It informed Rothermere about the photographic copies and hinted that Rothermere's relationship with Hitler would be seriously undermined should Stephanie's contract truly be terminated.

> You know my Lord that the F.[ührer] greatly appreciates the work the Princess did to help improve the relations between our countries. The work was made—and this, the Princess never ceased to state and repeat—on your behalf and on your instructions. It was done by her with great ability, assiduity and tact.... Considering the chivalrous character and magnanimity of the F., leave in my mind no doubt that he will grant her help in her fight to re-establish her personal honour, which was attacked while in your service. He will grant her the permission to use the above-mentioned correspondence as evidence to prove that she was working for you, as he will feel it will be a great help for a woman in a fight against a powerful man, but no doubt it will be very unpleasant for him and he will have a strong aversion against the fact that any correspondence of his should be read in court.[20]

Rothermere was furious at the blackmail plot cooked up by Stephanie and Wiedemann and didn't believe for a minute that Hitler would be amenable to their conspiracy. Rothermere threatened to expose their ruse to the Führer himself, but as it turns out, Hitler was already on to the couple.

* * *

Hitler had finally learned that his esteemed Princess was sleeping with Fritz Wiedemann, and he was furious at the scheming he suspected had been going on behind his back. This paranoia prompted Hitler's jealous inner-circle to go into overdrive, looking for any evidence that would get rid of both favorites once and for all.

Now that the Führer was receptive, he was presented with evidence from Adolf Eichmann's Department for Jewish Affairs that Stephanie was most definitely "half Jewess."[21] German Military intelligence, the *Abwehr*, had also been spying on the couple, and reporting back to Hitler. The *coup de grâce* was a report from SS Chief Heinrich Himmler showing "credible evidence" from an undercover agent of the German Secret Service in England that Princess Stephanie von Hohenlohe was working for British intelligence. What this "evidence" was, we do not know; nothing appears in the declassified MI5 files. Nevertheless, Hitler became enraged and ordered that the Princess be arrested immediately.

* * *

18. "One of these days there will be a big scandal" 163

The Führer had ceased to confide in his once close adjutant, Fritz Wiedemann, and Wiedemann felt as though his days alongside the high command were numbered.

"I just hung on until Hitler sent me into the wilderness," he said.[22]

On January 19, 1939, Hitler decided once and for all that Wiedemann was too dangerous to keep in Berlin. The Führer's excuse was that the adjutant had lost his nerve during the Jewish pogroms and that he had "no use for men in high positions, and in my immediate circle, who are not in agreement with my policies."[23]

Hitler summoned the man with whom he shared history dating back to the Great War, and summarily dismissed him as adjutant. However, Hitler offered Wiedemann a position as Consul-General to San Francisco—about as far away as he could think to send him at the time. Wiedemann accepted. According to *Time Magazine,* Wiedemann's mission was "to smooth ruffled US-German relations and sell the Nazi regime to an unsympathetic US."[24]

Hitler also admonished Wiedemann that he must stop seeing the Princess immediately because she was "under suspicion" and was being investigated by the Gestapo for possible espionage activity. Wiedemann vouched for the princess and her influence on British policy toward Germany, but Hitler would not be swayed. In his eyes, Princess Stephanie was now a traitor to the Nazi cause.

* * *

Stephanie's son Franzi was in residence at Leopoldskron Castle in the early spring of 1939 when he says it was "seized from the Hohenlohes without warning." He reports that he was forced to leave Salzburg without delay and was followed by the Gestapo to Munich "for an uncomfortable week"[25] before he was able to slip from Austria and into England.

When Wiedemann and Franzi got word to Stephanie that her life was in danger in the Reich, she fled to London, where she made do with the final check that Rothermere had written for her services. As she contemplated how she would make a living now that she had been shut out by both of her former employers, Hitler and Rothermere, word came that Franz Salvator, former Archduke of Austria and father of Stephanie's son, had died. He was buried in the same tomb as Marie Valerie at Wallsee-Sindelburg Cemetery. Of their 25-year relationship, Stephanie would write, "It was to remain a true and sincere friendship. One of those that only death can end."[26]

* * *

The Western powers were soon to learn that Hitler was in no way appeased by having Austria and the Sudetenland under his belt. He would move to take all of Czechoslovakia in order to "protect the Reich" from any unrest in the surrounding territory. His next goal was Danzig and the Polish Corridor—land also ceded in the Versailles Treaty of 1919. This plan was finally too much for the British and French to bear. They realized too late that Hitler's aims went far beyond merely uniting the German people; his goal was European domination.

On March 18, 1939, Anglo-German relations took a turn. The British cabinet endorsed Prime Minister Chamberlain's recommendation to change its policy toward Nazi Germany. No longer would Great Britain try to appease Hitler; England would now have to threaten war if Hitler refused to pull back his expansions. The French were also on board, agreeing to go to war if the Germans forcibly acted against Danzig or Poland. In April, Chamberlain announced to the House of Commons that Britain and Poland had agreed to sign a mutual assistance pact should either country be attacked "by a European power."[27]

In May, Hitler explained his intentions to a group of Germany's top military leaders gathered at the New Reich Chancellery.

"It is not Danzig that is at stake," he said. "For us it is a matter of expanding our living space in the East and making food supplies secure and also solving the problem of the Baltic States." Hitler said it was necessary "to attack Poland at the first suitable opportunity. "We cannot expect a repetition of Czechia. There will be war."

Gone was any talk of improving German-Anglo relations. Should conflict with the West be unavoidable, Hitler said, "then the fight must be primarily against England and France. The aim is always to bring England to its knees."[28]

American journalist William Shirer noted how Goebbels' propaganda machine was misleading the German people into absurdly false reasoning about the coming war. He wrote on August 10 after arriving back in Berlin to "the cockeyed world of Nazism": "Whereas all the rest of the world considers that the peace is about to be broken by Germany, that it is Germany that is threatening to attack Poland ... here in Germany, in the world the local newspapers create, the very reverse is maintained.... What the Nazi papers are proclaiming is this: that it is Poland which is disturbing the peace of Europe; Poland which is threatening Germany with armed invasion...."

Headlines by the Nazi-run press included "Complete Chaos in Poland—German Families Flee—Polish Soldiers Push to Edge of German

18. "One of these days there will be a big scandal" 165

Border!" and "This Playing With Fire Going Too Far—Three German Passenger Planes Shot At By Poles—In Corridor Many German Farmhouses in Flames!"

"You ask: But the German people can't possibly believe these lies?" Shirer wrote. "Then you talk to them. So many do."[29]

Still, the German people had no appetite for war, which Hitler understood, even as he moved inexorably toward that outcome. He pretended at diplomacy as "an alibi, especially for the German people, to show them that I have done everything to preserve peace," as the army was told to make preparations to attack Poland on September 1 at 4:30 a.m.[30]

At 11:15 a.m. on September 3, 1939, British Prime Minister Neville Chamberlain took to the airwaves. "This morning the British Ambassador in Berlin handed the German Government a final Note stating that, unless we heard from them by 11 o'clock that they were prepared at once to withdraw their troops from Poland, a state of war would exist between us," he said.

> I have to tell you now that no such undertaking has been received, and that consequently this country is at war with Germany.
>
> You can imagine what a bitter blow it is to me that all my long struggle to win peace has failed. Yet I cannot believe that there is anything more or anything different that I could have done and that would have been more successful.
>
> Up to the very last it would have been quite possible to have arranged a peaceful and honourable settlement between Germany and Poland, but Hitler would not have it. He had evidently made up his mind to attack Poland whatever happened, and although He now says he put forward reasonable proposals which were rejected by the Poles, that is not a true statement. The proposals were never shown to the Poles, nor to us, and, although they were announced in a German broadcast on Thursday night, Hitler did not wait to hear comments on them, but ordered his troops to cross the Polish frontier. His action shows convincingly that there is no chance of expecting that this man will ever give up his practice of using force to gain his will. He can only be stopped by force.
>
> We and France are today, in fulfilment [sic] of our obligations, going to the aid of Poland, who is so bravely resisting this wicked and unprovoked attack on her people. We have a clear conscience. We have done all that any country could do to establish peace. The situation in which no word given by Germany's ruler could be trusted and no people or country could feel themselves safe has become intolerable. And now that we have resolved to finish it, I know that you will all play your part with calmness and courage....
>
> Now may God bless you all. May He defend the right. It is the evil things that we shall be fighting against—brute force, bad faith, injustice, oppression and persecution—and against them I am certain that the right will prevail.[31]

* * *

Princess Stephanie undoubtedly listened to the address from her London hotel, but she was more concerned about how she would pay the rooming bill now that she no longer had any discernible income. Stephanie then hatched a plan that would set her up quite nicely if it succeeded; she would sue Lord Rothermere for breach of contract, claiming that he had guaranteed her a lifetime salary to act as his political emissary. She hoped that threatening to go public with Rothermere's Nazi dealings, especially now that Britain was at war with Germany, would force him into settling before embarrassing details were made public. She also made it clear that if she lost the case, she would publish her memoirs, which would include the Viscount's dealings with the Nazis. In addition to making money, Stephanie hoped to restore her reputation, which she believed had been tarnished back in 1933 when she had been accused of espionage and Rothermere had advised her to ignore the libelous story that had appeared in French newspapers. If her ex-husband, Prince Friedrich Franz von Hohenlohe-Waldenburg-Schillingsfürst, decided to strip her of her title on the grounds that her bad reputation were denigrating his family name, he could legally do so, which would destroy her social standing and any chance at future income. According to Stephanie's attorney, "The Royal Court of Budapest by its decree granting the divorce reserved for you the right to use his title and the name of your husband. This is an extraordinary privileged granted to the woman who has not been found guilty. Consequently there exists the obligation of the wife even after the dissolution of marriage—if she continues in using her former husband's name—to safeguard the reputation of the same. If she vilifies it—if she becomes unworthy to use the privilege that the law exceptionally granted to her on account of her not having been found guilty in the divorce—then the former husband is entitled to request the court to prohibit his former wife from the use of his name."[32]

And with Franz Salvator now gone, there might quite literally be no powerful men left on her side in Europe to help her should she once again be known as simply Stephanie Richter.

While she prepared her lawsuit and made plans to meet up with Fritz Wiedemann in the United States, Stephanie's file with British intelligence was growing by the day as they listened in on her telephone calls, and intercepted her letters and telegrams. Now that Great Britain was at war, there were questions as to whether she should be interned or at least questioned about her suspected Nazi collusion.

"We had no information that Hohenlohe has been intriguing in the interests of Germany in the past few weeks," one entry read, "but in the middle of August a friend in Austria begged her to use all of her efforts on Germany's behalf: 'I pray that you may—as hitherto—use your excellent contacts in Germany's interests. Only very few Germans know what they owe you for the maintenance of peace.'"[33]

Guy Liddell, the MI5 Director of counter-espionage, filed a detailed brief in October 1939, regarding Stephanie's desire to leave London.

> Princess Hohenlohe and her mother are both Hungarians [sic] and have now applied for a permit to proceed to the United States; firstly to visit Princess Hohenlohe's son, who is alleged to be seriously ill, and secondly to discuss certain legal matters.
>
> I am inclined to think that the real object of this visit may be: (1) to see Hans [sic] Wiedemann Hitler's envoy in San Francisco, whose mistress she was believed to have been for a considerable time; (2) fear of internment as one who, in the past, has had close connection with Nazi leaders. Alternatively, she may be intending to get some American crook lawyer to blackmail Rothermere from the other side of the Atlantic. She could very well threaten him with all sorts of publicity in the United States. It is, of course, also possible … that she has been offered a considerable sum to leave the country, so that when the case comes up, a settlement may be announced.
>
> Our view is that for the time being at any rate, she should not be given a permit to travel. We might later consider whether she should be given a no return permit.[34]

Rothermere's counsel deemed Stephanie's lawsuit a blatant attempt at blackmail and argued that it was in both the Viscount's and the nation's best interests for a trial not to go forward. One of Rothermere's attorneys, a Mr. Butler of the firm Charles Russell and Co. solicitors, approached British intelligence with the theory that she was a Nazi spy who should be expelled from the country. The MI5 files reflected his concerns:

> in Lord Rothermere's view the woman was a German agent and had probably been double-crossing him before he terminated his contract with her. He thinks it very undesirable that she should be permitted either to enter or remain in the country. Mr. Butler would like, if possible, to be informed if the Princess was at the present time in the United Kingdom and, if not, whether steps could be taken to refuse her admission.

The entry goes on to say that "M.I.5. are not pressing for her immediate internment" but that "her case will fall to be dealt with by the appropriate tribunal in due course."[35]

After much consideration, the British Home Office decided that it would be improper to intervene in the court case, and Lord Rothermere refused to settle on principle. Hohenlohe vs. Rothermere was set for trial in the High Court on November 8, 1939.

Interestingly, on September 4, the day after Britain declared war on Germany, Rothermere published a decidedly anti–Nazi editorial in the

Daily Mail that was in sharp opposition to the fawning letters to Hitler he had written for years: "We now fight against the blackest tyranny that has ever held man in bondage."

> This war was inevitable whether it began with Austria, Sudetenland, Bohemia, or Danzig. If it had not come over Danzig it would have come later upon some other issue.
> It became inevitable from the day Hitler seized power in Germany and began his criminal career by enslaving his own people. For his one aim since then has been gradually to enslave all others by the methods of brute force.[36]

Gone was the talk of "Adolf the Great," as Rothermere had referred to the Führer following the "bloodless solution of the Czechoslovakian problem."[37]

* * *

Newspapers in Great Britain and beyond ran with the story "A Princess Sues Lord Rothermere," in which all of the political machinations of the past several years would be publicly uncovered.

Stephanie managed to raise enough money to hire Theodore Goddard & Partners, who had represented Wallis Simpson in her second divorce to pave the way for her marriage to the former King Edward VIII.

On the first day of trial before Mr. Justice Tucker of the King's Bench Division, the Princess alleged that she had been engaged to act as a special foreign political representative in Europe for Lord Rothermere and *The Daily Mail*. She sued him for breach of contract and to vindicate her reputation due to libels that appeared in the French, German and Viennese Press, calling her "a spy, a vamp and an immoral person," from which Lord Rothermere did not protect her.[38]

Stephanie's barrister, Mr. Beyfus, began by explaining to the court how Stephanie had urged Rothermere to take up the cause of Hungary. He referred to the *Daily Mail* article, "Hungary's Place in the Sun," and how Rothermere became known as "The Little Father of Hungary" for his support of the flailing nation. The court heard that the Princess rejected the idea that Rothermere's son, Esmond, should be suggested as King of Hungary, and that she wanted to publish an account of the campaign to help the country in the *Daily Mail*. Beyfus told the court that Rothermere paid the Princess £5,000 not to do so, instead, proposing that she become his personal foreign political representative—not the representative of the newspaper.

"I can only think," said Mr. Beyfus, "that the adulation of the Hungarian public had gone to the head of Lord Rothermere. He told the Princess that he had decided to work for the restoration of the Hohenzollern and Hapsburg dynasties. He wanted to be a modern Warwick, the king-maker and to work on the European rather than the English field."

Beyfus reported that Rothermere offered the Princess £5,000 a year and expenses as a collaborator.

Rothermere's barrister, Sir William Jowitt, interrupted to say that the Viscount's counsel regarded the contract to be a social arrangement rather than a business one, that expired at the end of a definite period.

Beyfus continued: the Princess accepted the position and thereafter acted as his ambassadress to the ex-German Kaiser, the ex-Crown Prince, Hitler and the Regent and Prime Minister of Hungary, "almost as though he were a sovereign power himself, dealing with them on equal terms." Beyfus said that Rothermere had a "royal reception" in Germany and promised the Crown Prince that he would do everything in his power to restore the Hohenzollerns to the German throne.

Regarding the libels, Beyfus said Lord Rothermere forbade the Princess to take action against newspaper claims that she was arrested in France for espionage at a time when she was actually in America, and that Rothermere promised he would clear her name, which he did not.

Next, Beyfus spoke of the 1934 invitation the Princess obtained for Lord Rothermere to visit Hitler, stating that Rothermere received a royal reception and told Stephanie that Hitler should make her a duchess. Later, Rothermere suggested that the Princess should stay at less expensive hotels, the mixed messages, apparently, a sign of extreme cruelty on the part of the Viscount. Beyfus told the court that Stephanie said, "It is just torture to be with you. One day you give one the powers of a queen and another day you put one in the gutter."

Beyfus said this prompted an argument that ended with Rothermere promising to pay the Princess £5,000 a year for the rest of her life, adding, "I have never yet let a woman down." As if to prove that Rothermere meant to adhere to this verbal contract, Beyfus said, that over a period of five-and-a-half years, Rothermere paid the princess more than £51,000 (nearly $2.5 million in today's U.S. dollars).

Princess Stephanie next took the witness box, explaining how she had been the brains behind the Hungarian campaign and that when she first met Lord Rothermere he did not know that Bucharest and Budapest were two different cities. Journalists covering the trial reported laughter at this observation. The first day of court then adjourned.[39]

Even in the midst of military operations, Joseph Goebbels still made sure to watch the trial closely from Berlin to see what, if anything, damaging to the Reich might surface.

"In London a legal wrangle is in progress, Rothermere against the Princess Hohenlohe concerning an allowance that this 'lady' is demanding from his lordship," the propaganda minister wrote. "All kinds of painful revelations, including some to do with Wiedemann. Nevertheless, I don't believe that the Hohenlohe woman has been spying. It is true that she has intervened in our favor on many occasions."[40]

When he took the stand, Rothermere said that his campaign to improve Anglo-German relations occurred "before Hitler ran amok," and that he had been working to maintain peace in Europe. He retorted that he was "not a sovereign state yet," when asked if he had hired the Princess to act as his ambassador, and scoffed at the notion that he had agreed to support the Princess for life, saying, "There was no opportunity of 'giving' her money because she was always asking for it.... She was always pestering and badgering me, so I sent her away to Budapest and Berlin."[41]

Rothermere's barrister read in open court the "blackmail letter" that the team of Hohenlohe and Wiedemann had written threatening to go to Hitler if Rothermere didn't fall in line. When Sir William Jowitt asked the Princess if she had used the letter to pressure Lord Rothermere to continue paying her, she replied, "I have not."[42]

Jowitt then addressed the court, saying it would have been a simple matter for Lord Rothermere "to pay all, and more than all, this lady desires. He has deliberately not taken this course because the view which he seeks to present to the court is that the claim this lady is making is not an honest claim." Jowitt went on to say how very shocking it was that the Princess would have his client's letters photocopied by the Special Photographic Bureau of the Department of the German Chancellor. He closed with, "Who can say whether if Lord Rothermere had succeeded in the endeavours which he made [toward Anglo-German relations], we might not be in the position in which we are today."[43]

After six days of testimony, Mr. Justice Tucker ruled against Stephanie. The judge said her claim that Lord Rothermere promised a lifelong salary was without justification. Further, he found that Rothermere never contractually agreed to clear her name from damaging press reports.

In the end, the sensationalistic trial shredded both Stephanie's and Rothermere's reputations. The letters read in open court portrayed the Viscount as a near-traitorous Hitler sycophant, while the Princess could only be described as a wily and manipulative double-agent in her quest to extract as much money and favors as possible out of both Lord Rothermere and Adolf Hitler.

19

"Worse than ten thousand men"

—FBI report on Stephanie von Hohenlohe

In the days following the trial, as Princess Stephanie made her way into London's Ritz Hotel, a place where she had always been welcome as European royalty, four society ladies were holding court—the Duchess of Westminster, Lady Dufferin, Lady Stanley, and Mrs. Richard Norton. They were none too pleased to see this unwelcome "Mata Hari" in their midst who had helped to plunge their country into war with her Nazi intrigues. The women began grumbling over their lunch when one finally vociferated in Stephanie's direction: "Get out you filthy spy!"[1]

Stephanie knew her time in London was up, but where would she go with her limited funds? She decided to return to the well one last time, writing Lord Rothermere a theatrical letter meant to guilt him into helping her financially.

"I don't know if you planned to ruin me, but in any case you have succeeded," she wrote, glossing over the fact that it was she who brought the lawsuit against him.

> This letter to you is the culmination of your victory over me. I will try to be as unmelodramatic as possible, which is not easy, since you have turned my life into a horror-play. One kind word to me from you could have prevented everything. You never had a better or more devoted friend than me. I would have gone through fire for you, and my devotion to you was like that of a faithful dog. You knew that, you knew it very well. And you knew it when you came to court. It was the cowards around you, the ones who hate me, who confused your sense of justice and turned you against me, which, as you know, I do not deserve.
>
> Your barristers and solicitors, seventeen of them all told, and all your other friends, filled half the court when the case was being heard, while I was only accompanied by my 78-year-old mother, since my son has abandoned me, because he could no longer tolerate the passive resistance which arises from the allegation

that I am a spy, and from my reputation as a spy. You had millions, I only had £250—that was all I had left after my lawyers had milked me dry, and I had been forced to exist for two whole years without the income on which I had built my life. The fact that I am still in the land of the living today, is only due to my wanting to spare my boy from being the victim of a further sensation—his mother's suicide. But my indescribable misery will perhaps make me forget even this consideration.

Stephanie then told Rothermere about the financial offers she had received to write her memoirs, especially salacious details about the political intrigues she had carried out for him with the Führer. She passive aggressively said she hoped she would never have to lower herself enough to sell her story, but threatened that she would if she had to. Stephanie then asked Rothermere to guarantee her financial stability for the next three years for the sake of her son. She did her best to stab at Rothermere's conscience as she closed her letter: "You hold the lives of two human beings in your hands, that of a young man full of hope for the future, and mine, which you have robbed of any future—It is for you alone to decide what shall become of these two lives!"[2]

Rothermere answered Stephanie through an intermediary, Lady Ethel Snowden, agreeing to pay Stephanie's passage if she agreed to leave England for good. Stephanie answered that she would gladly leave the country, but she refused to return to Europe where war was raging and the Nazis were still looking to have her arrested. This fact was still fresh in her mind, as she recorded in her notes, "Gratitude of the Nazis: [I] was to have been arrested in Berlin a year ago."[3]

No, she and her mother would head to America, where Stephanie hoped to rekindle her relationship with Fritz Wiedemann in San Francisco. Wiedemann had been sending her forlorn love letters, complaining that he hadn't heard from anyone in Europe in a very long time, possibly because something was wrong with the mail system. "I have had no word from either my mother or my son for weeks, nor any message of any real significance. You don't write either. That's not very nice. One tries to piece together a picture of how things really sit. But perhaps it's better not to know. We still had that lovely time in Leopoldskron a year ago. They were really the last peaceful days one was able to enjoy. Here, nothing remains but waiting, waiting to see what happens and whether there is any sort of opportunity in which I can be of any use. The longer it lasts, the more unlikely it becomes."

At the end of the typewritten letter, he added in his own handwriting, "I also wanted to tell that I miss you very much! Lots of love, ever yours, Fritz."[4]

19. "Worse than ten thousand men" 173

Stephanie heading to America was not what Rothermere had in mind; he did not want her anywhere near the U.S. press where she might publish incendiary articles or even a book where she could do even more damage to the Rothermere name. If the Princess insisted on going to America, Rothermere would pay her legal bills, but he would not pay her travel passage.

Stephanie must have appealed to Wiedemann next, because she somehow found the money to pay for the 11-day trip across the Atlantic. She just had to wait for her exit permit to come through from the British authorities. The British government, however, was secretly mulling over whether she should be tried for treason for her Nazi collusion. If the Princess were allowed to come and go as she pleased inside the UK, she could further weaken the war effort. Her MI5 file reflected the concern: "It is of course quite possible that she will also work as some sort of propaganda agent for the Nazis. She is in any case a political intriguer and adventuress of the first water and should be treated with the utmost suspicion."

On their exit permit applications, both Stephanie and her mother listed the Viscountess Snowden of Dolphin Square and the Hungarian Legation as their two references. They also said their New York destination was the Waldorf Astoria Hotel. Further, both Stephanie and her mother were thoroughly searched before being allowed to board the Holland-America Liner. Stephanie gave the year of her birth as 1897, six years later than the actual date of 1891. Her mother could not escape truth, however, when the recording agent typed "corpulent" under "visible distinguishing marks."

Finally, it was decided that on November 23, 1939, Princess Stephanie and her 75-year-old mother would be granted their exit permits to proceed to America. However, Stephanie's permit contained the words "No Return." She had escaped internment and a trial for treason, but, as the MI5 files made clear: "She should not be allowed to land in the United Kingdom again."[5]

Stephanie did not let her financial difficulties stop her from making an elegant arrival in New York harbor several days before Christmas. A reporter with the *New York World-Telegram* described her ensemble: "Her auburn hair was combed straight back. She wore a silver-fox turban with a provocative pink rose perched on it, a three-quarter length silver-fox coat, a black dress of silk jersey (an Alix model), and black kid Perugia sandals with sky-blue platform soles. Gorgeous diamond ear-clips were fastened on her small, pretty ears, and a scintillating diamond clip lightened her dark dress."[6]

The tabloid press wasn't the only faction awaiting Princess Stephanie's arrival. MI5 had tipped off the FBI to the woman they suspected was far from finished with her Nazi past. A memorandum made its way through the bureau on Stephanie, saying, "She is known to have very close connections with high officials of the Third Reich, is described as being extremely intelligent, dangerous and clever, as an espionage agent to be 'worse than ten thousand men,' to reputedly be immoral, and capable of resorting to any means, even to bribery, to gain her ends."

One fact, the FBI got wrong, however.

"She became the lady friend of Archduke Leopold Salvator," the report said, "through whom she gained access to military circles during the World War and many of her 'connections' date from those days."[7] But Stephanie wouldn't have been satisfied with a second-rate Habsburg; she had targeted Archduke Franz Salvator, the husband of the Archduchess Marie Valerie, all those years ago. She had given birth to an illegitimate royal child, and even felt, for a brief moment, what it was like to live as an Archduchess herself in Schloss Leopoldskron, before it was ripped away. Becoming pregnant by the husband of the Emperor's daughter allowed Stephanie to become a Hohenlohe princess, which opened up the world of European society and diplomacy to her whims. Princess Stephanie von Hohenlohe had betrayed a litany of people—not the least of whom shared her Jewish blood—by the time she disembarked in America in 1939; but she most certainly felt as though she had been the one who had been forsaken.

Epilogue: "We recall the 'Princess' Hohenlohe"

—Josef Goebbels

Following the embarrassment and financial burden of the trial, Lord Rothermere began to have health problems, undoubtedly brought on by the crushing stigma left behind once his cozy relationship with Hitler had been revealed. The Viscount travelled to Bermuda to escape the London gossip, as well as to seek out warmer climes, but his health continued to deteriorate, and he was finally admitted to the King Edward VII Memorial Hospital. Rothermere never did fully recover, and one year after the trial, he was dead at the age of 72.

* * *

At about the same time, the British Secret Service pondered a telegram received from its representative in New York. The young man who had once looked to Fritz Wiedemann for help with joining the German Diplomatic Service was now requesting to work with the Allies.

"Princess Stephanie Hohenlohe's Son, Francis Josef, aged 23, who was at Oxford, wishes to return to England to do war work, such as driving an ambulance," it read.

> As you doubtless know, he is the apple of her eye and probably the only person for whom she has any real affection.
>
> Stephanie Hohenlohe is in a position to be useful and might certainly be so if her son was in the U.K. and under our control.
>
> Have you any objection?
>
> One cannot, however, neglect the possibility that this may be a move by the Gestapo to kill two birds with one stone, i.e., (1) to attempt to double-cross us through Princess Hohenlohe, and (2) to place an agent in the U.K....

The answer from MI5 was that they had nothing against Franzi himself, and had no objection to his presence in the U.K. They said they had no reason to fear his possible activities in Britain but would accept him in "with our eyes open."[1]

Franzi would not get a chance to make it back to the U.K., however, before U.S. authorities caught up with him and his mother. He was working as an artists' model in New York while Stephanie and her mother were out west living with Fritz Wiedemann and his family. Stephanie had been allowed to enter the United States as a private citizen, with no strings attached, despite all the information MI5 had forwarded to the FBI. The U.S. Immigration and Naturalization Service had opened case file 56,001-45 on Stephanie, which read: "NON-SECTARIAN ANTI-NAZI LEAGUE re whether Princess STEPHANIE HOHENLOHE will be allowed to enter as private citizen or required to register as propagandist for foreign Govt. as required by recent Act of Cong."[2] But any official talk of having Stephanie register as a propagandist went no further than that. Stephanie was able to move out to California without being detained, and the old team of Hohenlohe and Wiedemann got back to work, continuing their love affair under his wife's nose, as recorded by the FBI.

In a memorandum to President Franklin Delano Roosevelt, J. Edgar Hoover wrote, "On May 29, 1940, Princess Hohenlohe met Fritz Wiedemann at Fresno, California, and they spent that night together in a cabin in Sequoia National Park as 'Mr. and Mrs. Fred Winter,' of San Francisco, California." In another entry, Hoover was more straightforward about the tawdriness of the affair. "On September 3, 1940, Princess Hohenlohe, as Mrs. H. Warden, of Philadelphia, Pennsylvania, registered at the Palace Hotel, San Francisco. She checked out of the hotel on the same date an an immediate inspection of the room which she had occupied reflected that intimate relations had existed during the time that the room was occupied by "Mrs. Warden."

Hoover intimated that the couple had to be engaging in espionage activities for the Nazis, as "Princess Hohenlohe mentioned to Wiedemann that she has received two letters from 'Number 34 and Number 35' and requested instructions as to what Wiedemann wished to be done in the matter." The couple also hatched an incredible plan to attempt to broker peace between Germany and Britain, and set up meetings with diplomats on both sides to try to bring about an understanding.

"It is interesting to note," Hoover wrote, "that both conferences were dominated by Princess Hohenlohe and that in fact she proposed that she could approach Hitler as one possible solution toward effecting the proposed peace treaty."[3] How she planned to accomplish this, considering Hitler still had a warrant out for her arrest, Stephanie never did disclose.

Stephanie and Wiedemann did succeed at drumming up U.S. sympathy for the Nazi cause. Wiedemann had set up a foreign arm of the Nazi Party known as the *Auslands-Organisation,* or AO, in the United States for all pro–German supporters. According to MI5, AO was a "ready-made instrument for intelligence, espionage and ultimately for sabotage purposes," and the leading agents in the United States were Wiedemann and Princess Stephanie.[4] The AO's goal was to keep the United States out of the war in Europe and to do what it could to align German-American businesses with Deutschland. Wiedemann then created the German-American Business League whose members agreed to make purchases only from Germany, to boycott Jewish firms, and to solely employ Aryans. The League grew to include the owners of 1,000 companies across the United States, and Wiedemann addressed one gathering with the following speech: "You are citizens of the United States, which has allied itself with an enemy of the German nation. The time will come when you may have to decide which side to take. I would caution that I cannot advise you what to do, but you should be governed by your conscience. One duty lies with the Mother country, the other with the adopted country. Blood is thicker than ink.... Germany is the land of your fathers and regardless of the consequences, you should not disregard the traditional heritage which is yours."[5]

Photo of Princess Stephanie von Hohenlohe taken in 1940. She continued to help her lover Fritz Wiedemann's Nazi efforts once she landed in the United States. She would end up in custody once the U.S. Government caught on to the full extent of her espionage activities (author's collection).

In the midst of this Nazi propaganda work, Stephanie learned that her American visa was running out, and that she was up for deportation. Franzi gave a newspaper interview in her defense, in which he claimed she was not Jewish and never worked with the Nazis. Stephanie had hoped that Wiedemann would work to defend her honor and help her stay in the United States, but he simply told her to take the next boat to Lisbon. Stephanie was furious, but before she walked out on him for good in

December 1940, she reverted to old habits by demanding money. Wiedemann not only refused to pay; he presented her with a detailed bill for $3,003, that was enclosed in a farewell letter. "I cannot simply draw a line under the years, which thanks to you have been among the most wonderful and richest of my life. I know you will think it hypocritical if I say that whenever you call on me, I will be there for you as much as my resources permit.... You asked me for a sum of money, which I do not have. I can't just embezzle it.... I regret having given you a year ago my money set aside for emergencies.... Your shares and jewellery [sic] are worth several times what I have."[6]

Without Wiedemann's help, Stephanie next went all the way to the top, writing to President Roosevelt himself, imploring him to allow her to stay in the United States. When FDR read J. Edgar Hoover's report on Stephanie's activities within the United States, however, he was livid.

"That Hohenlohe woman ought to be got out of the country as a matter of good discipline," the President wrote to his Attorney General. "Have her put on a boat to Japan or Vladivostok."[7]

When Stephanie's attorney told her there was no way to stop her deportation, she threatened suicide and had to be transported to her deportation hearing in an ambulance and carried in on a stretcher. But since no country would agree to have her, Stephanie would have to be held in an Immigration and Naturalization Service detention center in San Francisco.

Now in her 50s, Stephanie managed to seduce the married Commissioner of the Immigration and Naturalization Service, Major Lemuel B. Schofield, who agreed to set her free in exchange for her help with anti–Hitler propaganda. The FBI followed the new couple to their love nest at the Raleigh Hotel in Washington, D.C., where, according to Hoover's report, they "indulged in a great deal of drinking on these occasions."[8]

The day after the Japanese attack on Pearl Harbor, when the United States formally entered the war, Stephanie was arrested once again and interned in the Gloucester City internment camp in New Jersey. She described the dreadful conditions.

> The living conditions there were appallingly unhygienic and inadequate in every way. Twenty women occupied a single room, which was filthy and also served as a dump for old furniture, dirty, worn-out mattresses, and mountains of dusty old papers. For weeks we had no bed-linen or hand-towels; instead we were given old rags. The floor was made of stone, icy cold and damp.
>
> The wind blew from all sides through the ten big windows, and most of the time the heating did not work. The doctor advised us: "Keep your feet off the floor if you don't want to catch pneumonia. This is no place for women."

We spent our time sitting on our beds, fully clothed, with our overcoats on. There was no furniture in the room except for our beds, a table and a bench. During the night the warders made the rounds twice and shone torches in our faces, to count us. Sleep was impossible under those conditions.

We had six drains in the room which, because of the faulty sewage system, flooded the room whenever it was high tide on the Delaware river. Sometimes the stench was unbearable.

I had to share the room with prostitutes and sluts with venereal disease....

For months on end our food consisted of nothing but beans, fatty meat and meat-balls. We didn't eat the fatty meat, and just the smell of the meat-balls made us ill.

For the first two months we weren't allowed to leave the room. After that we were able to spend about half an hour each day, except Saturdays and Sundays, on a dirty, covered balcony.[9]

Five months later, Stephanie was transferred to a German cell block of the Alien Detention Camp in Seagoville, Texas. Despite spilling as much information as she had on Hitler and his cronies to the Office of Strategic Services, J. Edgar Hoover made sure she was the very last German-speaking prisoner to be released at the end of the war on May 9, 1945, after four years of internment.

* * *

Franzi was arrested on February 16, 1942, and was held at Ellis Island for five months until he had a hearing in New York. He was then transferred to Camp McAlester, Oklahoma, then on to Camp Kennedy, Texas.

"Despite all their efforts, the FBI haven't been able to come up with anything against me," he wrote in a letter to his imprisoned mother.[10]

He was finally released on parole at the end of February 1944. According to U.S. enlistment records, Franzi was drafted into the U.S. Army on September 7, 1944, as a Private, although he was "not yet a citizen." His enlistment was "for the duration of the War or other emergency, plus six months, subject to the discretion of the President or otherwise according to law."[11] Wisely, the U.S. Government kept Franzi out of Europe; he was sent to the Pacific theater, where he fought until the end of the war.

On June 20, 1945, Princess Stephanie von Hohenlohe-Waldenburg-Schillingsfürst was added to Great Britain's Post War Black List. Such a stigma could not stop the indomitable Princess. She used her remarkable list of international contacts to become a magazine reporter, and was soon jet-setting again, interviewing the likes of Princess Grace of Monaco, the wife of the Shah of Iran, and Lady Bird Johnson. She also began writing her memoirs, which were never published, and she buried the hatchet with Fritz Wiedemann, helping him write his memoir, *The Man*

Who Wanted to Command. The book makes no mention of their love affair.

While in Geneva, Switzerland, in 1972, Stephanie complained of a stabbing pain in her abdomen and was diagnosed with a dangerous stomach ulcer; she did not survive surgery. Franzi had her buried in the mountain village cemetery of Meinier, Switzerland. The plaque at her grave includes the title that had been so important to her: S.A.S. ("Her Most Serene Highness") Princess Stephanie Hohenlohe. Her birth and death dates are 1905–1972, which would have made her 66 years old. In reality, she had been born in 1891, which made her true age 80.

* * *

On December 22, 1940, from an air-raid shelter in Berlin with warning sirens blaring through the thick concrete walls, Joseph Goebbels and Adolf Hitler sat discussing their plans of oppression and cruelty, as well as their own bloated grandeur. First they spoke of anti-Nazi theologian Friedrich Niemöller, whom they had imprisoned in Sachsenhausen concentration camp.

"Niemöller is asking for leniency," Goebbels wrote. "No question of it. Let him eat well, get fat, so that no one can mistake him for a martyr. But he won't be let loose on the human race again. He should have thought of that earlier."

Next, they spoke of their own prowess. "We discuss Prussia's mission in the creation of the Reich, which the Führer values very highly. But only a South German and a Catholic could have completed the great work of German racial unity."

And finally, from the relative safety of their bunker, the two chuckled about the once esteemed princess. "We recall the 'Princess' Hohenlohe, who has now been deported from the USA, quite penniless. Wiedemann became quite sexually infatuated with her."[12]

Of course, their information was faulty—Stephanie was never actually deported from the United States.

Four-and-a-half years later in the Führerbunker, the two would no longer be so smug. Talk had turned desperately to suicide and cremation, since Hitler was adamant that he "did not want to be put on display in some waxworks in Moscow."[13] On April 29, 1945, in a dank, underground room, Hitler had finally made Eva Braun his wife after the couple signed a document declaring that they were "of pure Aryan descent" and that there were "no hereditary impediments to their marriage."[14] Goebbels had signed as a witness.

As the Soviets descended on Berlin on the afternoon of April 30, Hitler bade his farewells to his staff, brushing off Magda Goebbels' last desperate suggestion that he leave Berlin and give them all a chance to escape death. Hitler then disappeared into his study with his new wife. Several minutes later, both Hitler and Eva Braun were dead at their own hands, slumped alongside one another on a small sofa; she had bitten into a cyanide capsule, while he had shot himself in the right temple.

Magda Goebbels now had to arrange for the murder of her six children aged between four and 12: Helga, Hilde, Helmut, Holde, Hedda, and Heide. She instructed the SS doctor to give each child a shot of morphine, then she crushed a cyanide capsule inside each of their mouths.

Magda and Joseph Goebbels then climbed up to the Chancellery garden, said their goodbyes, and bit into their own cyanide capsules. An SS guard fired into their slumped bodies to make sure they were gone. All of the sacrificial bodies were then burned to the best of the survivors' abilities with what little petrol they had left.

* * *

The Nazis murdered six million European Jews in the Holocaust. The Nuremberg Trials would hold some of them accountable for the horror. Twenty four of the highest-ranking leaders of the Third Reich were ushered before the International Military Tribunal in the Palace of Justice between November 20, 1945, and October 1, 1946.

Fritz Wiedemann was never tried for any of his Nazi activities or his association with Hitler. In fact, he testified against the Nazis in a 240-page report for the Office of Strategic Services on September 19, 1945, to be used in the Nuremberg Trials. He mentioned Princess Stephanie in the transcripts as being an important source of information for him when he was Counsel General in San Francisco. When his interrogators asked if in the early 1940s he thought the United States would go to war, he answered, "I was convinced that the United States would go to war. I tell you frankly I got during my stay in San Francisco many informations [sic] through my well known friend Princess Stephanie Hohenlohe."

The stenographer stopped him and asked how to spell the last name. Then the colonel interrogating Wiedemann asked more about the princess.

"She was living a long time in London and go-between [sic] from Rothermere to Hitler," Wiedemann said. "And I told Ribbentrop I was convinced that the United States would go to war."[15]

The U.S. Interrogators asked Wiedemann about Nazi spying activities, including microfilm, marking suitcases with "micro dots," and a complicated system of secret codes.

Of those found guilty at Nuremberg, 12 were sentenced to death; three were sentenced to life in prison; two were sentenced to 20 years; one was sentenced to 15 years; one was sentenced to ten years; three were acquitted; one was found medically unfit for trial; and one committed suicide before trial.

Although Hermann Göring was one of those sentenced to death, he escaped the hangman's noose by swallowing cyanide just hours before his scheduled execution. His body was cremated at Dachau and his ashes reportedly dumped in a garbage can.

Wiedemann was let go and quietly returned to his farm and family in Bavaria.

* * *

Out of the fire pit of two world wars, Austria has reclaimed her independence and the creative spirit that made her home to some of the greatest musicians, artists, and intellectuals of the past 300 years. Wiser now in hindsight to the history that brought them to this point, Austrians continue to honor their aristocratic past. In the mountainous region of the Salzkammergut, where the noble edelweiss are now considered endangered of becoming extinct due to climate change, the nearly 700-year-old Bad Ischl parish church of St. Nicholas endures. Each year, thousands of people line the same route where Archduchess Marie Valerie once rode in her wedding carriage to the church for her marriage to Franz Salvator. The onlookers are still happily under the auspices of the former Habsburg monarchy, if only for honorary ceremonies. Marie Valerie's descendants, who are now the proprietors of the Kaiservilla, lead the crowds up the road to St. Nicholas for Imperial Mass in honor of Emperor Franz Joseph's birthday each August 18th.

The remaining Habsburgs feel a weighty responsibility to preserve the Kaiservilla just as Emperor Franz Joseph left it for the last time in 1914. And, as long as there are Habsburg heirs to carry on these traditions, there will most certainly be those willing to learn from both the glories and the travesties of this slice of world history.

Appendix I: Marie Valerie's Diary, 1881-1890

Although Marie Valerie's diary has been published in German by Piper (Munich, 1998), it has not yet been published in English. Following are passages pertinent to this book that were translated into English specifically for this author's research.

1881

(Thirteen-year-old Marie Valerie meets her mother's cousin, King Ludwig II of Bavaria, for the first time. She refers to her brother Rudolf by his nickname, "Nazi," which had no political meaning at the time.)

18 June. Oh! The King is supposed to come to Possenhofen today to visit Mama. He had an enormous magnificent bouquet sent to her with the query, when might he visit her? But it must be in the evening and no one is allowed to look at him! ... but we will see him somehow anyway.

19 June. No, is it possible ... that ... o no! The King ... yesterday on 18 June 1881, yesterday I tell you, spoke to me ... only me out of all of the children! no ... no ... but actually, yes. So: yesterday the King was supposed to visit Mama in Possenhofen at 7 o'clock, and we (Amélie, Paula, Elisabeth, Countess Kornis, Siegfried, a Miss Tebr. and I) were watching from Count Angele's room. But there was honeysuckle growing up to the window and I said I would throw a sprig down to the King; everyone said, no, then Mama came and I called out to her and asked if I could. Mama said she would fetch jasmine (because there is a long story connected with jasmine and the King), but oh! while Mama was getting the jasmine, the King came into the schloss himself to look for her. There was a kerfuffle. We ran to Siegfried's balcony and Mama was already down below with the King and oh! she said that I, me alone, could come down so that she could introduce me, o, me, and only me to him. O! I can still hardly believe it! But I came trembling and Mama handed me the jasmine before the door and now this incredible thing should actually take place. And I didn't even have time to put on my gloves and my dress (it was still the brown linen one) was dirty and creased. But I came out anyway ... and gave him the jasmine with a very, very low curtsey! O! Great King, now you actually have the jasmine I gave you!!! He wanted to kiss my hand o! He asked me if Nazi was in Prague and I said: "Y...es!" He asked me if Gisela was here and I said: "No, she is in Munich." He asked me whom I was up there with, whether they were my cousins and I said "Y...es."

He speaks very fast and unclearly and felt as embarrassed as I did. Mama invited us to use informal pronouns with each and he said: "But if so, then both of us, right?" And then I gave another courtesy and left. Of course, I was inundated with questions back upstairs, what it was like, what he said etc. ...

1882

(Marie Valerie refers to herself here as a "backfisch," German for "fried fish.")

1 January. To the opera "Oberon." At the entrance to the opera house there was a policeman who opened the carriage gate. We went up the private staircase, which is very wide and beautiful, into a small blue (light blue) salon, where we set down our things, then over a couple of steps into our loge which is much bigger than our loge at the Burgtheater.

INVITATION TO AN ADOLESCENT'S BALL GIVEN BY HER IMPERIAL AND ROYAL HIGHNESS, THE SERENE ARCHDUCHESS MARIE VALERIE ON WEDNESDAY, 15TH OF JANUARY, 1882, FROM 5:30 P.M. UNTIL 10 P.M. ENTRANCE SOLELY VIA THE BELLARIA, THE EVENT IN THE ALEXANDER ROOMS.

After eating, I practiced reception curtsies for the ball until 3:30 p.m. How my poor backfisch heart pounded!... I—I Valérie, the ungainly backfisch, who has seen so few people in her life, am supposed to appear at a ball! I am supposed to dance with 16 men! To conduct myself properly and yet not forcedly. I am supposed to say something to all these strange girls!!!? Oh! and what if they're embarrassed too!? No, no, how frightful! How I can look forward to that. I was cold with fear ... and after a short discussion about the jewelry I was supposed to take, Feifalik came to comb my hair.... I went down admired by the entire household. I shook. Mama was already ready in her white dress, the one covered in black lace, and with corals round her neck and in her hair, and Papa at her side. They both thought I was beautiful and I did too, as I stood in front of the mirror for ages. And now we went into the great hall (not into the ballroom yet); where Aunt Mathilde and Uncle Karl (Ludwig) were standing with Margarete, Otto and Ferdinand…. Finally a man came who announced that everyone was there. My heart beat like a drum! I had to go in front with Gretel. Terrible thought, that each step was bringing us closer!!! Oh, now, now, now the door is opening—one—two—three—it has happened, we're there. O so many people But propriety! O, what a deep curtsey we did! What a sea of people! All the girls were dressed the same. No, not quite. And so now Zulimuli introduces them (the girls), the leader of the dance Heinrich Hoyos introduces the boys…. He was so confused that he had forgotten everyone's names and had to whisper "What's your name?" the whole time…. Heinrich Hoyos grabbed me and we were in full swing. My throat dried up because I was so scared … after surviving the first two rounds, I started having priceless conversations. I went around all the girls with Gretel and asked them about every imaginable rehearsed topic such as "Are you fond of dancing? Do you draw? Do you play piano? Are you also enjoying your time in Ischl?" and so on. It wasn't as hard as I was expecting, it was actually fun…. The supper was at 7:30, which was very fun, because all the boys made fun of poor Heinrich Hoyos and he endeavoured to defend himself. I believe he found the champagne and beer quite to his taste as he became very lively after the supper. Uncle Ludwig came to the cotillion, Count Goess, Countess Festetics, Landgravine Fürstenberg, Ida Ferenczy, Nopcsa, Count Stolberg, the bishop, Wiederhofer all watched…

13 May, Laxenburg. Then we saw the marital bed of Emperor Rudolf II—I don't know what a marital bed is—I don't believe the stuff Zulimuli told me—I guess backfisch aren't allowed to know.—It's frightfully short and only open from the sides and there are windows underneath at the end. I would die if I had to sleep there but I don't feel sorry for Emperor Rudolf II for having to sleep there because I hate him because he just locked himself away in his Hradschin with his astrologers and didn't care about poor Austria. I always worry that Rudolf will be like that. That would be too sad.

(The day of Marie Valerie's confirmation in the Catholic Church. The "he" she speaks of is the Archbishop of Vienna.)

4 June. When he finally started giving this wonderful speech, I cried because it made such a big impression on me when he said: "so that you will be worthy of your forebears." Oh! and I am so proud to be a Habsburg, there was really no other house like this one, so devout, upright, kind and complete …

(Crown Prince Rudolf turns 24.)

21 August, Ischl. Rudolf's birthday. At 11 o'clock there was a Holy Mass in which I prayed that he would one day become as good an Emperor as Papa. The good Lord can do anything—I do hope so—but it's also so nice to think that Papa is the best Emperor. I want to strive to be worthy of being his daughter…

15 September. O! I am going to pray for Mama and Papa so much now! I have such terrible fear. Mama has gone off this evening to Trieste, there is going to be a folk festival and an EXHIBITION! there and Papa insisted on going. (He has been traveling around these countries for a while now.) It is frightfully dangerous. The Italians want to have Trieste for themselves and hate Austria. They already threw a bomb at an Austria general when Uncle Karl was there and people are now afraid that…. O! No! I can't think bear to think about it, the good Lord must protect Papa…. He can't punish Papa for being too good to think ill of these terrible people. And Mama! … Mama, even though Papa doesn't want her to, is going there anyway and intends to protect him herself! O may the good Lord protect them both!

(Here, Marie Valerie writes of Count Eduard Taaffe, who was Minister-President of the Austrian portion of the Empire, called Cisleithania.)

20 September, Gödöllő. Mama and Papa (o how will I ever have enough gratitude for this) came back today, healthy and happy that it's over. Not until Mama, Uncle, Aunt and I were alone did we hear about the danger. O how I cried as I sat there on Mama's lap as she told us about it. Mama was so angry with Count Taaffe and the governor of Trieste if something had happened it would have been all their fault for calling Papa there. She also told them that she couldn't understand how they could take on such a responsibility. Yes! Such a responsibility! Because 2 Italians were found with bombs "as a greeting to the Emperor of Austria" as they confessed to it… "As the Emperor drove to the hospital, I just went with him," said Mama… "And in the carriage I sat on the landward side and let the Emperor sit on the seaward side, it probably wouldn't have helped much, but maybe a little bit." Uncle asked whether Papa noticed. "I don't know—I said it was because of the sun." No, I can hardly be surprised when I think of all Mama did. She was so angry at the traitorous Italians.

"I barely greeted them," she said. "They yell 'Eviva, eviva' the whole time and then they stab you in the back with a dagger. And amidst all the spectacle, there came a voice right by our carriage: 'God bless you!' At least that came from the heart!"

I had never seen Mama like that before. She had tears in her eyes and was still so angry with this awful rabble and Taaffe. O and I, how I cried and how I happy I was at the same time. O, when I have a husband I will try to sacrifice myself just like Mama. That his life would be dearer to me than my own. And o! How good the dear Lord was! O yes, He protected Papa. He takes special care of the House of Habsburg!

22 December. I dined with Mama, Papa, Aunt and Uncle at 6 o'clock yesterday evening. Uncle Gackel and Aunt Marie José are awfully sweet. Rudolf and Stephanie are coming today, that will probably end up being less cosy.

23 December. So I dined downstairs again yesterday evening with Papa, Mama, Rudolf and Stephanie, Uncle Carl Theodor and Aunt Marie José. Stephanie was too ridiculous again. She and Rudolf look at each other the whole time and then she talks as if she's already celebrated her silver wedding anniversary. Aunt Marie José is the complete opposite, Stephanie is almost nasty compared to her. When I saw her like that with her black dress, doe eyes and amusing small face, I wondered whether Rudolf does not envy Uncle this lovely, beautiful little wife? Stephanie is really something compared to her. So big, fat, yellow and blonde and in a hideous white satin dress.

But that's enough whining, Uncle Gackel and Aunt Marie José are leaving for Munich today, and then Stephanie will be even more the centre of attention.

1883

2 August. Mama wants me to speak Hungarian with Zummel.... Conversation between Mama and Papa that left me all in a tizz.

Mama: "Valérie keeps speaking German with Countess Kornis." Papa: "No? What? Valérie doesn't talk to Countess Kornis in Hungarian?" Mama: "No, never, she doesn't want to." Papa walked back and forth, smiling, and said rubbing his hands: "Ah—hm! That's very good—it's better she speaks German—very praiseworthy." And he laughed so kindly as he said it that my heart was all aflutter.—O, Papa and I always think the same even if I don't talk to him very much or uninhibitedly, there is still a love and respect that there are no words for—only sometimes, when Papa says something that comes right from my heart too, we look at each other with a smile as if had made a prior arrangement…

8 August. Later the Duke of Bragança arrived, actually the Crown Prince of Portugal—he wanted—oh woe, I am almost embarrassed to write it, he wanted to marry me. But they told him it wouldn't be possible … not at all pleasant, so small and fat and talks so loud: in a word, insufferable…

> *(Marie Valerie's mother presents the now 15-year old, with the highest ladies' order of the House of Austria.)*

25 August. I went to see Mama at 2:30 p.m. today, who said she had something marvelous to tell me. Since I am now so big.… After Mama kept me in suspense for an age, she finally took a velvet box and a likewise velvet book from her dressing table drawer—and—o my dear diary just think!!! It was—the Order of the Starry Cross.

27 August. At Mama's until 10 o'clock. I read to her while we were both having our hair combed.

> *(The "Queen" that Marie Valerie refers to is Stephanie's mother, Queen consort of the Belgians.)*

2 September, Schönbrunn. And so Stephanie has a little daughter.

Breakfast for four in Mama's salon: Mama, the Queen, Rudolf and I. We talked about Stephanie the whole time, she is said to have suffered a great deal and was also in danger at one point.—Rudolf slept a little on the floor next to her, and Stephanie said to Hofrat Braun: "I mustn't scream or I'll wake the Archduke" … Finally she called out: "Rudolf! You won't be angry with me if it's a girl, will you?" The little one was born at 5 minutes to 7. Stephanie is said to have cried and Rudolf said: "It doesn't matter—a daughter is much sweeter."

> *(Marie Valerie mentions the actress Katharina Schratt, who would become the Emperor's companion.)*

27 November. "Dorf und Stadt" at the Burgtheater. A new actress called Schratt was playing Lorle, she is very beautiful but not as sweet as Wessely.

1884

30 May. After the meal, Papa told me I could come over and I sat next him as quiet as a mouse for a good hour while he worked, smoking. It must have been some very important things because he only looked up once and even then, only to comment: "But you must be frightfully bored," to which of course I answered passionately: "O no Papa; it's so nice to sit here...." "My pleasure," he said and carried on working. Poor Papa! The way I saw him sitting so patiently in front of this pile of papers, without a word of complaint ... the way every man in government just passes on the effort and concerns higher and higher until it all ends up with the Emperor—and he, who can't pass it on to anyone higher than himself, takes it all on and patiently works through it, caring about the wellbeing of every individual. It is lovely to have such a father. At 8 o'clock, father bid me good night.

> *(Marie Larisch was a niece of the Empress Elisabeth. She was viewed with suspicion while at court and was completely banished by the Empress following Crown Prince Rudolf's murder-suicide at Mayerling in 1889.)*

21 June. Marie Larisch. One could almost find it a fault with her that she is even alive—is it not, after all, theft to eat, drink and sleep—and accomplish nothing? She lives each day blindly, is bored everywhere all the time and doesn't see her husband or children for months at a time ... Gisela—the opposite—that is no pointless living-each-day-in-the-moment—I hope I will be as virtuous a wife and mother as Gisela someday.

1886

11 March. A few days after arriving in Lacroma, Stephanie became sick due to a peritonitis infection. Poor Rudolf!... The most terrible thing for me is all the wicked thoughts that arise during this occasion and which are so difficult to banish. May the dear God rain blessing and grace on the two of them and let that which is best for Rudolf happen.

13 March. Mama is fond of the idea of Franz, it would be a comfort to her to be able to keep me so close all the time.

> *(Marie Valerie speaks of herself in the third person while contemplating her relationship with Franz Salvator.)*

14 July. Mama's favorite idea, to bring me and Franz together more often this summer so that we can get to know each other thoroughly (Love? No, fear, Valérie would then be married off as an Emperor's child without love). But with Franz: "I felt as though the first love of his childhood heart was dedicated to me..." Now Valérie senses that his childhood love has grown with him and has reached maturity. What a miracle, when I gaze up at him with moved gratitude, he who has not won the love of the Emperor's daughter but that of Valérie.

29 July. Second Toscana dinner in honor of the old grandmother.—The "whole gang," as Papa says, came too. Absolutely lovely dinner next to Franz.

Mama asked Franz about Männi. "Small, blond, red." Mama: "Does he seem bright?" Franz: "Hm—yes, I think so! But I've never understood him because he speaks such thick Saxon." Mama told me there had not been the slightest trace of scorn in Franz's reply and that he had looked particularly happy and contented—I wonder why?—I should find it very unpleasant if Franz thought he had the right to be so contented and at peace; I certainly give him no reason for it...

I am afraid this little matter preoccupies me far too much.

> ("Nino" was the nickname for Franz and Leopold Salvator's father, Archduke Karl Salvator, of the Tuscan branch of the Habsburgs. The "dear Saxon" referred to is Crown Prince Friedrich August of Saxony.)

4 October. Papa to Mama: "What does this mean now, you carting the WHOLE NINO BRICK around with you all the time?" Mama: "You mean what's going on between Leopold and Valérie?" "No, between Franz and Valérie, I noticed a long time ago that the two of them are on very good terms with each other. But I beg you, the boy and that dreadful old Nino—that would be a disaster." Then Mama explained everything to him. As Papa could think of nothing bad to say about Franz, he only expressed his annoyance with the Ninos in general, certainly set on by somebody, argued health, kinship: "She can't marry within the family again, where will we end up?" Finally, he set his hopes on the dear Saxon coming to Vienna in winter. "That would be so good and appropriate in every respect."—But Papa in his goodness will certainly not only consider appropriateness but also the inner happiness of his child, for which he always prays, after all.

11 October. In a letter from Amélie, an enclosure from Papa, declaring Friedrich August to the be the man with whom Valérie would be happy ... the image of Franz rose before me like a silent reproach, I saw his clear eyes gazing on me so deeply, so sadly and so questioningly.... Should I reject such a deep, true love, such a love as I will certainly never find again.... Should I make one boy unhappy, a boy I like through and through, on account of another boy, a strange one, to whom I am nothing and who is nothing to me, simply because he may perhaps be more educated?

16 October. Mädi doesn't understand that I'm not in love with Franz.... But my childhood adoration of Reinhart, my silly and really only imagined puppy love for Eugen (my respect and love for the Zerbel brother, who first taught me an appreciation for many things, will never die but doesn't enter into it, praise God) has robbed me of all confidence regarding a true, everlasting and deep love on my part, such that it will take a long time before I can trust myself to say with certainty: he is the one I love.

5 December. To my utter astonishment I found a postcard from Franz … ridiculous excitement, wonder if he will be at the Burgtheater, he knows that I often go there … the only place he can even see me. If he doesn't come, he shows an astonishing lack of interest.… Finally 7 o'clock.—Papa, Mama and I went over and, as well as Uncle and Aunt (Gackel), we found Aunt Elisabeth and Uncle Karl Ludwig. "Fabrikant"—followed by "Jugendliebe"—but Franz did not come. Aunt Marie José and I were in fits of laughter but deep down, I was not in the mood for it at all.… That Franz did not consider it worth the effort to seek his happiness.… Doubts about his love.

1890

28 July. All of Ischl is being decorated and is in uproar.

30 July. Arrival of Franz, with whom Mama wished to speak before the arrival of the guests.… Every moment that I don't dedicate to Mama is filled with farewells.… One of the most poignant moments was when Papa and Mama called Zummel to the table in the large hall where I gave her the truly very masterful double portrait by Fröschl of Franz and me. Dear Zummel then cried even more than on all the previous days, she sobbed and was not able to utter a word; Mama and I of course sobbed too and even Papa had tears in his eyes. Who could not treasure and love this precious, pure soul? … A second mother—and Mama is not jealous of her.

1 August. As our clock had stopped (!Franz?), it was already 10 o'clock when we got up, and while I was still getting dressed, I received a sweet letter from Papa and Mama … which moved me to tears … wrote to Mama and Zummel … my thoughts in gratitude to the dear ones … but I did not feel homesick. My darling husband cherishes and cares for me, always thinks only of me.… A hunter from Ischl brought a lovely bracelet from Emperor Wilhelm of white and black pearls.

5 August. Frequent letters to Papa and Mama.… A short, sweet letter from Feldafing from Mama, however she does not say much about herself. I have also spoken to Franz about my great desire to be a mother. He shares the same.

12 August, Bellagio. At the table d'hôte.... Lederer gave me a letter from Mama he had found at the post office and as I read this same letter under the tablecloth, I noticed for the first time that Mama only writes very general things ... and all at once I clearly understood what she had always told me, that she would consider me quite another person if I ever left ... this hurt me ... sadness amidst all the strange people, so far from everyone who surrounded me in my girlhood, that I had to fight with all my strength not to burst into tears at the table. Franz (who reads my every thought) ... noticed at once and arose from the table as soon as it was possible.

15 August. How can people say that husbands are less loving than bridegrooms?

24 November. Left Vienna in the morning with Mama, we separated in Amstetten.... Mama heading to Biarritz and then later further south.... Mama's turnaround a miracle like the awakening of Lazarus as so many unscrupulous people do everything possible to keep her in that state. It is such a bitter feeling to have to judge people from the heart like this, as I come to judge these dire relatives of the Viennese court even more year after year—as the instincts of my earliest childhood are proven even truer.

26 November. Papa in Wallsee ... such a cheerful mood that you see how happy he is to be with us again ... cheery, chatty dinner.

27 November. Papa received us first thing in the morning with the sobering news that he must leave today rather than tomorrow, as the agitation that has been in parliament for some time now had now spread to the streets and taken on quite serious dimensions ... too sad to see Papa constantly in fresh worries that cannot even let him have two days of peace.

29 November. After yesterday's news from Vienna that sounded truly alarming, where even the military had to get involved, the news today is that the demission of Badeni's cabinet have brought about a general calm. In any case, it is brewing everywhere in poor, multilingual Austria and it is probably only a matter of time as to when it comes to a more serious outbreak with grave consequences.

2 December. Even here ... flags were hung out to celebrate the beginning jubilee year, which, by the way, has begun in very sad circumstances in Prague and even with the imposition of martial law. Who knows what it will all bring for us at the 1848 commemoration. I can only bring myself to complain in that it must mean more to Papa as a bitter disappointment in his life that was so rich in suffering.

Appendix II: Stephanie von Hohenlohe's Draft Memoir Passage on Lord Rothermere's Tactics

In Stephanie Hohenlohe's draft memoir, on file at the Hoover Archives in Stanford, California, she tries to convince the reader that Lord Rothermere bullied her into serving as his European ambassador. Although never published, the memoir is neatly typed and has gone through several rounds of editing with pencil, as well as blue and red ink. In this passage, she refers to "the life-long dear friendship of Archduke Franz Salvator" as well as her reasons for remaining a "good Austrian monarchist" even though she later helps Hitler overthrow Austria in the *Anschluss*. Sections that have been crossed out by Stephanie or her editor but are still legible are printed here in italics.

* * *

[A]t the time I had no legal or business experience of any kind whatsoever, and I accepted the three lines, assuring me of three substantial payments, with sincere satisfaction and without the slightest misgivings. Addressing me as "Dear Princess Stephanie of Hohenlohe" bewildered me more than the omission of mentioning my services and expenses. However, I had no reason during the ensuing three years to regret my naïve trustfulness. Our oral agreement of July 1932 was executed fully. Salaries and expenses were paid to me punctually, and the financial differences between Lord Rothermere and me, which finally led to court proceedings in 1939, had nothing to do with this particular and peculiar contract. I have quoted Lord Rothermere's letter of agreement merely to illustrate the simplifying imperiousness of his methods, and to reveal the psychological uneasiness which prevented him from stating the services, for which he obliged himself to pay so heavily. He was not ashamed of establishing a diplomatic link of his own with the "royal personages and statesmen" he had in those men and women. But in his subconsciousness he probably wished to remain able to deny anything and everything in any unforeseen eventuality, and, last not least [sic], he desired to usurp all credit for achievement. This had been manifest during the five preceding years in his relations with Hungary, when he had succeeded in obscuring the origin of his campaign, and in keeping my name completely in the dark. He was willing to renumerate [sic] me handsomely for my political services, but I was to have no place in the sun of his glory. As I had derived a great deal of happiness from being able to be useful to my country and its dynasty, and as I had no desires for publicity and no political ambitions of my own, I did not resent Lord Rothermere's vanity and his puerile egotism. I was perfectly content to remain the unknown woman behind the illustrious man *who was trying to pull the royal strings of Europe.*

At any time before 1932 I might have seriously hesitated to accept Lord Rothermere's offer. I had been living in apparently unassailable security in a charming house in Paris, *I had employed eight servants*, great comfort and a good deal of luxury had been my happy lot. But the turbulent years of 1930 and 1931 had changed all that. The financial crashes in America, Austria, Holland and Germany had turned the carefree lotus-eater into a trembling leaf. My security had unaccountably yet irretrievably vanished, and if in the Daily Mail's phraseology "Europe was seething with unrest," so was I. All my life I had been gaily unemployed, provided with an utterly unearned yet highly welcome income. It was fortunate that in the circumstances of 1932 I proved to be employable. With high hopes I embarked on my romantic career *in secret diplomacy* and I was inwardly proud of the transition from a dreaming amateur *in politics* into a well-paid professional.

My qualifications for the tasks involved were perhaps more visible to Lord Rothermere than to myself. My political and economic notions at the time were probably the shallow sentiments and prejudices of the class I had married into, and thus they harmonized easily with the views of my employer. Fraulein Stephanie Richter of Vienna who had married Fuerst Friedrich Francois Augustin Marie Hohenlohe-Waldenburg-Schillingsfuerst and Mr. Harold Sidney Harmsworth of London, who had become the first Viscount Rothermere of Hemsted, were politically of the same ilk; they were congenial conservatives. Similar social circumstances produce the same phenomena on the Danube as on the Thames. My widely-flung social connections in France, Austria, Hungary and Germany were known to Lord Rothermere, and he must have realized that I could easily build bridges into otherwise inaccessible quarters. He also credited me, rightly or wrongly, with political instinct, journalistic flair, insight and judgement [sic]. Looking back upon the last nine years I cannot possibly feel that he was right—but there it was. Finally, thinking so highly of himself as he did, he must have thought that "Her Serene Highness, the Princess Stephanie Hohenlohe-Waldenburg-Schillingsfuerst" would make his proper representative amongst the "royal personages and statesmen" on the continent. I tried, I tried hard to live up to his expectations.

In several lengthy conversations Lord Rothermere acquainted me more deeply with his political and economic ideal and with the suggestions I was to make on his behalf to those key figures abroad. He looked upon Europe with monumental simplicity. In his favourite words–"the continent was seething with economic and political unrest." Now was the moment, and only now, to solidify the social and political structures of the mid–European nations by restoring their exiled monarchs to their thrones. A return of the Hapsburgs [sic] and the Hohenzollerns to their God-given functions would pacify the world and revive its prosperity.

A "return of the Hapsburgs" was enough to intoxicate me. In an electrifying flash my girlhood in Vienna re-appeared [sic] in my mind and filled my heart with longing and nostalgia. Could that golden age really be brought back? Could the present Vienna, that sad ghost of what was once the gaiest [sic] city of Europe, really regain its high spirits, its loveliness, its melody? During my last visits to Vienna the city had seemed to me an awesome God's-acre, indecently populated by poor and exhausted remnants. Of all its world-famous churches, palaces and monuments only the age-old gothic dome of St. Stephen appeared to me [sic] have retained its beauty and dignity, and to be somehow expressive of the spirit of the place, as it was expressive, differently though, of the spirit of its builders, the Babenbergs. All the other architectural dreams of the Vienna of the Renaissance, the Baroque and the Rococo were just doleful reminders of an exuberance that was gone, vanished, evaporated. They were out of place, out of time, out of tact.... The city of the baroque par excellence had been turned into a veritable cemetery, but, alas, the baroque is a grating style in a graveyard ...

Truly, Lord Rothermere's eloquence was not required (sixteen years later) to turn me into a Hapsburg (propagandist) believer.

If my birth and youth in Vienna, if the friendly kindness of the old Emperor Francis Joseph, or his successor Emperor Charles, of Archduchess Maria Theresia [sic], and the life-long dear friendship of Archduke Franz Salvator had not made me a good Austrian monarchist, all the wiles of all the Press [sic] lords could certainly not have succeeded. Lord Rothermere found no complexes in me to overcome. If he could have looked into my heart he would have seen there the ancient slogan of the Hapsburgs: A.E.I.O.U. "Austriae es imperare orbi universo." ("Alles Erdreich ist Oesterreich untertan.")

* * *

In spite of this psychological readiness of mine to fall in with the ambitious plans of Lord Rothermere, I soon discovered to my own dismay that a certain critical inclination, a mental impatience, a questioning contrariness began to possess my mind, while His Lordship was lecturing. Or the various conversations we had in that sunny July of 1932 were not really conversations; they were rather a summer course in the political and economic theories of Lord Rothermere. He was instructing me, and I was listening. But my enforced silence was only superficial; inwardly I was hurling rebelling questions at him and, sometimes, answering them to my own satisfaction. When he proclaimed that Central Europe was "seething with economic unrest: in consequence of the shackles of the unjust and ignominious peace treaties of 1919, that ghastly unemployment was driving the civilized masses into the arms of that Eastern monster: communism," I was thinking of England and her unemployed, and I found that if any country was seething at the time America was seething most, and that her armies of unemployed were bigger, relatively and absolutely, than any. And yet, neither England nor America had lost a war, neither England nor America were shackled by unjust and ignominious peace treaties, neither England nor America seemed to be tumbling into the nightmare of communism. When Lord Rothermere maintained that the restoration of the monarchists would "stabilize the social structure" and cure all economic ills, I was thinking that the return of the unemployed Hohenzollerns would be a solution of their employment problem, but not of that of the workers, and that America had not lost a dynasty at all, at least not recently, and that her vast unemployment could certainly not be eliminated by a restoration of the Hannoverians [sic]. It also occurred to me that the labour market was something infinitely complex. According to my prospective employer ten to fifteen million men in their best years had been killed in the four years of the war, and yet the labour markets of Europe seemed infinitely less absorbent than before. Was this perhaps due to the fact that ten million men are not only ten million producers but also ten million consumers and providers? When Lord Rothermere was banging his right fist into his left palm emphasizing again and again that *now* was the moment for action, that it was *now* that the restoration of the monarchies should be brought about, that it was now and only now that a powerful rampart against Bolshevism could be erected in Germany, I was trying in vain to shut out of my mind the memories of innumerable advertisements in which mesmerizing eyes or forefingers were exhorting the readers to send in their orders now, to buy the cosmetics in question *now*, to send for the miraculous emetics n-o-w.

Although that particular month in the history of Europe, July 1932, suited me personally to perfection for the beginning of any campaign whatsoever, I could never appease or eliminate the torturing question why the right moment had arrived just then for the opening shots in a monarchist restoration movement. Why July 1932 and not July 1927, or 1926, or 1924!?! O why not—perish the thought!—July 1949!!! I remember too well the two abortive attempts of the late Emperor Charles to regain the throne of Hungary in 1921. All the explanations which had been given for his dismal failures were stressing the point of the "wrong moment." The attempts were "premature, the time was not ripe, the proper time had not come yet," and so on and so forth. I shuddered at the thought that Lord Rothermere might be repeating the mistakes of the last Hapsburg, that July 1932 was possibly not the right moment, that it was perhaps not *now* but much much later when that highly desirable retrograde movement should be set into motion. My days and my nights were infested with that unanswerable everlasting question: why now?!!

Appendix III: Stephanie von Hohenlohe on Lord Rothermere and Nazi Leaders

In this passage from her unpublished memoirs, Stephanie von Hohenlohe accuses Lord Rothermere of playing into the hands of Adolf Hitler's Propaganda Minister Joseph Goebbels.

* * *

Within a period of two weeks or so Lord Rothermere did his very best to impress upon my mind his political notions about practically every European issue of the time. He supplemented his doctrinal-monologues by copious readings from old and recent articles and statements of his, and I never left him without being presented with pamphlets, reprints and press cuttings, repeating, accentuating and emphasizing the oral lecture that I had just received. I was to carry his messages and present his views to various august personages on the continent, and he took infinite pains to prepare me thoroughly. It is difficult to imagine that any ambassador ever received more minute instructions from his Foreign Office, than I was provided with by Lord Rothermere. Towards the end of our "conversations" my mind was a veritable arsenal of Daily Mail points of view and arguments.

The ever-recurring leitmotiv of all his perorations was the curse of communism. The Red menace was his bête noire. He was the most perfect specimen of the capitalist with bolshevism on the brain. Whatever was happening in any corner of the world, detrimental to the interests of his class, was due to the diabolical machinations of the monsters of Moscow. The dimensions of his Russophobia were more frightening than its primary cause could ever have been. Leninism had to be destroyed, if Christianity, civilization, humanity, decency, family life and the Daily Mail were to survive. All his other political emotions, his monarchism, his championship of the Hohenzollerns, the Hapsburgs, Hungary and Germany, his hostility towards Tschecho-Slovakia, Poland and Roumania spring from the central impulse of his tempestuous anti-bolshevism. The "new Europe" that he wanted to create, that he saw emerging from the chaos of two decades (and which was really nothing but the good old Europe of his youth) was to be "a rampart, a bulwark, a bastion, a fortress, a Maginot line [sic] against the rising tide of the red terror." As he had selected Germany and Hungary to become the holders of the white fortress against the fiends from the Red East, France and the Little Entente were to be sacrificed. With the heroic resignation of a new Abraham he was willing to deliver the new composite Isaak to the bidding of the new God, well knowing that this time the transaction would have to be carried out in earnest. Sadly he recollected that his brother, Lord Northcliffe, and he himself had been the godfathers, if not the fathers of Tschecho-Slovakia and Poland, but he was determined to face the facts and to conform to the new age, which demanded a new orientation. No matter how completely a dramatic situation may repeat itself in the history of humanity, the psychology of the participant changes. Whereas the obedient servant of the one and only God in the old testament is not reported to have found it necessary to discover suddenly that little Isaak was really an intolerably vicious brat, Lord Rothermere convinced himself that Benes was an insufferable firebrand, that Prague was a hotbed of subversive intrigue, and that the Tsecho-Slovak army had grown to recklessly provocative proportions. (In 1932!) In equally fine indignation he attacked the "spirit of Locarno," the "organized humbug of the League of Nations," the "gang of old men that was ruining the British Empire and Europe," and, last not least [sic], if somewhat disconnectedly, the "holy Alliance" of the first quarter of the 19th century.

(It never occurred to me at the time that Lord Rothermere's scintillating political shop-window contained nothing but second-hand goods. When, some time later, I heard the same statements, the same accusations, the same arguments, the same bombast and the same invectives from the fanatical mouth of one Adolf Hitler, it seemed at first as if the Fuehrer had been hypnotized by the Daily Mail. It did not take long, however, to realize the true sequence of events, and to give credit where credit belonged. The copyright in this ideology was Adolf

Hitler's, of course, and not Lord Rothermere's. If the propaganda ministry under Dr. Goebbels was the sender non plus ultra, Northcliffe House in the good old city of London was the receiving station par excellence. They were wishing, wanting, waiting for the bulletins of the limping doctor).

Chapter Notes

Prologue

1. Stephanie Hohenlohe, *Draft memoir*, Stephanie zu Hohenlohe-Waldenburg-Schillingsfürst files, Hoover Archives, Stanford, California.
2. Ibid.
3. Martha Schad, *Hitler's Spy Princess: The Extraordinary Life of Stephanie von Hohenlohe* (Stroud: Sutton, 2004), 7.
4. *Memorandum on Stephanie von Hohenlohe for U.S. President Franklin D. Roosevelt*, Franklin D. Roosevelt Presidential Library and Museum, Marist University, October 28, 1941.

Chapter 1

1. Count Egon Corti, *Elizabeth, Empress of Austria* (New Haven: Yale University Press, 1936), 416.
2. Marie Valerie von Osterreich, *Das Tagebuch de Lieblingstochter von Kaiserin Elisabeth 1878–1899* (Munchen: Piper Verlag GmbH, 2005), 89.
3. "The Dower of an Emperor's Daughter," *Edinburgh Evening News*, April 24, 1890.
4. Brigitte Hamann, *The Reluctant Empress: A Biography of Empress Elisabeth of Austria* (New York: Alfred A. Knopf, 1986), 335.
5. Marie Valerie von Osterreich, *Das Tagebuch de Lieblingstochter von Kaiserin Elisabeth 1878–1899* (Munchen: Piper Verlag GmbH, 2005), 233.
6. "A Regal Marriage," *Pittsburg Dispatch*, July 31, 1890, 5.
7. Count Egon Corti, *Elizabeth, Empress of Austria* (New Haven: Yale University Press, 1936), 419.
8. Brigitte Hamann, *The Reluctant Empress: A Biography of Empress Elisabeth of Austria* (New York: Alfred A. Knopf, 1986), 341.
9. *Recollections of a Royal Governess* (New York: D. Appleton, 1916), 163. (Anonymous.)
10. Marie Valerie von Osterreich, *Das Tagebuch de Lieblingstochter von Kaiserin Elisabeth 1878–1899* (Munchen: Piper Verlag GmbH, 2005), 117.
11. U.S. House of Representatives, House Documents, Vols. 11–12, Vol. 226 (Washington, D.C.: U.S. Government Printing Office, 1866), 374.

Chapter 2

1. Marie Valerie von Osterreich, *Das Tagebuch de Lieblingstochter von Kaiserin Elisabeth 1878–1899* (Munchen: Piper Verlag GmbH, 2005), 237.
2. Ibid.
3. Ibid.
4. Ibid.
5. Ibid.
6. "People of Literary Fame," *Tombstone Epitaph*, September 20, 1891.
7. "Royal Composers," *The Jasper News*, November 7, 1908.
8. Marie Valerie von Osterreich, *Das Tagebuch der Lieblingstochter von Kaiserin Elisabeth 1878–1899* (Munchen: Piper, 1998), 94.
9. Brigitte Hamann, *The Reluctant Empress: A Biography of Empress Elisabeth of Austria* (New York: Alfred A. Knopf, 1986), 332.
10. Charlotte Zeepvat, *From Cradle to Crown: British Nannies and Governesses at the World's Royal Courts* (Stroud: Sutton, 2006), 43.
11. Ibid., 50.
12. Warwickshire County Record Office, *Letter from Empress Elisabeth of Austria to*

Lady Mary Throckmorton, November 4, 1868, CR1998/SS/5/14/1–14.

13. England & Wales, *National Probate Calendar (Index on Wills and Administrations), 1858–1966, for Mary Elizabeth Frances Throckmorton.*

14. *Recollections of a Royal Governess* (New York: D. Appleton, 1916), 129. (Anonymous.)

15. The Milton Keynes Heritage Association, *Letter from Empress Elisabeth to Mary Throckmorton,* http://www.mkheritage.co.uk/eoa/docs/throckmorton.html.

16. *Maria Valerie and Mary Throckmorton,* Warwickshire County Record Office, http://apps.warwickshire.gov.uk/api/documents/WCCC-863–397.

17. "Queen Elisabeth and Gödöllő," *Royal Palace of Gödöllő,* http://www.kiralyikastely.hu/page.58.elisabeth_and_godollo.

18. *Ibid.*

19. "Princess Aglaë von Auersperg," *The Illustrated American,* November 26, 1892.

20. Brigitte Hamann, *The Reluctant Empress: A Biography of Empress Elisabeth of Austria* (New York: Alfred A. Knopf, 1986), 180.

21. Marie Valerie von Osterreich, *Das Tagebuch de Lieblingstochter von Kaiserin Elisabeth 1878–1899* (Munchen: Piper Verlag GmbH, 2005), 17.

22. *Ibid.,* 16.

23. Brigitte Hamann, *The Reluctant Empress: A Biography of Empress Elisabeth of Austria* (New York: Alfred A. Knopf, 1986), 333.

24. *Ibid.,* 231.

25. Count Egon Corti, *Elizabeth, Empress of Austria* (New Haven: Yale University Press, 1936), 280.

26. Marie Valerie von Osterreich, *Das Tagebuch de Lieblingstochter von Kaiserin Elisabeth 1878–1899* (Munchen: Piper Verlag GmbH, 2005), 21.

27. Brigitte Hamann, *The Reluctant Empress: A Biography of Empress Elisabeth of Austria* (New York: Alfred A. Knopf, 1986), 231.

28. *Ibid.,* 317.

29. *Ibid.,* 248.

30. Warwickshire County Record Office, *Telegram from Marie Valerie of Austria to Lady Mary Throckmorton, December 27, 1888,* CR1998/SS/5/14/1–14.

Chapter 3

1. "The Subtle Distinction: Court Ball and Ball at Court," *The World of the Habsburgs,* http://www.habsburger.net/en/chapter/subtle-distinction-court-ball-and-ball-courtl.

2. *Ibid.*

3. Count Egon Corti, *Elizabeth, Empress of Austria* (New Haven: Yale University Press, 1936), 340.

4. Marie Valerie von Osterreich, *Das Tagebuch de Lieblingstochter von Kaiserin Elisabeth 1878–1899* (Munchen: Piper Verlag GmbH, 2005), 90.

5. *Ibid.*

6. *Ibid.*

7. Brigitte Hamann, *The Reluctant Empress: A Biography of Empress Elisabeth of Austria* (New York: Alfred A. Knopf, 1986), 335.

8. *Ibid.,* 323.

9. Marie Valerie von Osterreich, *Das Tagebuch de Lieblingstochter von Kaiserin Elisabeth 1878–1899* (Munchen: Piper Verlag GmbH, 2005), 41.

10. Brigitte Hamann, *The Reluctant Empress: A Biography of Empress Elisabeth of Austria* (New York: Alfred A. Knopf, 1986), 342.

11. *Ibid.*

Chapter 4

1. Rudolf Stoiber und Boris Celovsky, *Stephanie von Hohenlohe: Sie liebte die mächtigen der welt* (Berlin: F.A. Herbig Verlagsbuchhandlung, 1988), 54.

2. *Ibid.*

3. Karina Urbach, *Go Betweens For Hitler* (Oxford: Oxford University Press, 2015), 218.

4. Prince Franz Hohenlohe, *Steph: The Fabulous Princess* (London: New English Library, 1976), 8.

5. Jim Wilson, *Nazi Princess: Hitler, Lord Rothermere and Princess Stephanie von Hohenlohe* (Stroud: The History Press, 2011), 30.

6. Open Plaques, 12 Park Lane, Parktown, Johannesburg, South Africa, http://openplaques.org/places/za/areas/johannesburg/plaques?id=unphotographed.

7. Stephanie Hohenlohe, *Draft memoir,* Hoover Archives, Standford, California, 7.

Chapter 5

1. Walter C. Langer, *A Psychological Analysis of Adoph Hitler: His Life and Legend* (Washington, D.C.: M.O. Branch, Office of Strategic Services, 1943, declassified on March 12, 1968), 234.

2. Adolf Hitler, *Mein Kampf* (New York: Houghton Mifflin, 1999), 7.
3. *Ibid.*, 9.
4. James Giblin, *The Life and Death of Adolf Hitler* (New York: Houghton Mifflin Harcourt, 2002), 5.
5. *Ibid.*, 6.
6. Adolf Hitler, *Mein Kampf* (New York: Houghton Mifflin, 1999), 14–15.
7. Ian Kershaw, *Hitler: A Biography* (New York: W.W. Norton, 2008), 5.
8. Adolf Hitler, *Mein Kampf* (New York: Houghton Mifflin, 1999), 18.
9. August Kubizek, *The Young Hitler I Knew: The Memoirs of Hitler's Childhood Friend* (Yorkshire: Frontline Books, 2011), 32.
10. *Ibid.*, 33.
11. *Ibid.*, 30.
12. *Ibid.*, 66.
13. *Ibid.*, 69.
14. Adolf Hitler, *Mein Kampf* (New York: Houghton Mifflin, 1999), 23–24.
15. Werner Maser, *Hitler's Letters and Notes* (New York: Bantam, 1976), 10.
16. Brigitte Hamann, *Hitler's Vienna: A Portrait of the Tyrant as a Young Man* (New York: I.B. Tauris, 2014), 30.
17. Adolf Hitler, *Mein Kampf* (New York: Houghton Mifflin, 1999), 19.
18. Brigitte Hamann, *Hitler's Vienna: A Portrait of the Tyrant as a Young Man* (New York: I.B. Tauris, 2014), 32.
19. Adolf Hitler, *Mein Kampf* (New York: Houghton Mifflin, 1999), 20.
20. James S. Olson, *Bathsheba's Breast: Women, Cancer, and History* (Baltimore: Johns Hospiks University Press, 2005), 94.
21. Adolf Hitler, *Mein Kampf* (New York: Houghton Mifflin, 1999), 18.

Chapter 6

1. Martha Schad, *Kaiserin Elisabeth und ihre Töchter* (München: Piper Verlag GmbH, 2002), 155.
2. Brigitte Hamann, *Hitler's Vienna: A Portrait of the Tyrant as a Young Man* (New York: I.B. Tauris, 2014), 375.
3. Count Egon Corti, *Elisabeth, Empress of Austria* (New Haven: Yale University Press, 1936), 425.
4. Brigitte Hamann, *The Reluctant Empress: A Biography of Empress Elisabeth of Austria* (New York: Alfred A. Knopf, 1986), 363.
5. Martha Schad, *Kaiserin Elisabeth und ihre Töchter* (München: Piper Verlag GmbH, 2002), 155–156.
6. *Ibid.*, 156.
7. Hamann, *The Reluctant Empress*, 370.
8. Telegram from Marie Valerie to Lady Mary Throckmorton, September 13, 1898, The National Archives, Warwickshire County Records Office, CR1998/GS/6.
9. Marie Valerie von Osterreich, *Das Tagebuch de Lieblingstochter von Kaiserin Elisabeth 1878–1899* (Munchen: Piper Verlag GmbH, 2005), 311.
10. Count Egon Corti, *Elisabeth, Empress of Austria* (New Haven: Yale University Press, 1936), 489.
11. Hamann, *The Reluctant Empress*, 371.
12. Letter to Mrs. Mary Throckmorton, December 13, 1898, The National Archives, Warwickshire County Records Office, CR1998/GS/5.
13. The Milton Keynes Heritage Association, http://www.mkheritage.co.uk/eoa/docs/throckmorton.html.
14. Constantin Christomanos, *Elisabeth von Österreich. Tagebuchblätter von Constantin Christomanos* (Vienna, 1899), 84.
15. Hamann, *The Reluctant Empress*, 373.
16. *Ibid.*
17. *Ibid.*, 374.

Chapter 7

1. Brigitte Hamann, *Hitler's Vienna: A Portrait of the Tyrant as a Young Man* (New York: I.B. Tauris, 2014), 356.
2. *Ibid.*, 162.
3. Adolf Hitler, *Mein Kampf* (New York: Houghton Mifflin, 1999), 21.
4. *Ibid.*, 34.
5. Reinhold Hanisch, "I Was Hitler's Buddy," *The New Republic*, April 5, 12, 19, 1939.
6. *Ibid.*
7. Hamann, *Hitler's Vienna*, 275.
8. George V. Strong, *Seedtime for Fascism: Disintegration of Austrian Political Culture, 1867–1918* (New York: Routledge, 1998), 124.
9. Adolf Hitler, *Mein Kampf* (New York: Houghton Mifflin, 1999), 55.
10. Amos Elon, *The Pity of It All: A Portrait of the German-Jewish Epoch, 1743–1933* (New York: Macmillan, 2003), 224.
11. Hamann, *Hitler's Vienna*, 146.
12. Adolf Hitler, *Mein Kampf* (New York: Houghton Mifflin, 1999), 24.
13. Stephanie Hohenlohe, *draft memoir*, Hoover Archives, Standford, California.

14. Ibid.
15. Martha Schad, *Kaiserin Elisabeth und ihre Töchter* (München: Piper Verlag GmbH, 2002), 184.
16. Brigitte Hamann, *The Reluctant Empress: A Biography of Empress Elisabeth of Austria* (New York: Alfred A. Knopf, 1986), 314.
17. Ibid., 316.
18. Hohenlohe-Waldenburg-Schillingsfürst, Stephanie Juliana, Prinzessin zu Collection, box 3, folder 3, Hoover Institution Archives.

Chapter 8

1. S.L.A. Marshall, *American Heritage History of World War I* (Newbury, MA: New Word City, 2014).
2. Alan Palmer, *Twilight of the Habsburgs: The Life and Times of Emperor Francis Joseph* (New York: Grove Press, 1994), 324.
3. Emperor Franz Joseph, *To my people! Emperor Franz Joseph's proclamation—Declaration of War*, July 28, 1914, British Library, http://www.bl.uk/collection-items/to-my-people-emperor-franz-joseph.
4. Ibid.
5. Marie Valerie von Osterreich, *Das Tagebuch der Lieblingstochter von Kaiserin Elisabeth* (Munchen: Piper, 1998), 18.
6. Adolf Hitler, *Mein Kampf* (New York: Houghton Mifflin, 1999), 161.
7. Ibid., 16.
8. Werner Maser, *Hitler's Letters and Notes* (New York: Bantam, 1976), 10.
9. Ibid., 30.
10. Ian Kershaw, *Hitler: A Biography* (New York: W.W. Norton, 2008).
11. Werner Maser, *Hitler's Letters and Notes* (New York: Bantam, 1976), 45–45.
12. "Christmas Gifts for the Troops," *Sunderland Daily Echo and Shipping Gazette*, December 11, 1914.
13. "Christmas Gifts for the Troops," *Western Mail*, December 11, 1914.
14. The Austrian Red Cross Archives, *Papers Telating to Archduchess Marie Valerie and Archduke Franz Salvator as Patrons, 1914–1917*.
15. The University of Innsbruck, *Certificate of Honorary Doctorate of Medicine Conferred upon Archduke Franz Salvator*, March 1916; Letter between Dr. Hormann and Baron von Lederer on Behalf of Franz Salvator, May 19, 1916.
16. Jim Wilson, *Nazi Princess: Hitler, Lord Rothermere and Princess Stephanie von Hohenlohe* (Stroud: The History Press, 2011), 31.

17. The British National Archives, MI5 files, "Princess Stephanie Marie von Hohenlohe-Waldburg-Schillingfurst," KV 2/1696–1697, 1928–1939.
18. Prince Franz Hohenlohe, *Steph: The Fabulous Princess* (London: New English Library, 1976) 20.
19. Stephanie Hohenlohe, Draft memoir, Hoover Archives, Standford, California.
20. Ibid.
21. Prince Franz Hohenlohe, *Steph: The Fabulous Princess* (London: New English Library, 1976) 20.
22. Ibid., 21.
23. Stephanie Hohenlohe, Draft memoir, Hoover Archives, Standford, California.

Chapter 9

1. James and Joanna Bogle, *A Heart for Europe—The Lives of Emperor Charles and Empress Zita of Austria-Hungary* (Leominster: Gracewing, 1990), 63.
2. United States Conference of Catholic Bishops, "Prayer of Commendation," http://www.usccb.org/prayer-and-worship/bereavement-and-funerals/prayers-for-death-and-dying.cfm.
3. "Threatening Symptoms," *Birmingham Gazette*, November 23, 1916.
4. Rudolf Stoiber und Boris Celovsky, *Stephanie von Hohenlohe: Sie liebte die mächtigen der welt* (Berlin: F.A. Herbig Verlagsbuchhandlung, 1988), 57.
5. "St. Stephen Scene of Splendor at Franz Joseph's Funeral," *The New York Times*, December 1, 1916.
6. Stephanie Hohenlohe, Draft memoir, Hoover Archives, Standford, California.
7. James and Joanna Bogle, *A Heart for Europe—The Lives of Emperor Charles and Empress Zita of Austria-Hungary* (Leominster: Gracewing, 1990), 66.
8. "Francis Joseph's 'Conscience Money' to Soldiers," *Sheffield Evening Telegraph*, December 15, 1916.
9. Harry Slapnicka, *The Fate of the Ischl Kaiservilla After the Death of Emperor Franz Joseph* (Oberösterreichischer Musealverein—Gesellschaft für Landeskunde, 2000).
10. Adolf Hitler, *Mein Kampf* (New York: Houghton Mifflin, 1999), 159.
11. *Evening Star* (Washington, D.C.), November 22, 1916.
12. James and Joanna Bogle, *A Heart for Europe—The Lives of Emperor Charles and*

Empress Zita of Austria-Hungary (Leominster: Gracewing, 1990), 64.
  13. Hohenlohe-Waldenburg-Schillingsfürst, Stephanie Juliana, Prinzessin zu Collection, box 3, folder 3, Hoover Institution Archives.
  14. Werner Maser, *Hitler's Letters and Notes* (New York: Bantam, 1976), 51.
  15. *Ibid.*
  16. *Ibid.*, 86–87.
  17. Volker Ullrich, *Hitler: Ascent 1889–1939* (New York: Alfred A. Knopf, 2016), 59.
  18. Werner Maser, *Hitler's Letters and Notes* (New York: Bantam, 1976), 54–55.
  19. *Ibid.*, 87.
  20. *Ibid.*, 56.
  21. Ian Kershaw, *Hitler: A Biography* (New York: W.W. Norton, 2008), 54.
  22. Thomas Weber, *Hitler's First War* (New York: Oxford University Press, 2010), 57.
  23. *Ibid.*, 63.
  24. Werner Maser, *Hitler's Letters and Notes* (New York: Bantam, 1976), 88.
  25. Adolf Hitler, *Mein Kampf* (New York: Houghton Mifflin, 1999), 165.
  26. Ian Kershaw, *Hitler: A Biography* (New York: W.W. Norton, 2008), 56.
  27. Thomas Weber, *Hitler's First War* (New York: Oxford University Press, 2010), 155.
  28. Adolf Hitler, *Mein Kampf* (New York: Houghton Mifflin, 1999), 159.

Chapter 10

  1. Stephanie Hohenlohe, *Draft memoir*, Hoover Archives, Standford, California.
  2. Hohenlohe-Waldenburg-Schillingsfürst, Stephanie Juliana, Prinzessin zu Collection, box 3, folder 3, Hoover Institution Archives.
  3. Thomas Weber, *Hitler's First War* (New York: Oxford University Press, 2010), 171.
  4. Volker Ullrich, *Hitler: Ascent 1889–1939* (New York: Alfred A. Knopf, 2016), 67.
  5. Hohenlohe-Waldenburg-Schillingsfürst, Stephanie Juliana, Prinzessin zu Collection, box 3, folder 3, Hoover Institution Archives.
  6. "From the Declaration of Relinquishment Signed by Emperor Karl on 11 November 1918," *The Last Days of the Monarchy*, Habsburger.net, http://ww1.habsburger.net/en/chapters/last-days-monarchy.
  7. Prince Franz Hohenlohe, *Steph: The Fabulous Princess* (London: New English Library, 1976), 23.
  8. Adolf Hitler, *Mein Kampf* (New York: Houghton Mifflin, 1999), 202.
  9. Thomas Weber, *Hitler's First War* (New York: Oxford University Press, 2010), 221.
  10. Adolf Hitler, *Mein Kampf* (New York: Houghton Mifflin, 1999), 203.
  11. *Ibid.*, 204.
  12. *Ibid.*, 202.

Chapter 11

  1. "Austrian Archduchess in Switzerland," *Manchester Evening News* December 23, 1918.
  2. Bertita Harding, *Lost Waltz: A Story of Exile* (Indianapolis: Bobbs-Merrill, 1944), 48.
  3. British National Archives, *Marie Valerie Letter*, December 28, 1919.
  4. *Evening Star* (Washington, D.C.), October 22, 1922, 11.
  5. Austrian National Archives, *Letter from Marie Valerie to Baron Lederer,* April 23, 1920.
  6. *Ibid.*
  7. Austrian National Archives, *Letter from Marie Valerie to Baron Lederer*, May 3, 1920.
  8. *Ibid.*
  9. Austrian National Archives, *Letter from Marie Valerie to Baron Lederer*, May 15, 1920.
  10. Austrian National Archives, *Letter from Marie Valerie to Baron Lederer*, May 3, 1920.
  11. Bertita Harding, *Lost Waltz: A Story of Exile* (Indianapolis: Bobbs-Merrill, 1944), 43.
  12. *Ibid.*, 44.
  13. *Ibid.*, 49.
  14. *Ibid.*, 71.
  15. James and Joanna Bogle, *A Heart for Europe—The Lives of Emperor Charles and Empress Zita of Austria-Hungary* (Leominster: Gracewing, 1990), 131–132.

Chapter 12

  1. Stephanie Hohenlohe, *Draft memoir*, Hoover Archives, Standford, California.
  2. Karina Urbach, *Go Betweens for Hitle* (Oxford: Oxford University Press, 2015), 223.
  3. Martha Schad, *Kaiserin Elisabeth und ihre Töchter* (München: Piper Verlag GmbH, 2002), 184.
  4. Austrian National Archives, *Prayer Card for Marie Valerie Following Her Death*, 1924.
  5. Edward Peters, *A Modern Guide to In-*

dulgences: Rediscovering This Often Misinterpreted Teaching (Chicago: Liturgy Training Publications, 2008), 13.
  6. Martha Schad, *Kaiserin Elisabeth und ihre Töchter* (München: Piper Verlag GmbH, 2002), 184.
  7. Volker Ullrich, *Hitler: Ascent 1889–1939* (New York: Alfred A. Knopf, 2016), 166.
  8. Karina Urbach, *Go Betweens for Hitler* (Oxford: Oxford University Press, 2015), 165.
  9. Peter Ross Range, *1924: The Year That Made Hitler* (New York: Little, Brown, 2016), 19.
  10. *Ibid.*, 20.
  11. Ian Kershaw, *Hitler: A Biography* (New York: W.W. Norton, 2008), 74.
  12. Peter Ross Range, *1924: The Year That Made Hitler* (New York: Little, Brown, 2016), 20.
  13. Ian Kershaw, *Hitler: A Biography* (New York: W.W. Norton, 2008), 74–75.
  14. Peter Ross Range, *1924: The Year That Made Hitler* (New York: Little, Brown, 2016), 27.
  15. *Ibid.*, 29–30.
  16. Volker Ullrich, *Hitler: Ascent 1889–1939* (New York: Alfred A. Knopf, 2016), 139.
  17. Peter Ross Range, *1924: The Year That Made Hitler* (New York: Little, Brown, 2016), 60.
  18. *Ibid.*, 2.
  19. Volker Ullrich, *Hitler: Ascent 1889–1939* (New York: Alfred A. Knopf, 2016), 148.
  20. *Ibid.*, 150–151.
  21. *Ibid.*, 158.
  22. Peter Ross Range, *1924: The Year That Made Hitler* (New York: Little, Brown, 2016), 137.
  23. Volker Ullrich, *Hitler: Ascent 1889–1939* (New York: Alfred A. Knopf, 2016),162.

Chapter 13

  1. Karina Urbach, *Go Betweens for Hitler* (Oxford: Oxford University Press, 2015), 225.
  2. Prince Franz Hohenlohe, *Steph: The Fabulous Princess* (London: New English Library, 1976), 37.
  3. James and Joanna Bogle, *A Heart for Europe—The Lives of Emperor Charles and Empress Zita of Austria-Hungary* (Leominster: Gracewing, 1990), 129.
  4. *Ibid.*, 137.
  5. Viscount Rothermere, *My Campaign for Hungary* (London: Eyre and Spottiswoode, 1939), Chapter Two.
  6. *Ibid.*, Chapter One.
  7. Katalin Kadar Lynn, "Strange Partnership: Lord Rothermere, Stephanie von Hohenlohe and the Hungarian Revisionist Movement," *The Independent Scholar* (The National Coalition of Independent Scholars, 2012), 7.
  8. Viscount Rothermere, *My Campaign for Hungary* (London: Eyre and Spottiswoode, 1939), Chapter Three.
  9. Jim Wilson, *Nazi Princess: Hitler, Lord Rothermere and Princess Stephanie von Hohenlohe* (Stroud: The History Press, 2011), 38.
  10. Martha Schad, *Hitler's Spy Princess: The Extraordinary Life of Stephanie von Hohenlohe* (Stroud: Sutton, 2004), 89.
  11. Viscount Rothermere, *My Campaign for Hungary* (London: Eyre and Spottiswoode, 1939), Chapter 8.
  12. *Ibid.*
  13. Stephanie Hohenlohe, Draft memoir, Hoover Archives, Standford, California.
  14. Martha Schad, *Hitler's Spy Princess: The Extraordinary Life of Stephanie von Hohenlohe* (Stroud: Sutton, 2004), 23.
  15. *Ibid.*, 23.
  16. *Ibid.*, 25.
  17. Harold Sidney Harmsworth Rothermere (Viscount), *My Campaign for Hungary* (London: Spottiswoode, 1939), 17.
  18. The British National Archives, MI5 files, "Princess Stephanie Marie von Hohenlohe-Waldburg-Schillingfurst," KV 2/1696–1697, 1928–1939.
  19. *Ibid.*
  20. Memorandum on Stephanie von Hohenlohe for U.S. President Franklin D. Roosevelt, Franklin D. Roosevelt Presidential Library and Museum, Marist University, October 28, 1941.
  21. Martha Dodd, *My Years in Germany* (London: Victor Gollancz, 1939), 223–224.
  22. Viscount Rothermere, *The Daily Mail*, July 10, 1933.
  23. https://www.kz-gedenkstaette-dachau.de/index-e.html.
  24. Bella Fromm, *Blood & Banquets: A Berlin Diary 1930–38* (New York: Touchstone, 1990), 119.

Chapter 14

  1. Martha Schad, *Hitler's Spy Princess: The Extraordinary Life of Stephanie von Hohenlohe* (Stroud: Sutton, 2004), 29.
  2. Heinrich Heine, *Heinrich Heine's gesammelte Werke 1893* (Berlin: G. Grote, 1893), 11.

3. Karina Urbach, *Go Betweens for Hitler* (Oxford: Oxford University Press, 2015), 235.
4. Martha Dodd, *My Years in Germany* (London: Victor Gollancz, 1939), 60.
5. Martha Schad, *Hitler's Spy Princess: The Extraordinary Life of Stephanie von Hohenlohe* (Stroud: Sutton, 2004), 30.
6. Martha Dodd, *My Years in Germany* (London: Victor Gollancz, 1939), 59–60.
7. *Memorandum on Stephanie von Hohenlohe for U.S. President Franklin D. Roosevelt*, Franklin D. Roosevelt Presidential Library and Museum, Marist University, October 28, 1941.
8. Karina Urbach, *Go Betweens for Hitler* (Oxford: Oxford University Press, 2015), 238.
9. Jim Wilson, *Nazi Princess: Hitler, Lord Rothermere and Princess Stephanie von Hohenlohe* (Stroud: The History Press, 2011), 49.
10. Karina Urbach, *Go Betweens for Hitler* (Oxford: Oxford University Press, 2015), 218.
11. Martha Schad, *Hitler's Spy Princess: The Extraordinary Life of Stephanie von Hohenlohe* (Stroud: Sutton, 2004), 31–32.
12. *Ibid.*, 33.
13. *Ibid.*, 30.
14. *Ibid.*, 35.

Chapter 15

1. "Prince with the Dyed Hair Worked for Nazis at Oxford," press clipping from the British National Archives, MI5 files, "Princess Stephanie Marie von Hohenlohe-Waldburg-Schillingfurst," KV 2/1696–1697, 1928–1939.
2. Martha Schad, *Hitler's Spy Princess: The Extraordinary Life of Stephanie von Hohenlohe* (Stroud: Sutton, 2004), 99–100.
3. Adolf Hitler, *Mein Kampf* (New York: Houghton Mifflin, 1999), 3.
4. Volker Ullrich, *Hitler: Ascent 1889–1939* (New York: Alfred A. Knopf, 2016), 492.
5. Ian Kershaw, *Hitler: A Biography* (New York: W.W. Norton, 2008), 313.
6. Bella Fromm, *Blood & Banquets: A Berlin Diary 1930–38* (New York: Touchstone, 1990), 171.
7. Volker Ullrich, *Hitler: Ascent 1889–1939* (New York: Alfred A. Knopf, 2016), 493–494.
8. Bella Fromm, *Blood & Banquets: A Berlin Diary 1930–38* (New York: Touchstone, 1990), 175.
9. Volker Ullrich, *Hitler: Ascent 1889–1939* (New York: Alfred A. Knopf, 2016), 474.
10. Bella Fromm, *Blood & Banquets: A Berlin Diary 1930–38* (New York: Touchstone, 1990), 177.
11. Peter Carlson, "American Journalist Dorothy Thompson Underestimates Hitler," *American History Magazine*, August 6, 2015.
12. Bella Fromm, *Blood & Banquets: A Berlin Diary 1930–38* (New York: Touchstone, 1990), 180.
13. Martha Schad, *Hitler's Spy Princess: The Extraordinary Life of Stephanie von Hohenlohe* (Stroud: Sutton, 2004), 35.
14. G. Ward Price, *Extra-Special Correspondent* (London: George G. Harrap & Co., 1957), 155.
15. *Ibid.*, 155–156.
16. Karina Urbach, *Go Betweens for Hitler* (Oxford: Oxford University Press, 2015), 241.

Chapter 16

1. Martha Schad, *Hitler's Spy Princess: The Extraordinary Life of Stephanie von Hohenlohe* (Stroud: Sutton, 2004), 95.
2. *Ibid.*, 35.
3. Karina Urbach, *Go Betweens for Hitler* (Oxford: Oxford University Press, 2015), 240.
4. Walter C. Langer, "Interview with Princess Stephanie von Hohenlohe: June 28, 1943 at Alien Detention Camp, Seagoville, Texas," *Hitler Source Book* (Washington, D.C.: M.O. Branch, Office of Strategic Services, 1943, Declassified on March 12, 1968).
5. Jim Wilson, *Nazi Princess: Hitler, Lord Rothermere and Princess Stephanie von Hohenlohe* (Stroud: The History Press, 2011), 70.
6. United States Holocaust Memorial Museum, "The Nuremberg Race Laws," https://www.ushmm.org/outreach/en/article.php?ModuleId=10007695.
7. Bella Fromm, *Blood & Banquets: A Berlin Diary 1930–38* (New York: Touchstone, 1990), 205.
8. Jim Wilson, *Nazi Princess: Hitler, Lord Rothermere and Princess Stephanie von Hohenlohe* (Stroud: The History Press, 2011), 69.
9. Martha Schad, *Hitler's Spy Princess: The Extraordinary Life of Stephanie von Hohenlohe* (Stroud: Sutton, 2004), 50.
10. Martha Dodd, *My Years in Germany* (London: Victor Gollancz, 1939), 212.
11. Martha Schad, *Hitler's Spy Princess: The Extraordinary Life of Stephanie von Hohenlohe* (Stroud: Sutton, 2004), 51.
12. Bella Fromm, *Blood & Banquets: A Berlin Diary 1930–38* (New York: Touchstone, 1990), 202.

13. Martha Schad, *Hitler's Spy Princess: The Extraordinary Life of Stephanie von Hohenlohe* (Stroud: Sutton, 2004), 38.
14. Stephanie zu Hohenlohe-Waldenburg-Schillingsfürst files, Hoover Archives, Stanford, California.
15. Jim Wilson, *Nazi Princess: Hitler, Lord Rothermere and Princess Stephanie von Hohenlohe* (Stroud: The History Press, 2011), 74.
16. Martha Schad, *Hitler's Spy Princess: The Extraordinary Life of Stephanie von Hohenlohe* (Stroud: Sutton, 2004), 40.
17. Ibid., 41.
18. Werner Maser, *Hitler's Letters and Notes* (New York: Bantam, 1976), 372.
19. Martha Schad, *Hitler's Spy Princess: The Extraordinary Life of Stephanie von Hohenlohe* (Stroud: Sutton, 2004),
20. Prince Franz Hohenlohe, *Steph: The Fabulous Princess* (London: New English Library, 1976), 107.
21. Stephanie zu Hohenlohe-Waldenburg-Schillingsfürst files, Hoover Archives, Stanford, California.
22. Volker Ullrich, *Hitler: Ascent 1889–1939* (New York: Alfred A. Knopf, 2016), 709.
23. Ibid., 709–710.

Chapter 17

1. Volker Ullrich, *Hitler: Ascent 1889–1939* (New York: Alfred A. Knopf, 2016), 711.
2. Ibid., 709.
3. Ibid., 712.
4. Bella Fromm, *Blood & Banquets: A Berlin Diary 1930–38* (New York: Touchstone, 1990), 266.
5. Volker Ullrich, *Hitler: Ascent 1889–1939* (New York: Alfred A. Knopf, 2016), 714–715.
6. William L. Shirer, *The Rise and Fall of the Third Reich: A History of Nazi Germany* (New York: Simon & Schuster, 2011), 336.
7. Ibid., 343.
8. Volker Ullrich, *Hitler: Ascent 1889–1939* (New York: Alfred A. Knopf, 2016), 716.
9. G. Ward Price, *Extra-Special Correspondent* (London: George G. Harrap & Co., 1957), 228.
10. Volker Ullrich, *Hitler: Ascent 1889–1939* (New York: Alfred A. Knopf, 2016), 717.
11. G. Ward Price, *Extra-Special Correspondent* (London: George G. Harrap & Co., 1957), 228.
12. Volker Ullrich, *Hitler: Ascent 1889–1939* (New York: Alfred A. Knopf, 2016), 717.
13. G. Ward Price, *Extra-Special Correspondent* (London: George G. Harrap & Co., 1957), 229.
14. Bella Fromm, *Blood & Banquets: A Berlin Diary 1930–38* (New York: Touchstone, 1990) 267.
15. Martha Schad, *Hitler's Spy Princess: The Extraordinary Life of Stephanie von Hohenlohe* (Stroud: Sutton, 2004), 47.
16. Ibid., 48.
17. Jim Wilson, *Nazi Princess: Hitler, Lord Rothermere and Princess Stephanie von Hohenlohe* (Stroud: The History Press, 2011), 76.
18. Walter C. Langer, "Interview with Princess Stephanie von Hohenlohe, June 28, 1943 at Alien Detentioon Camp, Seagoville, Texas," *Hitler Source Book* (Washington, D.C.: M.O. Branch, Office of Strategic Services, Declassified on March 12, 1968).
19. Jim Wilson, *Nazi Princess: Hitler, Lord Rothermere and Princess Stephanie von Hohenlohe* (Stroud: The History Press, 2011), 76.
20. "Friend of Hitler," *Evening Standard*, July 21, 1938.
21. Martha Schad, *Hitler's Spy Princess: The Extraordinary Life of Stephanie von Hohenlohe* (Stroud: Sutton, 2004), 91.
22. The British National Archives, MI5 files, "Princess Stephanie Marie von Hohenlohe-Waldburg-Schillingfurst," KV 2/1696–1697, 1928–1939.
23. Karina Urbach, *Go Betweens for Hitler* (Oxford: Oxford University Press, 2015), 251.
24. Prince Franz Hohenlohe, *Steph: The Fabulous Princess* (London: New English Library, 1976), 126–127.
25. Martha Schad, *Hitler's Spy Princess: The Extraordinary Life of Stephanie von Hohenlohe* (Stroud: Sutton, 2004), 92.
26. Prince Franz Hohenlohe, *Steph: The Fabulous Princess* (London: New English Library, 1976), 127.

Chapter 18

1. Karina Urbach, *Go Betweens for Hitler* (Oxford: Oxford University Press, 2015), 259.
2. Ibid., 260–261.
3. Prince Franz Hohenlohe, *Steph: The Fabulous Princess* (London: New English Library, 1976), 119.
4. Martha Schad, *Hitler's Spy Princess: The Extraordinary Life of Stephanie von Hohenlohe* (Stroud: Sutton, 2004), 89.
5. Bella Fromm, *Blood & Banquets: A Berlin Diary 1930–38* (New York: Touchstone, 1990), 279.

6. Volker Ullrich, *Hitler: Ascent 1889–1939* (New York: Alfred A. Knopf, 2016), 734.
7. *Ibid.*, 736.
8. *Ibid.*, 735.
9. *Ibid.*, 738.
10. Bella Fromm, *Blood & Banquets: A Berlin Diary 1930–38* (New York: Touchstone, 1990), 263.
11. Martha Schad, *Hitler's Spy Princess: The Extraordinary Life of Stephanie von Hohenlohe* (Stroud: Sutton, 2004), 103.
12. *Ibid.*
13. Bella Fromm, *Blood & Banquets: A Berlin Diary 1930–38* (New York: Touchstone, 1990), 282–283.
14. Ian Kershaw, *Hitler: A Biography* (New York: W.W. Norton 2008), 456.
15. *Ibid.*, 457.
16. *Ibid.*, 458–459.
17. Martha Schad, *Hitler's Spy Princess: The Extraordinary Life of Stephanie von Hohenlohe* (Stroud: Sutton, 2004), 114.
18. Jim Wilson, *Nazi Princess: Hitler, Lord Rothermere and Princess Stephanie von Hohenlohe* (Stroud: The History Press, 2011), 134.
19. Prince Franz Hohenlohe, *Steph: The Fabulous Princess* (London: New English Library, 1976), 116.
20. Karina Urbach, *Go Betweens for Hitler* (Oxford: Oxford University Press, 2015), 266
21. Jim Wilson, *Nazi Princess: Hitler, Lord Rothermere and Princess Stephanie von Hohenlohe* (Stroud: The History Press, 2011), 132.
22. Martha Schad, *Hitler's Spy Princess: The Extraordinary Life of Stephanie von Hohenlohe* (Stroud: Sutton, 2004), 105.
23. Jim Wilson, *Nazi Princess: Hitler, Lord Rothermere and Princess Stephanie von Hohenlohe* (Stroud: The History Press, 2011), 131.
24. *Ibid.*, 132.
25. Prince Franz Hohenlohe, *Steph: The Fabulous Princess* (London: New English Library, 1976), 128.
26. Stephanie Hohenlohe, Draft memoir, Stephanie zu Hohenlohe-Waldenburg-Schillingsfürst files, Hoover Archives, Stanford, California.
27. Ian Kershaw, *Hitler: A Biography* (New York: W.W. Norton, 2008), 482.
28. *Ibid.*, 486–487.
29. William L. Shirer, *The Rise and Fall of the Third Reich: A History of Nazi Germany* (New York: Simon & Schuster, 2011), 564.
30. Ian Kershaw, *Hitler: A Biography* (New York: W.W. Norton, 2008), 507.
31. BBC Archive, "The Transcript of Neville Chamberlain's Declaration of War," September 3, 1939, http://www.bbc.co.uk/archive/ww2outbreak/7957.shtml?page=txt
32. Karina Urbach, *Go Betweens for Hitler* (Oxford: Oxford University Press, 2015), 265.
33. The British National Archives, MI5 files, "Princess Stephanie Marie von Hohenlohe-Waldburg-Schillingfurst," KV 2/1696–1697, 1928–1939.
34. *Ibid.*
35. *Ibid.*
36. Prince Franz Hohenlohe, *Steph: The Fabulous Princess* (London: New English Library, 1976), 113–114.
37. Jim Wilson, *Nazi Princess: Hitler, Lord Rothermere and Princess Stephanie von Hohenlohe* (Stroud: The History Press, 2011), 85.
38. Martha Schad, *Hitler's Spy Princess: The Extraordinary Life of Stephanie von Hohenlohe* (Stroud: Sutton, 2004), 115.
39. "A Princess Sues Lord Rothermere," *The Leeds Mercury*, November 9, 1939.
40. Fred Taylor, ed., *The Goebbels Diaries, 1939–1941* (New York: G.P. Putnam's Sons, 1983), 49.
41. Martha Schad, *Hitler's Spy Princess: The Extraordinary Life of Stephanie von Hohenlohe* (Stroud: Sutton, 2004), 116.
42. Jim Wilson, *Nazi Princess: Hitler, Lord Rothermere and Princess Stephanie von Hohenlohe* (Stroud: The History Press, 2011), 143.
43. *Ibid.*, 144.

Chapter 19

1. Jim Wilson, *Nazi Princess: Hitler, Lord Rothermere and Princess Stephanie von Hohenlohe* (Stroud: The History Press, 2011), 144.
2. Martha Schad, *Hitler's Spy Princess: The Extraordinary Life of Stephanie von Hohenlohe* (Stroud: Sutton, 2004), 118–119.
3. *Ibid.*, 106.
4. Letter from Fritz Wiedemann to Stephanie von Hohenlohe, November 21, 1939, Stephanie zu Hohenlohe-Waldenburg-Schillingsfürst files, Hoover Archives, Stanford, California.
5. The British National Archives, MI5 files, "Princess Stephanie Marie von Hohenlohe-Waldburg-Schillingfurst," KV 2/1696–1697, 1928–1939.
6. Martha Schad, *Hitler's Spy Princess: The Extraordinary Life of Stephanie von Hohenlohe* (Stroud: Sutton, 2004), 122.
7. Memorandum on Stephanie von Hohenlohe for U.S. President Franklin D. Roo-

sevelt, Franklin D. Roosevelt Presidential Library and Museum, Marist University, October 28, 1941.

Epilogue

1. The British National Archives, MI5 files, "Princess Stephanie Marie von Hohenlohe-Waldburg-Schillingfurst," KV 2/1696–1697, 1928–1939.
2. U.S. Subject Index to Correspondence and Case Files of the Immigration and Naturalization Service 1903–1959, File 56,001–45: Princess Stephanie Hohenlohe.
3. *Memorandum on Stephanie von Hohenlohe for U.S. President Franklin D. Roosevelt*, Franklin D. Roosevelt Presidential Library and Museum, Marist University, October 28, 1941.
4. Jim Wilson, *Nazi Princess: Hitler, Lord Rothermere and Princess Stephanie von Hohenlohe* (Stroud: The History Press, 2011), 155.
5. *Ibid.*, 156.
6. Karina Urbach, *Go Betweens for Hitler* (Oxford: Oxford University Press, 2015), 276.
7. Martha Schad, *Hitler's Spy Princess: The Extraordinary Life of Stephanie von Hohenlohe* (Stroud: Sutton, 2004), 145.
8. *Memorandum on Stephanie von Hohenlohe for U.S. President Franklin D. Roosevelt*, Franklin D. Roosevelt Presidential Library and Museum, Marist University, October 28, 1941.
9. Martha Schad, *Hitler's Spy Princess: The Extraordinary Life of Stephanie von Hohenlohe* (Stroud: Sutton, 2004), 152.
10. Martha Schad, *Hitler's Spy Princess: The Extraordinary Life of Stephanie von Hohenlohe* (Stroud: Sutton, 2004), 156.
11. United States National Archives, World War II Army Enlistment Records, 1938–1946, Francis J. Hohenlohe.
12. Fred Taylor, ed., *The Goebbels Diaries, 1939–1941* (New York: G.P. Putnam's Sons, 1983), 215.
13. Ian Kershaw, *Hitler: A Biography* (New York: W.W. Norton, 2008), 954.
14. Werner Maser, *Hitler's Letters and Notes* (New York: Bantam, 1976), 196.
15. Colonel Richard P. Heppner, Lt. Colonel William S. Crawford, Captain Franklin M. Stone, and Lt. Guy Martin, Nuremberg, International Military Tribunal, 1945-09-19. "The Testimony of Fritz Wiedemann/Headquarters/Office of Strategic Services/China Theater/TOP SECRET," Ithaca, Cornell University Law Library.

Bibliography

The Austrian Red Cross Archives. *Papers Relating to Archduchess Marie Valerie and Archduke Franz Salvator as Patrons.* 1914–1917.

Bogle, James, and Joanna. *A Heart for Europe—The Lives of Emperor Charles and Empress Zita of Austria-Hungary.* Leominster: Gracewing, 1990.

The British National Archives. MI5 files. "Princess Stephanie Marie von Hohenlohe-Waldburg-Schillingfurst." KV 2/1696–1697, 1928–1939.

The British National Archives. Warwickshire County Records Office. *Telegram from Marie Valerie to Lady Mary Throckmorton, September 13, 1898.* CR1998/GS/6; *Letter to Mrs. Mary Throckmorton, December 13, 1898.* CR1998/GS/5.

Burgtheater Vienna. http://www.burgtheater.at/Content.Node2/home/eninfo/English_Information.at.php.

Carruthers, Bob, dir. *Hitler: A Journey Through His World* (1 hour, 27 minutes). Total Content Digital-Studio, 2010.

Chamberlain, Geoffrey. "British Maternal Mortality in the 19th and early 20th Centuries." *Journal of the Royal Society of Medicine* 9, no. 11 (November 2006). http://www.ncbi.nlm.nih.gov/pmc/articles/PMC1633559/#ref23.

"Christmas Gifts for the Troops." *Sunderland Daily Echo and Shipping Gazette,* December 11, 1914.

"The Coming Royal Marriage." *Hull Daily Mail,* June 17, 1890; August 18, 1910.

Corti, Count Egon. *Elisabeth, Empress of Austria.* New Haven: Yale University Press, 1936.

"The Crown Prince of Portugal." *Derby Daily Telegraph,* November 1, 1883.

"The Czarewitch." *The Sheffield Daily Telegraph,* August 15, 1887.

d'Almeida, Fabrice. *High Society in the Third Reich.* Malden, MA: Polity Press, 2008.

Dodd, Martha. *My Years in Germany.* London: Victor Gollancz, 1939.

Elon, Amos. *The Pity of It All: A Portrait of the German-Jewish Epoch, 1743–1933.* New York: Macmillan, 2003.

"Empress Eugenie Enjoys Last Favor of Joseph." *Bisbee Daily Review,* July 12, 1906.

Evening Star (Washington, D.C.), November 22, 1916.

FDR Library. *Memorandum Regarding: Princess Stephanie Hohenlohe Waldenburg. October 28, 1941.* http://docs.fdrlibrary.marist.edu/PSF/Box3/A31A01.html.

Fromm, Bella. *Blood & Banquets: A Berlin Diary 1930–38.* New York: Touchstone, 1990.

Giblin, James. *The Life and Death of Adolf Hitler.* New York: Houghton Mifflin Harcourt, 2002.

Gödöllő Royal Palace. http://www.kiralyikastely.hu/.

Hall, Allan. "Hitler's House to Go on Sale with £2m Price Tag—but Authorities Fear It Could Become Fascist Shrine." *The Daily Mail,* November 4, 2009. http://www.dailymail.co.uk/news/article-1225268/Hitlers-house-goes-sale-2m-price-tag-authorities-fear-fascist-shrine.html.

Hamann, Brigitte. *Hitler's Vienna: A Portrait of the Tyrant as a Young Man.* New York: I.B. Tauris, 2014.

Hamann, Brigitte. *The Reluctant Empress: A Biography of Empress Elisabeth of Austria.* New York: Alfred A. Knopf, 1986.

Hanisch, Reinhold. "I Was Hitler's Buddy." *The New Republic,* April 5, 12, 19, 1939.

Harding, Bertita. *Lost Waltz: A Story of Exile*. Indianapolis: Bobbs-Merrill, 1944.

Heine, Heinrich. *Heinrich Heine's gesammelte Werke 1893*. Berlin: G. Grote, 1893.

Heppner, Colonel Richard P., Lt. Colonel William S. Crawford, Captain Franklin M. Stone, and Lt. Guy Martin. Nuremberg, International Military Tribunal, 1945-09-19. "The Testimony of Fritz Wiedemann/Headquarters/Office of Strategic Services/China Theater/TOP SECRET." Ithaca, Cornell University Law Library.

Hitler, Adolf. *Mein Kampf*. New York: Houghton Mifflin, 1999.

Hohenlohe, Prince Franz. *Steph: The Fabulous Princess*. London: New English Library, 1976.

Hohenlohe, Stephanie. *Draft memoir*. Hoover Archives, Stanford, California.

"House of Habsburg, Habsburg-Lorraine." *Encyclopaedia Britannica*. http://www.britannica.com/topic/House-of-Habsburg/Habsburg-Lorraine.

"An Imperial Wedding." *The Watertown Herald*, August 2, 1890. http://nyshistoricnewspapers.org/lccn/sn85054447/1890-08-02/ed-1/seq-3.pdf.

James, Edward T., Janet Wilson James, and Paul S. Boyer, eds. *Notable American Women, 1607-1950: A Biographical Dictionary, Volume 2*. Cambridge: Belknap Press, 1971.

Joseph, Emperor Franz. *To My People! Emperor Franz Joseph's Proclamation—Declaration of War*. July 28, 1914. British Library. http://www.bl.uk/collection-items/to-my-people-emperor-franz-joseph.

Judson, Pieter M. *The Habsburg Empire: A New History*. Cambridge: Belknap Press, 2016.

Kershaw, Ian. *Hitler: A Biography*. New York: W.W. Norton, 2008.

Koda, Harold, and Andrew Bolton. *Poiret*. New Haven: Yale University Press, 2007.

Kubizek, August. *The Young Hitler I Knew: The Memoirs of Hitler's Childhood Friend*. Yorkshire: Frontline, 2011.

Langer, Walter C. *A Psychological Analysis of Adoph Hitler: His Life and Legend*. Washington, D.C.: M.O. Branch, Office of Strategic Services, 1943, Declassified on March 12, 1968.

Large, David Clay. *The Grand Spas of Central Europe: A History of Intrigue, Politics, Art, and Healing*. Lanham, MD: Rowman & Littlefield, 2015.

Leicester Daily Mercury, June 16, 1890.

Loudain, Irvine. "Maternal Mortality in the Past and Its Relevance to Developing Countries Today." *The American Journal of Clinical Nutrition* 72, no. 1 (July 2000). http://ajcn.nutrition.org/content/72/1/241s.full.

Lynn, Katalin Kadar. "Strange Partnership: Lord Rothermere, Stephanie von Hohenlohe and the Hungarian Revisionist Movement." *The Independent Scholar* (The National Coalition of Independent Scholars, 2012).

MacDonogh, Giles. *1938: Hitler's Gamble*. New York: Basic Books, 2011.

"Marriage of Archduchess Valerie." *The Sheffield Daily Telegraph*, August 1, 1890.

Marshall, S.L.A. *American Heritage History of World War I*. Newbury, MA: New Word City, 2014.

Maser, Werner. *Hitler's Letters and Notes*. New York: Bantam, 1976.

McIntosh, David. *The Unknown Habsburgs*. Falkoping, Sweden: Rosvall Royal Books, 2000.

The Milton Keynes Heritage Association. *Letter from Empress Elisabeth to Mary Throckmorton*. http://www.mkheritage.co.uk/eoa/docs/throckmorton.html.

Murad, Anatol. *Franz Joseph and His Empire*. New York: Twayne, 1968.

Official Kaiservilla Home Page. https://www.kaiservilla.at.

Olson, James S. *Bathsheba's Breast: Women, Cancer, and History*. Baltimore: Johns Hopkins University Press, 2005.

Palmer, Alan. *Twilight of the Habsburgs: The Life and Times of Emperor Francis Joseph*. New York: Grove Press, 1994.

Peters, Edward. *A Modern Guide to Indulgences: Rediscovering This Often Misinterpreted Teaching*. Chicago: Liturgy Training Publications, 2008.

Pittsburg Dispatch, July 31, 1890.

Price, G. Ward. *Extra-Special Correspondent*. London: George G. Harrap & Co., 1957.

"Princess *Aglaë* von Auersperg." *The Illustrated American*, November 26, 1892.

Range, Peter Ross. *1924: The Year That Made Hitler*. New York: Little, Brown, 2016.

Range, Regina Christiane. "Agency in the Everyday: Subversive Discourses in the Work of Gina Kaus." In *Exile and*

Everyday Life: Yearbook of the Research Centre for German and Austrian Exile Studies. Boston: Brill, 2015.

Range, Regina Christiane. *Positioning Gina Kaus: a transnational career from Vienna novelist and playwright to Hollywood script-writer.* PhD thesis, University of Iowa, 2012. http://ir.uiowa.edu/etd/3515.

Recollections of a Royal Governess. New York: D. Appleton, 1916.

Rothermere, Viscount. *My Campaign for Hungary.* London: Spottiswoode, 1939.

"A Royal Betrothal." *Bury Free Press.* June 26, 1886.

Sacré Coeur Pressbaum. http://sacrecoeur.scp.ac.at.

"St. Stephen Scene of Splendor at Franz Joseph's Funeral." *The New York Times,* December 1, 1916.

Schad, Martha. *Hitler's Spy Princess: The Extraordinary Life of Stephanie von Hohenlohe.* Stroud: Sutton, 2004.

Schad, Martha. *Kaiserin Elisabeth und ihre Töchter.* München: Piper Verlag GmbH, 2002.

Schloss Schönbrunn. "Schönbrunn Zoo." http://www.schoenbrunn.at.

Shirer, William L. *The Rise and Fall of the Third Reich: A History of Nazi Germany.* New York: Simon & Schuster, 2011.

Sinclair, Andrew. *Death By Fame: A Life of Elisabeth of Austria.* London: Constable, 1998.

Slapnicka, Harry. *The Fate of the Ischl Kaiservilla After the Death of Emperor Franz Joseph.* Oberösterreichischer Musealverein—Gesellschaft für Landeskunde, 2000.

Strong, George V. *Seedtime for Fascism: Disintegration of Austrian Political Culture, 1867–1918.* New York: Routledge, 1998.

"Tattle from Truth." *Dundee Evening Telegraph,* December 4, 1912.

Taylor, Fred, ed. *The Goebbels Diaries, 1939–1941.* New York: G.P. Putnam's Sons, 1983.

"Threatening Symptoms." *Birmingham Gazette.* November 23, 1916.

Ullrich, Volker. *Hitler: Ascent 1889–1939.* New York: Alfred A. Knopf, 2016.

The United States Holocaust Memorial Museum, www.ushmm.org.

Urbach, Karina. *Go Betweens for Hitler.* Oxford: Oxford University Press, 2015.

von Osterreich, Marie Valerie. *Das Tagebuch der Lieblingstochter von Kaiserin Elisabeth.* Munchen: Piper, 1998.

"Whole Family at Bedside." *Ottumwa* (Iowa) *Semi-Weekly Courier,* November 24, 1916.

Wackerow, Charlotte. "Some Traits of Character." In *Zeichen der Myrte: Erinnerungs-Blätter aus Anlass der Vermählung Marie Valerie mit Franz Salvator von Toscana.* Wien: Alfred Holder, 1890.

Wallsee-Sindelburg. "History." http://www.wallsee-sindelburg.gv.at/.

Warwickshire County Record Office. *Letter from Empress Elisabeth of Austria to Lady Mary Throckmorton.* CR1998/SS/5/14/1–14. November 4, 1868; *Maria Valerie and Mary Throckmorton.* http://apps.warwickshire.gov.uk/api/documents/WCCC-863–397; *Mary Throckmorton-Order of St. Elizabeth, First Class.* CR1998/GS/4.

Weber, Thomas. *Hitler's First War.* New York: Oxford University Press, 2010.

Wilson, Jim. *Nazi Princess: Hitler, Lord Rothermere and Princess Stephanie von Hohenlohe.* Stroud: The History Press, 2011.

Winter, Ludwig. *WWI Photographic Album: Thermal Spa Pro Patria Postyen* (photograph album recording the visit of the Archduke Franz Salvator to the Military Hospital for Wounded Soldiers at the Spa of Posteyen). Osler Library of the History of Medicine, McGill University. May 30, 1916.

The World of the Habsburgs. Http://www.habsburger.net.

Zeepvat, Charlotte. *From Cradle to Crown: British Nannies and Governesses at the World's Royal Courts.* Stroud: Sutton, 2006.

"Zigeunerbaron-Quadrille (Gypsy Baron Quadrille) op. 422." Johann Strauss Edition, Vol. 45. http://www.naxos.com/mainsite/blurbs_reviews.asp?item_code=8.223245&catNum=223245&filetype=About%20this%20Recording&language=English.

Index

Abetz, Otto 118
Academy of Visual Arts, Vienna 39
Acton, Sir John 21
Adlon Hotel, Berlin 121, 135, 159
Alfonso XIII, King 96
Alice, Hereditary Grand Duchess of Hesse 21
Andrássy, Count Gyula 19
"The Angel of Wallsee" 67
Anschluss 89, 146, 147, **150**, 151, 153, 156
Aryan 104, 122, 129, 137, 151, 177, 180
Auersperg, Aglaë or Aglaja 22–23
Augustianian Church, Vienna 13
Auslands-Organisation (AO) 177
Austrian National Theater 28
"The Austrian Question" 144
Austrian Red Cross 67, 68, 69, 79, 80, 86, 88
Austrian Republic 91
Austro-Fascism 130
Austro-Hungarian Compromise 19
Austro-Hungarian Empire 4, 19, 42, 57, 58, 61, 76, 113

The Battle of the Marne 89–90
The Battle of the Somme 72, 83, 85
Bavaria 19
Bavaria, Prince Leopold of (Gisela's husband) 10
Beau Rivage Hotel, Geneva 44
Beer Hall Putsch 101, 105–106, 135, 160
Berchtold, Count Leopold 61
Berghof 142, 146, 158
Berlin 69, 85, 104, 112, 119, 120, 121, 124, 126, 134, 135, 152, 157, 159, 163, 164, 172
Bishop of Linz 14
Bloch, Dr. Eduard 40, 103, 149
Bolshevik 102, 104
Bosnia 58, 61
Bourbon-Sicily, Princess Marie Teresa of 28
Braganza, Prince Miguel of 10

Branau on the Inn, Austria (also Braunau am Inn) 35, 65
Braun, Eva 141–142
Brownshirts 130
Bruckner, Anton 12
Brussels, Belgium 116
Buchenwald 144, 161
Buda, Hungary 19, 100
Budapest, Hungary 96, 97, 112, 114, 115, 116
Bülow, Bernhard von (Secretary of State) 138
Bürgerbräukeller Beer Hall 105
Burgtheater 28, 55, 58

Cadogan, Alexander 156
Carinthia 23
Chamberlain, Neville 157, 158, 159, 164, 165
Charles VI, Holy Roman Emperor 26, 57
Chotek, Sophie (also Duchess of Hohenberg) 58; assassination 59
Christian Social Party 52, 98
Christmas Truce of 1914 83
Christomanos, Constantin 46
Church of the Capuchin Friars 45, 75
Churchill, Winston 141
Clarissa, Countess Komis von Göncz-Ruszka ("Zummel") 12
Communism 119
Corfu, Greece 51–52
Crown of Saint Stephen
Crown Prince of Saxony 10, 28
Crown Prince Wilhelm 117, 119, 121

Dachau 120, 161
The Daily Mail 110, 113, 114, 119, 134, 135, 136, 148, 168
Daladier, Édouard 159
Danzig 164
Department for Jewish Affairs 162
Diadem of Hortense 95

Index

Dodd, Martha 119; description of Ribbentrop 139; impressions of Hitler 122–123
Dodd, William Edward (U.S. Ambassador to Germany) 119, 133
Dollfuss, Engelbert (Austrian chancellor) 129, 130, 146

Edward VIII, King 168
Eichmann, Adolf 162
Elisabeth Marie, Archduchess ("Erzi," daughter of Rudolf) 11, 22, 75; flower girl in MV's wedding 12; reaction to father's death 12
Empress Elisabeth of Austria and Queen of Hungary 8, 75; acts as matchmaker for MV and FS 28–29; assassination 44; blamed Stephanie for Rudolf's death 30; *Cercle* at the Court Ball 27; comments that FS will be MV's husband 27; crowned Queen of Hungary 19; depression after Rudolf's death 12; disapproval of Crown Princess Stephanie 29; emotions 11; George Raab painting *20*; and Katharina Schratt 55; letter to Mary Throckmorton 21; mourns losing MV 9; relationship with Erzi 12; smothering relationship with MV 23; views on marriage 10; on visiting MV at Lichtenegg 42; wedding poem 10
Empress Maria Theresa 26, 57
Engelhardt, Lt. Col. Philipp 82
Esterházy, House of 97, 116

Fascism 119
Fascist Party 125
Fascisti Party 104
Federal Bureau of Investigation (FBI) 118, 174, 176, 179
Festetics, Marie 25
Francis Stephen of Lorraine 26
Franz Ferdinand 12, *60*; assassination 58–59
Franz Joseph (emperor of Austria and King of Hungary) 3, *48*, 51, 54, 182; crowned King of Hungary 19; death 73; declares war on Serbia 62; discourages MV's relationship with FS 9; dislike of Court Ball 27; funeral 74; learns of Franz Ferdinand's assassination 57; learns of wife's assassination 44,; photograph with young Archduke Otto *59*; rules jointly with Karl 72; stops Rudolf's annulment 30; war maneuvers *62*; wartime schedule 68; welcomed all nationalities inside empire 52; will 75
Franz Salvator 3, 153; appearance at wedding 14; dances with Marie Valerie at Court Ball 27; death 163, 166, 174, 182; difference between SR and MV 53–54; in dress officer's uniform *19*; father of Stephanie Richter's child 4; honeymoon 17; meets Stephanie Richter 34; notices Marie Valerie 27; portrait with MV *47*, *63*; reaction to Agnes's death 44; reaction to MV's death 101; receives honorary doctorate 68–69; remarries 129; takes SR to Kaiservilla 54; Tuscan branch of Habsburgs 26; as vice-patron of the Red Cross 68; wedding day *9*
Franz Xaver Winterhalter 11
Frischauer, Willi 156–157
Fromm, Bella 120, 130, 133, 138, 140, 147, 151, 154, 157, 159–160

Geneva, Switzerland 44
German-American Business League 177
German National Socialist Party 125
German Red Cross 144
German Workers' Party 103
Gestapo 151, 163
Gisela, Archduchess 10, 51, 67, 92, 93; appearance 11; inheritance of Elisabeth's estate 45–46; in MV's diary 23; at MV's wedding 12; royal wedding 13
Gizycki, Count Josef 34
Gmunden, Austria 31, 32
Göding 28
Gödöllő Palace 20, 22
Goebbels, Joseph 123, 131, 135, 140–141, 147, 148, 158, 159, 164, 169–170, 180–181
Goebbels, Magda 135, 140, 181
Göring, Hermann 104, 105, 135, 146, 147, 152, 182
Graf, Ulrich 106
The Great War 103, 104, 132, 163
Grynszpan, Herschel 160
Gutmann, Lt. Hugo 87, 103

Habsburg, Otto von *59*, *77*, 112, 116, 147
Habsburg, House of 9, 12, 15, 26, 27, 30, 31, 34, 35, 39, 40, 51, 57, 58, 64, 66, 68, 74, 75, 88, 89, 91, 92, 94, 112, 116, 146, 153, 168, 174, 182
Haffner, Sebastian 104
Halifax, Lord 144, 154, 156–157
Hanfstaengl, Ernst ("Putzi") 104, 137; jealous of Stephanie 138
Hanisch, Reinhold 51
Harmsworth, Esmond 115, 134
Harmsworth, Harold Sidney (1st Viscount Rothermere, also Lord Rothermere) 110, *111*, 113; ceases to associate with Stephanie 161; death 175; decides

to restore monarchy 116; hosts dinner for Hitler 135; invited to Berlin 126; named candidate for king 115; pays bonus 123; publishes *Hungary's Place in the Sun* 113; sued for breach of contract 166–170; travels to Obersalzberg 140; urges support for Fascism 119; writes anti–Nazi editorial 167–168
Hearst, William Randolph 137
Heine, Heinrich 51, 122
Heldenplatz 151
Hepp, Ernst 83
Hermés Villa 15, 46
Hess, Rudolf 104, 133
Hesse, Prince Philip of 147–148
Himmler, Heinrich 149, 151, 162
Hindenburg, Paul von 131–132
Hitler, Adolf 5, *102*; Anschluss 148–151; awarded Iron Cross Second Class 82; becomes dispatch runner 81; becomes Nazi propagandist 104; Beer Hall Putsch 105–106; birth 35; budding nationalism 37; comes to support Leuger; consolidates power 132; death of Edmund 37; death of father 37; on death of Franz Joseph 76; dislike of work 38; dog Foxl 84; early politics 51; enamored with Stephanie 125; fails to register for Austrian military 64–65; father's abuse 36; friendship with Gustl 38; infatuation with Stefanie Isak 38; injured during Battle of the Somme 72; invites Stephanie to Nuremerg Rally 138; Iron Cross First Class 87; in Landsberg Prison and trial 106–107; learns of Stephanie-Wiedemann affair 162; learns of surrender 89; letter to Frau Popp 65–66; letter to Rothermere 124; letter to Stephanie 144; marries Eva Braun 180; meets with Neville Chamberlain 158; mother dies 40; orders Dollfuss assassination 131; orders Stephanie's arrest 162; orders "The Night of the Long Knives" 130; physical description during Great War 81; registers for First Bavarian Infantry Regiment 64; rejected from art school 39; relationship with Göring 152; sells paintings 50; sends Wiedemann to San Francisco; suicide 181; talent for speaking 102; travels to Vienna 38; views on women in politics 121; works with Reinhold Hanisch; writes about desire for pure Germany 83
Hitler, Alois (also Alois Schicklgruber) 35–36
Hitler, Alois, Jr. 36

Hitler, Edmund 37
Hitler, Klara (also Klara Poelzl) 35, 36; cancer diagnosis 40
Hitler, Paula 37
Hitler Youth 118
Hofbräuhaus 104
Hofburg Palace 3, 22, 26, 27, 46, 51, 55, 56, 61, 68, 151
Hohenlohe, Franz Joseph (Franzi) Rudolf Hans Wriand Max Stefan Anton von 3, *128*, 177; arrested 179; comments on FS using influence 70, 88, 94, 97, 110, 116; doubt he was a Hohenlohe 5; forced to leave Leopoldskron 163; letter to Wiedemann 129; at Oxford 127; wants to work with Allies 175
Hohenlohe, Prince Konrad 74
Hohenlohe, House of 4
Hohenlohe-Waldenburg-Schillingsfürst, Friedrich Franz von 4, 56; files for divorce 97, 166; gambling debts 5; reported spy 69
Hohenlohe-Waldenburg-Schillingsfürst, Stephanie 3, 69, *141*, *177*; account of Franz Joseph's funeral procession 74; adversarial relationship with Ribbentrop 138–139; attempts to mourn Franz Joseph at Hofburg 73–74; awarded Nazi Gold Medal of Honour 152; blacklisted 179; death 180; describes internment camp 178; describes looting 79; describes trenches 80; describes wartime Vienna 86; description as she landed in New York 173; discusses Hungary 111; divorces 97; on FS death; given credit for Munich Agreement 159; gives birth 69; honeymoon 69; hostesses dinner party for Hitler 135; impressions of Hitler 122–123; invited to Obersalzberg 140; letter to Hitler 142; letters to Rothermere 161, 171; loses dual citizenship 96; meets Lord Rothermere 110; meets the ex–Kaiser 117; meets Wiedemann 119; moves to Italian front 77; named Honorary Aryan 53; negotiates contract with Rothermere 117; physically repulsed by Hitler 125; praised by Horthy 115; receives Leopoldskron; remains in touch with FS 127; runs international salon 98; stationed at the Russian front 71; sues Rothermere 166–170; trains as Red Cross nurse 69; waits out the end of the war 88; wedding 4; works with Wiedemann in U.S. 177
Hohenzollern, House of 116, 117, 168
Holocaust 181
Hoover, J. Edgar 176, 178, 179

Index

Horthy, Miklós (Admiral) 112, 113, 115, 157
Hungarian Soviet Republic 97
Hungary 19, 22, 110, 112, 113, 116, 118
Hungary's Place in the Sun 113

The Illustrated American 23
Imperial Order of Saint Elisabeth 46
Infanta Blanca of Spain (wife of Leopold Salvator) 66, 94–96
Isak, Stefanie 38; receives letter from Hitler 39
Ischl, Austria (also Bad Ischl) 8, *13*, 16, 22, 26, 31, 41, 47, 54, 57, 61, 63, 75, 92, 182

"The Jewish Question" 51, 103, 141

Kaiservilla 10, 13, *14*, 22, 26, 41, 43, 47, 59, *61*, *62*, 63, 75, 92, 182
Karl Franz Joseph Ludwig Hubert Georg Otto Maria (also Emperor Karl I of Austria and King of Hungary) 58, 60, 61, 63, 72, *74*, 78, 88, 115, 147; becomes Emperor 76; "Easter Bid" 112; exile and death on Madeira 112; and Franz Ferdinand's funeral 61; leaves Austria 89; negotiates with Spain 96; relinquishes affairs of state 89
Karl Ludwig, Archduke (Emperor Franz Joseph's brother) 57
Karl Salvator, Archduke (Franz Salvator's father) 26; gifts FS Wallsee Castle 42
Kaus, Gina 32
Koerber, Dr. Ernest von (Austrian minister-president) 73
Kristallnacht 160
Krobatin, Alexander Freiherr von (minister of war) 68
Kubizek, August ("Gustl") 38, 39
Kuranda, Robert 34

Lainzer Tiergarten 15
Lake Traunsee 31
Landsberg Prison 106, 135
Lederer, Baron von 69, 93–94
Leonding, Austria 36, 149
Leopold John, Archduke 26
Leopold of Bavaria (Gisela's husband) 10, 92
Leopold Salvator (brother of Franz Salvator) 26, 28, 66, *67*, 94–96, 174
Leopoldskron Palace *153*, 163, 174
Lichtenegg Castle 42
Liddell, Guy 167
Linz, Austria 36, 40, 65, 135, 148
List, Col. Julius von 65

List Regiment 65, 85
The Little Entente 118
Lucheni, Luigi 44
Ludendorff, Erich (General) 104–106, 134, 135
Lueger, Dr. Karl 52

Madeira, Portugal 112
Magyars 19
The Man Who Wanted to Command 180
Mariahilferstrasse 149
Maria Theresa, Archduchess (sister of Franz Salvator) 69, *70*, 149, 163, 174, 182
Marie Antoinette Brooch 95
Marie Immaculata of Bourbon–Two Sicilies (Franz Salvator's mother) 12, 26, 28
Marie Valerie, Archduchess 3, *9*; appearance 11; Baby Agnes dies after birth 43; becomes a citizen of the Republic 91; begins keeping diary 23; birth 19; childhood and relationship with governess 22; comments on FS's mother; death and funeral 100–101; description of Rudolf's death 12; dressed for costume ball *18*; at dying father's bedside 73; family photo with 8 children *43*; on father's Golden Jubilee appearance 47; feelings on Katharina Schratt 55; financial concerns after the war 93; forced to speak Hungarian 24; German nationalism 18; honeymoon 17; on hopes for a 10th child 41; impressions of FS at the Burgtheater 29; inheritance of Elisabeth's estate 45–46; names first child after her mother 42; not obliged to marry 17; observations on Stephanie as Rudolf's wife 29; as Patron of the Red Cross 67; photographic portrait with FS *63*; portrait of MV and FS *47*; pregnant with 10th child 41; reaction to mother's assassination 45; relationship with Aglaë Auersperg 22–23; remembers father's birthday celebration at Ischl 63; renunciation ceremony 15; resentment of Hungary 25; resents women like MV 53; Rustimo mentioned in diary 24; on Stephanie after Rudolf's death 30; on strong Catholic faith 42; supports German nationalism 52; talk of the Pragmatic Sanction 57; telegram to Mary Throckmorton announcing engagement 25; tensions with Gisela 93; thoughts on the Kaiservilla 14; wedding day 8; worry over father's nerves 46–47; writes about sad family

life 25; writes to Mary Throckmorton's sister 91–92
Marie Valerie Poor Hospital and Old People's Home 67
Marxist 102, 104
Masaryk, Jan 156, 157
Mata Hari 32
Mauthausen 151
May T. 12, 22
Mayerling 11
Medill, Joseph 34
Mein Kampf 101, 102, 122, 129, 137
Mensdorff, Countess Viktoria 116
Metternich, Prince Klemens von 33
Metternich, Princess Franziska (Fanny) von 33–34
MI 5 110, 117, 154, 162, 167, 173, 174, 175–177
Mitford, Unity Valkyrie 138, 141–142
Morgenstern, Samuel 50
Müllner, Josef 66
Münchener Post 106
Munich, Germany 64–65, 67, 83, 92, 102, 104, 105, 106, 135, 137, 158, 160, 163
Munich Agreement 158
Mussolini, Benito 104, 130, 146, 148, 159

National Observer 104
National Socialist German Workers' Party *(Nationalsozialistische Deutsche Arbeiterpartei)* 103, 117
Neurath, Baron von 135
Nicholas II, Tsar 34
"Night of the Long Knives" 119, 130
Nuremberg Laws 138
Nuremberg Rally 138
Nuremberg Trials 181

Obersalzberg 140, 146
Offensee, Austria 16
Ostmark 149

Paar, Count Eduard 57
Palais Leopold 67, 92
Patterson, Eleanor Medill 34
Pearl Harbor 178
Polish Corridor 164
Pope Pius XV 68
Popp, Joseph 65, 81, 82
Pragmatic Sanction of 1713 26
Prague 23
Price, George Ward 134, 148, 149, 151
Princip, Gavrilo 59

Queen Marie Antoinette of France
Queen Marie of Naples (Empress Elisabeth's sister) 20
Queen Victoria 4

Rajecz, Stephan Burián von (Austrian Foreign Minister) 72
Rath, Ernst vom 160
Rax Mountains 60
Reich Chancellery 121, 122, 135, 152, 153
Reichenau 60
Reichstag 118
Reinhardt, Max (also Maximilian Goldmann) 137, 153–155
Revolutions of 1848 53
Ribbentrop, Annelies von 135
Ribbentrop, Joachim von 135, 138–139, 146, 156–157
Richter, Johannes Hans 31, 33
Richter, Ludmilla (mother of Stephanie Richter) 31
Richter, Stephanie Maria Veronika Juliana (also Stephanie von Hohenlohe) 30, 31, 49, 53, 69; approves of Emperor's relationship with Katharina Schratt 56; becomes a beauty queen 33; and Count Gizycki 34; decides to marry a prince 33; description 32; escapades with FS 54; and half-sister Gina Kaus 32; loses paternal support 33; meets FS 34; style 54
Risenfels, Melanie Freiin von 129
Röhm, Ernst 130
Romanov, Tsarevich Nikolai 10
Rome Protocols 130
Roosevelt, Pres. Franklin Delano 176, orders Stephanie's deportation 178
Rudolf, Crown Prince 11, 57; addiction 29; disapproval of MV's engagement 29; marriage to Stephanie of Belgium 29; in MV's diary 23; royal wedding 13; sexually transmitted disease 29; suicide 30
Rustimo 24–25

Sachsenhausen 161
Saint Nicholas (Parish Church of Ischl) 10, 11, 14, 75, 182
Saint Stephen's Cathedral 68
Salzburg, Austria 65, 153, 154
Salzkammergut region of Austria 31, 44
Sarajevo 58
Schad, Martha 55
Schleicher, Elisabeth von 130
Schleicher, Kurt von 130
Schmidt, Dr. Paul 141, 144
Schofield, Major Lemuel B. 178
Schönbrunn Palace 44, 51, 55, 63, 68, 72, 88, 89, 149
Schratt, Katharina 55, 73
Schushnigg, Kurt von (Austrian Chancellor) 130, 146–148, 151

Index

Schutzstaffel (SS) 120, 130, 136, 144, 149, 151, 162
Schwarzenbergplatz 66, 67
Seipel, Dr. Ignaz 98
Serbia 57, 62, 67
Seyss-Inquart, Arthur 147, 148
Shirer, William 164
Simon, Hans 32
Simpson, Wallis 168
Snowden, Lady Ethel 172
Socialist 104
Sonnermann, Emmy 135
Sophie, Archduchess (Emperor Franz Joseph's mother) 12
Stephanie, Crown Princess (also, Stephanie of Belgium) 11, 23, 29, 30, 67
Storm Troopers 104, 105
Stosstrupp 1917 141
Strauss, Eduard 27
Strauss, Johann 27
Strauss Orchestra 27
Sudetenland 155, 156, 157, 158, 164
Swastika 104
Sztáray, Irma (Empress Elisabeth's attendant) 44

Taft, Pres. William Howard 34
Tennant, E.W.C. 135
Theresienstadt 161
Thimig, Helene 155
Third Reich 118, 147, 174, 181
Thompson, Dorothy 132–133
Throckmorton, Lady Mary (governess) 14, 20–22, 25, 45, 46, 91
Treaty of Saint-Germain-en-Laye 113
Treaty of Trianon 111, 113, 118
Treaty of Versailles 113, 136, 164
Trench warfare **80**

Ullstein Press 120
U.S. Office of Strategic Services 138, 152, 179
University of Innsbruck 68
Unter den Linden 121

Vetsera, Mary (Rudolf's mistress) 11
Vienna for the Past Sixty Years 53
Vienna's Iron Soldier 66

Wagner 130
Wallsee Castle 41, 46, 53, 67, 86, **99**
Wallsee-Sindelburg Cemetery 163
Weimar Republic 92, 104, 118, 133
Wiedemann, Fritz 81, 85, 87, **143**, 151, 154, 159, 163, 175; affair discovered by Ribbentrop 139; affectionate letter to Stephanie 140; becomes lovers with Stephanie 125; blackmail letter to Rothermere 162; letter from Franzi 129; letter to Stephanie from San Francisco 172; meets with Lord Halifax 156; physical description 119; recommends Stephanie to Hitler 121; testifies against Nazis 181; works with Stephanie in U.S. 177; writes memoir 179
Wiener, Max 31
The Wife Takes a Flyer 32
Wilhelm II, Emperor 51, 62, 116
Wilhelminenberg Castle 66, 94
Wilhelmstrasse 158
Wilson, President Woodrow 87
Wurmbrandt, Count Karl 79

Ypres, Belgium **79**

Zita of Bourbon-Parma (also Empress of Austria and Queen of Hungary) 60, 61, 72, 76, **77**, 96, 112, 116, 147
Zuckerkandl, Dr. Otto 71